The Most Dangerous
Man in Britain?

The Most Dangerous Man in Britain?

The Political Writings

Tony Benn

Foreword by Melissa Benn

VERSO
London • New York

This collection first published by Verso 2025
This book contains materials previously published in a variety of works by Tony Benn
© Estate of Tony Benn, 1964–2011
Foreword © Melissa Benn 2025

The manufacturer's authorised representative in the EU for product safety (GPSR)
is LOGOS EUROPE, 9 rue Nicolas Poussin, 17000, La Rochelle, France
Contact@logoseurope.eu

All rights reserved
The moral rights of the authors have been asserted

1 3 5 7 9 10 8 6 4 2

Verso
UK: 6 Meard Street, London W1F 0EG
US: 207 East 32nd Street, New York, NY 10016
versobooks.com

Verso is the imprint of New Left Books

ISBN-13: 978-1-80429-829-9
ISBN-13: 978-1-80429-830-5 (US EBK)
ISBN-13: 978-1-80429-831-2 (UK EBK)

British Library Cataloguing in Publication Data
A catalogue record for this book is available from the British Library

Library of Congress Cataloging-in-Publication Data

Names: Benn, Tony, 1925–2014, author. | Benn, Melissa, author of foreword.
Title: The most dangerous man in Britain? : The political writings / Tony
  Benn ; foreword by Melissa Benn.
Description: First hardback edition. | London ; New York : Verso is the
  imprint of New Left Books, 2025. | 'This book contains materials
  previously published in a variety of works by Tony Benn' – T.p. verso. |
  Includes bibliographical references.
Identifiers: LCCN 2024058197 (print) | LCCN 2024058198 (ebook) | ISBN
  9781804298299 (hardback) | ISBN 9781804298305 (US ebk)
Subjects: LCSH: Benn, Tony, 1925–2014 – Speeches. | Benn, Tony,
  1925–2014 – Correspondence. | Politicians – Great Britain – Interviews. |
  Politicians – Great Britain – Correspondence. | Labour Party (Great
  Britain) – History – 20th century. | Socialism – Great Britain – History. |
  Great Britain – Politics and government – 20th century. | Great
  Britain – Politics and government – 21st century.
Classification: LCC DA591.B36 A5 2025 (print) | LCC DA591.B36 (ebook) |
  DDC 941.085092 [B] – dc23/eng/20250113
LC record available at https://lccn.loc.gov/2024058197
LC ebook record available at https://lccn.loc.gov/2024058198

Typeset in Fournier by MJ & N Gavan, Truro, Cornwall
Printed and bound by CPI (UK) Ltd, Croydon CR0 4YY

Contents

Foreword by Melissa Benn   ix

I. The British State
1. On the Power of the Crown   3
2. Democratic Rights or Ancient Traditions?   6
3. The Common Ownership of Land   18
4. The Disestablishment of the Church of England   21
5. Power, Parliament and the People   28

II. The Many Faces of Democracy
6. A Socialist Reconnaissance   37
7. Developing a Participating Democracy   54
8. The Politician Today   62
9. How Democratic Is Britain?   67
10. Rights under Capitalism   90
11. Democracy and Marxism   97

III. Industry
12. The Case for Workers' Control   113
13. A Ten-year Industrial Strategy for Britain   121
14. The Miners' Strike   129

15.	Argument for Full Employment	133
16.	On 'Outsourcing'	139
17.	The IT Generation	142

IV. Britain in the World

18.	For Sanctions against South Africa	151
19.	European Unity: A New Perspective	154
20.	The Falklands Factor	163
21.	After Enniskillen	168
22.	Why We Should End Nuclear Weapons	173
23.	Iraq: A Speech Against Bombing	180
24.	The Crisis in Kosovo	187
25.	On the Real Nature of Global Capitalism	192
26.	After the Bombing	199

V. The Radical Tradition

27.	Christianity as a Revolutionary Doctrine	205
28.	Marxism and the Labour Party	214
29.	The Levellers and the English Democratic Tradition	221
30.	Listening to the New Generation	233
31.	A Woman's Place	237
32.	The Political Struggle for Equality	246

VI. Politics after Politics

33.	Last Speech to the House of Commons	253
34.	Anti–Iraq War Speech	258
35.	The Idealism of the Old	260
36.	The Last Interview with Melissa Benn	263

Selected Bibliography   273

Foreword

Melissa Benn

Few British politicians of the modern age have possessed the ability to attract so much attention and turn it to so many radical purposes as my late father, Tony Benn. At the height of his fame, he rarely ventured out in public without a debate or discussion sparking up between him and some stranger – sometimes a small crowd would gather to listen. It could be irritating as a teenager to go to Boots with him or settle in for a rare Saturday-night family outing only to end up a surly bystander to a spirited discussion about the end of colonialism or the vagaries of industrial policy. Train journeys were a particular hazard – he even coined a name for these informal seminars that so often occurred whenever he was on the move: the socialist train carriage. More than ten years after his death, his pithy soundbites and video extracts of his most passionate speeches regularly circulate on social media forums such as X and TikTok. None of his influential and accomplished peers, from Roy Jenkins to Tony Crosland, provoke anything like the same degree of contemporary popular interest.

What was his (very public) secret? Beyond the power of his commitment to socialist ideas, I believe the explanation lies in the fusion of a forceful and uncompromising moral personality, a continuous and lively engagement with changing social and economic forces, and an unusual ability to captivate and motivate audiences, plus the wider society's enduring and unhealthy English fascination with social class. My father came into politics in the post-war period (when class identities were even more pronounced than they are today) possessing all the conventional markers of a privileged, if progressive, background. His father, William Benn, and both his grandfathers were Liberal MPs. William was a government whip in the Liberal government of 1910–15. He left the Liberal Party to join Labour in 1927, after which he served as Secretary of State for India from 1929–1931; he subsequently refused to join Ramsay MacDonald's National Government. In 1942, King George VI gave William a peerage on the recommendation of Prime Minister Winston Churchill, who wanted to increase Labour's representation in the Lords amid a wartime coalition. Churchill took the advice of his deputy prime minister, Clement Attlee, on who the new peer should be; William was subsequently appointed Secretary of State for Air in the 1945 government.

Following a conventional Establishment education – Westminster School and then a degree in politics, philosophy and economics at Oxford University – my father served as an officer in the Royal Air Force and then worked as a producer at the BBC (with a short spell as a hilariously inept commentator at Wimbledon). He was elected to Parliament in 1950, when he was just twenty-five years old, making him the youngest MP in the House. In 1960, after the death of his father, and following the wartime death in 1944 of his beloved elder brother, Michael, who would have entered the Lords and inherited William's peerage, Tony automatically inherited the peerage. He fought for three years to renounce the title so that he could remain an MP, the political job he always most prized, eventually succeeding with the passage of the Peerage Act 1963.

For many, then, this conventional upper-class origin, yet rather unusual journey, infused his later turn to radical politics with the air of a latter-day Thomas More; the eloquent public man confidently defying the modern-day equivalents of monarchs and other powerful elites. The press loved to remind readers that he was born Anthony Neil Wedgwood Benn and was, for a brief period, Viscount Stansgate, and to suggest that his later preference for the simpler 'Tony Benn' was mere affectation, along with his pint tea mugs, teetotalism and omnipresent pipe. Many of his parliamentary colleagues, including those on the left, shared, if largely in exasperated and mocking tones in private, a view of 'Wedgie' as the bright, young hope of post-post-war Labour who had lurched towards an irresponsible socialism. This lurch had earned him the hostile soubriquet 'the most dangerous man in Britain' (although it was, somewhat bizarrely, novelist and poet Kingsley Amis who first came up with the term).

Much later he was designated a 'national treasure', a title conferred on him, he used to say, by an Establishment who now judged him a 'harmless, old gentleman'. I suspect that those who saw him in February 2003 address the 2-million-strong march in Hyde Park against the proposed invasion of Iraq or watched him challenge, live on the BBC, the rather bewildered female presenter who tried to stop him from broadcasting details of the Gaza appeal in 2008 would have good reason to quibble with that description. (As one below-the-line commenter on the exchange, still available on YouTube, observed: 'That, my friends, is one badass old man.') He was one of the few public figures to emerge not just unscathed but with his reputation enhanced following an interview with the TV satirist Ali G. His own writings, particularly his diaries and the short autobiographical volumes that he published later on in his life, increasingly emphasised his uncommon insider-outsider trajectory and himself as a distinct *personality*: that mix of unassailable confidence, easy wit and moral courage, plus an endearing streak of eccentricity revealed in his love of all manner of gadgets and his alarming habit of sometimes setting fire to his own clothes, through a failure to properly douse his tobacco pipe before putting it back in his pockets. As a human being, and as a father, he was huge fun, warm, tolerant and immensely loveable; he knew it and could turn it to good uncynical account.

However, something important risks getting lost in this concentration on his character, his background or even his mid-life turn to greater radicalism; and that is the chance for us to develop a deeper and truer understanding of a mainstream Labour politician of the mid-twentieth century. He was keenly aware of the changing currents of the nation and the globe, often predicting, with unnerving accuracy, the shifting nature of the economy, culture and the state; he developed an analysis of the ills of post-post-war British society that challenged both the presiding managerialism and monetarism of the period; and he also took up, and fought for, a vast number of important causes. My father was not a great theorist or intellectual nor even much of a reader; he was instead a pragmatic, inventive, exceptionally hard-working, quick-thinking public man who instinctively grasped the workings of the key institutions at the top of British society and was educated and socialised to feel at home within them. However, being an MP and minister did not further confirm any sense of innate superiority; instead, it introduced him to the wider world, to the lives, experiences and demands of those traditionally excluded from power – those from the trade union movement, women's liberation, the Black Power movement, student activism – all of which had a profound impact on him. In *The Searchers*, a sympathetic account of the political histories of five key figures on the modern Labour left, journalist Andy Beckett describes how, in May 1968, Tony sat, incognito, at the back of a series of meetings-cum-lectures put on by students who had set up the Free University of Bristol. He listened intently to debates on the Vietnam War, Black Power and the subject of revolution, writing in his diary afterwards that it made him realise how little real thinking he had done about politics for several years. Both this action and reaction were typical of him (apart from the going-unnoticed bit). He was an outspoken opponent of racism, supporting the Bristol Bus

Boycott of the early '60s after local trade unions refused to agree to the employment of black drivers or conductors; the leader of that boycott, Paul Stephenson, remained a friend for life. One of the accusations regularly levelled against him was that he romanticised or sentimentalised the lives and aspirations of the less privileged. For all his human blind spots (including an inability to sympathise with more materialist ambitions in others, and a tendency as he aged to lump all marginalised groups together), what most interests and moves me now is the *attempt* itself – the continual effort to remain curious about, and open to, the experiences and political analyses of others, and then to use the tools of his acknowledged privilege to challenge established narratives and structures.

In the first half of his parliamentary life, he showed considerable skill at the kind of steadfast political work that the German sociologist Max Weber perceptively characterised as the 'strong and slow boring of hard boards'. The new MP for Bristol South East entered Parliament eager to observe, and learn, its byzantine rules; in his early years, he kept himself apart from the left/right camps led by Nye Bevan and Hugh Gaitskell respectively, lobbying discreetly and energetically on the issues he cared about, and forging the incremental advances that are the stuff of day-to-day politics. He played a key role, for example, in organising Labour opposition to the great Suez misadventure of Anthony Eden's premiership. In just one day alone (31 October 1956), his diary records him organising a meeting in his Bristol constituency, lobbying the United Nations Association, persuading the Movement for Colonial Freedom to book Trafalgar Square for a Labour Party meeting, imploring Labour Party HQ to begin a national campaign, drafting a petition to be presented in the House, and persuading the Arab Society and the Labour Club at Oxford University to merge forces and hold not two, but a single public meeting on the Suez question, all of which helped to persuade Gaitskell to finally declare his 'complete and utter opposition' to the war. The keen young MP, who had already helped the Labour Party to modernise its media messaging, also led negotiations with the BBC to enable Gaitskell (who did not even own a television set) to record a broadcast setting out the opposition's case against Eden's actions. Meeting at the Labour leader's house to work on the text of that recording, he confided to his diary, 'I really felt that at that moment I was in the centre of the world.' Such is the draw – and drug – of life at the political top, and he always thrived when occupying a central role in the big political issues of the day.

As mentioned before, following his father's sudden death in 1960, he automatically became Viscount Stansgate and was barred from the House of Commons. There began his long battle to remain as a member of Parliament, an experience that gave him his first taste of genuine political outsiderness. I dimly recall the dark clouds that this period cast over our household, but it is only as an adult that I can grasp the desperately lonely slog and the economic anxiety that he – the main breadwinner for a family of four young children – must have experienced during those years. I can now also fully appreciate his skill and determination in representing himself in court, right up to the High Court, in order to change the law, and help bring into being the Peerage Act 1963: a piece of legislation which enabled members of the House of Lords to renounce their titles (but not in perpetuity). He renounced his own title twenty-two minutes after the Act came into force, declaring, 'I am the first man in history who, by Act of Parliament, is prevented from receiving a hereditary peerage. I am statutorily immunised.' Three weeks later he once again took up his seat in the Commons.

Growing up, we liked to hear about the ins and outs of the peerage case, and to look at the many political cartoons which were hung along the brick walls of the back corridor of his basement office, along with a framed copy of Churchill's letter of support, offering a financial contribution of £5 (a sum I always thought rather paltry). Without doubt, the peerage battle deepened my father's knowledge, and distrust, of the British constitution, particularly the brute reality of rigid deference to established laws and institutions, symbolised by the monarchy, and the long reach of political patronage via the

Crown prerogative. He wrote that 'in order to sit in Parliament I had to tell seventeen lies under oath', while as a privy counsellor 'there was another oath in which I pledged myself to support the monarch against "foreign prelates, potentates and powers", but this one was administered, that is read to me, and required no assent by me. It was like having an injection.' His prime allegiance, he always asserted, was to his constituents, not to the Crown. He was also an early critic of an unelected House of Lords, opposing the automatic right of bishops to sit in the second chamber; more generally, he was scathing towards the ossified hierarchical structure represented by dukes, marquises, barons and so on, and the mass of 'minor honours' dispensed in the name of the long-disappeared empire. It was, he argued, a kind of 'grace and favour' democracy, and led to his drawing up of the Commonwealth of Britain Bill, in which he tried to codify democratic constitutional change – many elements of which are still relevant today.

The experience of being in government only radicalised him further. In 1964, appointed Postmaster General, he proposed removing the queen's image from stamps. In the end, he only managed to shrink the monarch's head, but he did succeed in introducing a range of beautiful commemorative stamps, specially commissioned from the artist David Gentleman. In 1966, as Minister for Technology (or MinTech as it was widely known), he came to appreciate the technological developments of what he called 'the third industrial revolution', and how these developments were changing the relationship between government and citizen. These ideas found careful expression in his 1970 Fabian pamphlet *A Socialist Reconnaissance*, written after Labour's defeat that same year. In the 1974 Labour government, he became Secretary of State for Industry, a position through which he championed the often controversial Anglo-French airline project Concorde and began to seriously develop plans for extension of public control beyond the existing nationalised industries to a range of ailing private companies. Arguing for new forms of planning agreements for industry and schemes for wider workers' participation, he encouraged creative experiments such as cooperative production at the Triumph Meriden motorcycle factory and the drawing up of the Lucas Plan at Lucas Aerospace in Birmingham. As he argued in 1971, the person 'who actually has to do a job of work on the factory floor, or in a foundry, or in a shop or office, is the best person to know how his or her work should be organised'. As a Shadow Minister of Industry, Tony had also publicly supported the Upper Clyde Shipbuilders in Glasgow in their campaign for state rescue. Despite many of these policies appearing to honour the pledge in the 1974 Labour manifesto that 'the British People, both as workers and consumers, must have more control over the powerful private forces that at present dominate our economic life', Prime Minister Harold Wilson was becoming impatient regarding the radical proposals being put forward by his industry minister and demoted him to energy. Largely undaunted, Tony pioneered new projects such as the creation of an Energy Commission (he called it a kind of 'energy Parliament') and negotiated a number of complicated contracts that helped bring North Sea oil revenues to Britain. In his ministerial office, he put up a map of the United Kingdom, hung upside down, to make the point that London was not the centre of the UK, especially in the light of North Sea/ Scottish oil reserves. Within Cabinet, he was beginning to make the case for an Alternative Economic Strategy, building on the ideas of radical economists of the period who believed there was a third way between rigid centralised economic systems and the unjust anarchy of free market models.

By all accounts, he was an excellent minister but, for him, the greater gift of public office was, once again, the insight it gave him into new territories of experience, from the workings of government to the true roots of national industrial decline. He questioned the genuine independence of the civil service which he believed too frequently obstructed projects, particularly those that Labour politicians had been elected to implement (his diaries record his clashes with more than one powerful Permanent Secretary). He was an advocate of 'free thought and independent enquiry' among the civil service and security services; as early as 1956 he was arguing with typical playful exaggeration that 'far from dismissing any member of the Foreign Office who had read Karl Marx, my inclination would be to dismiss anyone who had not read Karl Marx'. Growing contact with the trade unions altered his views of the balance of power between workers and employers, the nation-state and capital. He foresaw the growth of multinationals and the dangers they posed to more egalitarian and redistributive national economies. An early enthusiastic adopter of the Common Market, he became critical of the ways in which bureaucrats in Brussels constrained British sovereignty. Increasingly convinced that the modern citizen was no longer satisfied with merely voting in a managerial-style government every five years, whether Labour or Conservative, he began to push for greater democracy at a number of levels. He advocated referenda on the major issues of the day and campaigned for greater accountability of Labour MPs and ministers to the grassroots membership of the party as a way to ensure that radical policies were not watered down in government.

As his radicalism – and his fame – grew from the early '70s onwards, my father became the target of a viciously hostile press. He was routinely derided and denounced as a member of the 'loony left' and, according to a *Guardian* analysis of press treatment of him, published shortly after his death, he was consistently 'demonised in highly slanted news, articles, editorials and cartoons'. (Fellow left-wing Labour MP Michael Meacher believed that much of the vitriol emanated from the right wing of the Labour Party.) During the 1974 general election campaign, for example, the *Daily Express* published a cartoon representing him as Adolf Hitler; on the day of the 1984 by-election in Chesterfield, in which he stood as the Labour candidate (after boundary changes, he had lost his Bristol seat in the 1983 general election), the *Sun* ran a feature headlined 'Benn on the couch: a top psychiatrist's view of Britain's leading leftie', in which the article claimed him to be 'a Messiah figure hiding behind the mask of the common man ... greedy for power and willing to do anything to get it'. The piece appeared to draw on the verdict of an American psychiatrist who subsequently admitted that his comments were never supposed to be taken seriously and that he had only offered a hypothetical opinion on a politician whom he had never met. My father later joked to a National Union of Journalists (NUJ) conference that 'there were 16,000 readers of the *Sun*' in Chesterfield, but even so 'the Labour vote went up'.

His comments to the NUJ conference were characteristic of one of the ways he dealt, in public at least, with the constant stream of misinformation and hostility: mocking his tormentors, and in so doing appearing to deny them their power. But that was hardly the whole story; he knew that the press coverage was highly damaging, and the pressure of constant attacks could make him seem harsh and humourless, feeding the already distorted media picture of him as an intolerant authoritarian. Arguably, the sustained propaganda of this period affected my mother, Caroline (herself lampooned as Lady Macbeth), and our family even more negatively than it did him; we possessed no right of reply nor had access to any public platform from which to counter misinformation. Some of my most vivid memories of my teenage years involve a sense of diffuse but distinct fear and mistrust; in addition to the constant press attacks, our phones were tapped (as my father half-joked in a speech to the Commons in 1992, 'my telephone is the only remaining link that I have with the British Establishment'), our rubbish sifted through. For a while, we had a policeman guarding our door. On the first day of my O-levels, I left the house to face a bank of photographers, some of whom chased me up the road, shouting aggressive and suggestive remarks; there were rumours of kidnapping threats against us children. In short, no member of our immediate family was left unmarked by those years. I certainly have no truck with those who argue that such behaviour is harmless or that the media themselves are part of a 'here today, gone tomorrow' culture (or what used to be called 'tomorrow's fish and chips paper'). When the media have someone in their sights, they can, in ways both crass and subtle, diminish, distort or even destroy them: but most importantly of all they have the power to *define* an individual in the public eye for decades to come. I saw it happen once with my father and I watched it happen all over again during Jeremy Corbyn's leadership of the Labour Party from 2015 to 2019; it will take future historians to strip the prejudice and vitriol away from perceptions of the left in both periods of modern history and establish a more balanced picture.

So were the seeds of the second and, in many ways, the most significant part of my father's political life planted; he began to use whatever platform was available to him to elaborate on his socialist, democratic, anti-imperialist analysis; to exercise a politics of conscience; to make the case for a very different set of social arrangements, rather like his heroes, the Levellers and Diggers of the seventeenth century, who he thought were (ultimately) more influential than Cromwell. As he argued in a speech in the mid-'70s, 'politics is really about education, and not about propaganda. It is about teaching more than management. It is about ideas and values and not only about Acts of Parliament, political institutions, and ministerial office.' He would use elections of all kinds – national or intra-party – to launch and explicate his ideas; if he had won his 1981 campaign against Denis Healey for the deputy leadership of the Labour Party, he and the left would have been in pole position to push through significant structural and policy changes in the party. Some of his later bids for Labour Party office had a more symbolic feel, such as his decision to stand against Neil Kinnock for the leadership of the party in 1988; a bid that many close to him thought a largely pointless exercise that risked merely underlining the weakness of the left.

As his influence within the higher echelons of the Labour Party began to dwindle, he increasingly sought an audience outside Parliament. His immersion in socialist thought came relatively late; he did not read the *Communist Manifesto* in full until my mother, Caroline, a radical intellectual in her own right, sneaked it into his Christmas stocking one year. Always eclectic in his approach, Tony picked up ideas as he went along, be it from radical political economists such as Francis Cripps or Stuart Holland or fellow MP and friend Alan Simpson, an early climate change campaigner and articulate opponent of globalisation. Caroline was his most stringent critic and wisest special adviser. Both his parents had a deep influence on his political thinking; he got his internationalism and deep commitment to parliamentary democracy from his father, William, and his interest in Christian thought – particularly the teachings of Jesus Christ – from his mother, Margaret, an ecumenical Christian and one of the earliest campaigners for women in the priesthood. He and I clashed, in various spirited ways, particularly over feminism when I was a teenager in the early '70s. I launched a poster campaign criticising what I saw as the unfair division of domestic labour in our household; he counter-leafleted in the hallways. He was a fast learner, able to grasp where injustices lurked under what many, particularly the powerful, deemed the natural order of things.

His gift for impassioned public argument turned him into a kind of secular preacher. Vocal solidarity with the oppressed, wherever they were, national or international, became ever more important to him as he resolutely supported a wide range of causes and campaigns. Long before many, including those within his own party, he understood that the so-called terrorists of today – Nelson Mandela in South Africa or Martin McGuinness in Northern Ireland – would become the statesmen of tomorrow. The Miners' Strike of 1984–5 was for him a seminal conflict, pitting the destructive and exploitative forces of the state and capitalism against the just might of the organised industrial working classes. He did not equivocate in his support for the striking miners or their leader, Arthur Scargill, and he always took an equal and eager interest in the emerging voices of miners' wives and families. Until his mid-eighties, when a series of small strokes slowed him down considerably, he travelled the length and breadth of the country, fuelled only by tea, Mars bars and bananas (of which he ate so many that he was briefly hospitalised with suspected potassium poisoning), speaking to crowded halls. His audiences were not just made up of those in sympathy with his radical politics; he also attracted many curious citizens of Middle England, who were surprised to enjoy the company of such an apparently reasonable man. He would travel to any picket line or demonstration, however far away, if he felt he could be of use. One of my favourite photographs of my father and mother shows them surrounded by masked rows of members of the English Collective of Prostitutes (ECP) during the ECP's occupation of the Holy Cross Church, Kings Cross, to protest 'police illegality and racism' against sex workers. (Not your usual publicity shot; certainly not your conventional family snap.) He was a forceful and leading opponent of the Falklands War and the joint US–UK assault on Iraq in 2003. In his late seventies, he became a highly visible, and therefore effective, president of the Stop the War Coalition.

Reflecting on the many dimensions of his dynamic life, it is clear that the tough-minded pragmatist, the innovative minister and the eloquent idealist were all important and ineradicable parts of his political make-up; I have often wondered how he might have sought to integrate these different aspects of himself if he had ever won the leadership of the Labour Party. He knew full well, and analysed in some detail, the 'formidable array of opposition' that would face any incoming socialist government. He often said that had he ever become leader of the Labour Party or prime minister, it would probably have ended in the manner imagined by his erstwhile political comrade and fellow MP Chris Mullin in his popular 1982 novel, *A Very British Coup*; at the book's close, left-wing prime minister Harry Perkins is forced out of office through a mix of deliberate press and security service manipulation and interference.

One is inevitably drawn back, time and again, to Tony's life: to both the high and low dramas and to the details of his politics. This volume, published in the centenary year of his birth, tries to do something different: to gather some of his seminal speeches and articles, and to showcase arguments that still have considerable power and, in some cases, have become more relevant as we move into what may be the most dangerous phase in global human history since the Second World War. With over sixty-five active years in public life, Tony's output was enormous; he delivered thousands of speeches and wrote hundreds of articles, a selection of which are here edited and organised around six key themes: 'The British State', 'The Many Faces of Democracy', 'Industry', 'Britain in the World', 'The Radical Tradition' and 'Politics after Politics'. A brief sense of the context framing each selected piece is provided, but here, at least, we can read his contributions free of the distorting prejudices of his detractors and, in particular, the embedded factionalism of Labour politics, whose frictions and failures are – oh so wearyingly! – always laid at the door of the left. Following its convincing election victory in 2024, one can only hope that the Labour Party will discover once again that it needs its left flank more than it needs to reflexively embrace cartoonish representations of many of its most influential socialist representatives as part of some Establishment-pleasing exercise.

I have two distinct hopes for this volume. The first is that it lays to rest a few myths, not just about my father but about the left in general – that collection of clichés and half-truths, laden with the usual lazy adjectives ('maniacal', 'unrealistic', 'destructive'), that I have observed, with mounting irritation, being disseminated throughout my own political lifetime. Time, too, to set aside the conventional-verging-on-simplistic narrative of a once decent, moderate chap who took a reckless swerve in mid-life from the steady middle of the political road to the hard-left shoulder, a shift often presented as a form of mental instability or immature recklessness. Reading so many of his early speeches and articles, it is clear how much of his radicalism was present from the start: his support for the various movements for colonial freedom, his early unequivocal opposition to South African apartheid, his rejection of McCarthyism in the US and his outspoken protests against Soviet incursions into Eastern Europe. As a young MP, active in campaigns against the hydrogen bomb, he quietly resigned from his first official post as a Parliamentary Private Secretary (PPS) when he realised that he would never be able to sanction the deployment of such a horrific weapon. The loss of so many lives at Hiroshima and Nagasaki haunted him, although he did not become a full-throated advocate of unilateral nuclear disarmament until later in his life.

The contributions gathered here also illustrate how ahead of their time he and many of his fellow socialists were. In 1968 he made a speech about broadcasting in which he broadly defended the role of the BBC but also argued for greater, and more diverse, public access to the media; to him, broadcasting was always too important to be left in the hands of the professional broadcasters. The speech caused a furore; for several days he was relentlessly attacked by colleagues and journalists, among others. Today, his argument seems not only completely obvious but to have perceptively anticipated a major shift in the role and structure of the media itself, including the growth of the Internet and social media, in which he took an eager if discerning interest towards the end of his life. He was also an early critic of the unaccountable power of the media in general, and how it worked to silence or distort radical critics. As early as 1971 he was examining, and endorsing, many of the claims of the women's movement while foreseeing how the movement might change the role of men, who have, he wrote, rather intriguingly, 'always been generous to themselves, in approving their own lifestyles'. Other ideas put forward in the speeches of the '60s and '70s still feel ahead of their time, such as his thinking around workers' control, industrial democracy and the Alternative Economic Strategy (AES); and his suggestion, for example, that the state itself should become an entrepreneur anticipates, by nearly half a century, the arguments of a number of influential contemporary economists. He was a vigorous supporter of freedom of information. He warned against the dangers of privatisation and globalisation long before many others. This volume also features several pieces on the anomalies and absurdities of the British constitution, including the case against an unelected second chamber. Progress on this issue has been slow and uneven. The 1997 Labour government first got rid of the bulk of hereditary peers; the 2024 Labour government is committed to abolishing the remaining ninety-two. It is at least no longer the case that, as Tony once argued, an attack on the hereditary peers is seen as an attack on the monarchy itself; however, no political leader has yet dared to go further and reform the honours system or to limit the powers, and extraordinary tax advantages, of the Crown.

My second hope is that this volume will inspire a new, and younger, audience. Tony understood that politics, and forms of political expression, must inevitably change with the times; we are all products of, and shaped by, the age in which we live. At the same time, principles tend to ricochet from era to era, altered – sometimes completely transformed – by specific political contexts. A belief in national sovereignty was at the heart of left-wing opposition to the then Common Market (now the European Union) only to be appropriated and poisoned by a form of far-right nationalism during the 2016 Brexit debate. Similarly, left criticism of the interference of the civil service found twisted expression in the disastrous and short-lived premiership of Liz Truss. Other causes do not change in their essentials. An early supporter of Israel, my father came to unequivocally oppose the occupation and oppression of the Palestinians; were he alive today, he would be in the forefront of those forcefully speaking out against the razing to the ground of Gaza by Benjamin Netanyahu's right-wing government, while emphatically rejecting the suggestion that such opposition is a form of anti-Semitism.

Helping to gather and edit these pieces, and reflecting upon what was, by most measures, an exceptional life, I feel only renewed admiration for his energy and eloquence, his wit and inventiveness, his thoughtfulness as well as his ability to retain his humanity under the severest provocation; but most of all I am moved by, and take great pride in, his bravery. He called out injustice wherever he saw it, and he was greatly – and rightly – loved for that singular fearlessness. Ultimately, however, he would have wanted his life and his ideas to exist not as any kind of example or guide but as a *resource* for those still fighting for the causes to which he gave his life: peace, social and economic justice, democracy and tolerance. He was an incurable optimist, a man who could write, as he entered his eighty-fifth year, that 'I am quite content to admit that I have still not decided what to do when I grow up'. He spoke often of the importance of hope – especially for the powerless – even if that same hope was perpetually dashed. He would have wanted his life and ideas to serve as a reminder that 'there is no final victory, as there is no final defeat. There is just the same battle. To be fought, over and over again.' This is the man, after all, who asked that the words 'He Encouraged Us' be carved onto the headstone that sits above his ashes: a request that we, his family, have gladly honoured.

Thanks to Ruth Winstone, Jad Adams, Joshua Benn, Hilary Benn and Stephen Benn for helpful comments on various drafts of the foreword.

I. The British State

1
On the Power of the Crown

In a letter to his grandchildren in 2010, Benn sets out the issues of the prerogatives of the Crown and how it pervades every level of the state.

When the United States came into being it threw out King George III and set up a republic, blowing up the medieval structure of class which still exists in Britain.

The legitimacy of that monarchy in Britain is based on military victory or conquest – whether by the Romans, William the Conqueror or the Wars of the Roses – and on the hereditary system in which the eldest son or daughter of successful conquerors has carried on the family line and possessions down to the present day.

This system is a constitutional monarchy, under which the people are allowed to elect the House of Commons but the Crown is hereditary and the Lords, which were once hereditary, are now ennobled by appointment, using the so-called Crown prerogative.

Here is the secret of the modern system: although the person of the monarch has no political power, the Crown has great powers and these powers are exercised in practice by the prime minister. That explains why every prime minister ends up supporting the Crown.

The prime minister appoints ministers, peers, archbishops and bishops by using the Crown prerogative and that same prerogative gives him or her the right to sign treaties and make a host of appointments – judges, police chiefs and army commanders. By using these prerogatives the prime minister escapes all responsibility to the elected House of Commons for the use made of them.

While the prime minister needs the Crown to be able to accept these appointments, the Crown relies on the political system to protect and ensure its survival. That is the deal that lies at the heart of our system of government. It is sometimes said that Britain does not have a written constitution, but of course it does and I can repeat it in full.

> I swear by almighty God that I will bear faithful and true allegiance to HM Elizabeth the Second, her heirs and successors, according to law.

Everyone in authority has, on appointment or election, to swear a similar oath. As a member of Parliament, on each of the seventeen elections I won, I had to swear that oath, even though my allegiance was never to the queen but to my constituents, whom I represented, to my colleagues and to my conscience. As a result, in order to sit in Parliament I had to tell seventeen lies under oath. As a privy counsellor there was another oath in which I pledged myself to support the monarch against 'foreign prelates, potentates and powers', but this one was administered, that is read to me, and required no assent by me. It was like having an injection.

Those who have sworn that oath include Roy Jenkins, Neil Kinnock and Peter Mandelson, all three of whom on appointment to the European Commission had to swear another oath that they would not be influenced by the interests of any government in the European Union.

It is in this way that the Crown has accommodated itself to the development of political democracy in order to survive, by conveying upon prime ministers the powers of the monarch.

But the Crown's social role is still crucial, despite all the changes and reforms of Parliament, because it continues to exist in the class structure of society: the dukes, marquises, earls, viscounts, barons, baronets and knights stand in their set place in the hierarchy, while under them is a lesser hierarchy which manifests itself in the mass of minor honours given to good and faithful servants: the recipients of CBEs, OBEs and MBEs – long after the British Empire has gone.

So important is the Crown to what I call the Establishment that the latter is ready to sacrifice a king to sustain the institution, as happened when Edward VIII was forced to abdicate because of an inappropriate marriage which it was thought might weaken public support for the Crown. And that could happen again.

When the British Empire ended, and the Commonwealth was set up in a mixture of nostalgia and arrogance, the king or queen was named in perpetuity as the head of that Commonwealth – which is why the present queen is queen of Canada, Australia and New Zealand, and why the presidents of India, Pakistan and South Africa seem happy to recognise the continuing authority of the British Crown in the Commonwealth.

It has no political or constitutional status, and it is strange that the heads of other Commonwealth countries do not insist that the title Head of the Commonwealth should rotate like the presidency of the European Union.

2
Democratic Rights or Ancient Traditions?

Is the British constitution, which has evolved over centuries, fit for purpose? Are the freedoms enshrined here based upon an understanding of rights or inherited traditions? In an excerpt from Common Sense *(1993), Benn sets out what a new constitution might look like, and the obstacles that might stand in its way.*

The British political system is so steeped in hierarchy that real progress is hindered at every point and the British people are perceived in the late twentieth century as quaint subjects of a discredited Crown; and as Britain draws close to the twenty-first century its people still enjoy no entrenched rights in their constitution, not even the right to vote: only obligations.

This lack of any guaranteed rights is underlined by the subservient status of the British people. The British constitution has entrenched this subservience by describing the people in law as subjects. The term 'citizen' itself was very controversial when, after the French Revolution, the words of the *Marseillaise*, '*Aux armes, citoyens*', struck terror into the hearts of Edmund Burke and the Tories and Whigs.

Once the concept of rights was recognised in France, the fear of the governing class was that this would inevitably lead to disturbing social changes in Britain, as it did. Three Conservative secretaries of state resigned in 1867 when the Reform Act, which extended the vote to include a small number of urban working-class men, was passed, describing it as 'a political betrayal which has no parallel in our annals'.

Rights and constitutions affect a country's economic, cultural and political life. They grant and set limits to power and its abuse; they define relationships between the individual and the government; and they determine the freedoms a citizen can enjoy. They are the fundamental elements which underlie the objectives of society.

The French constitution embraces 'liberty, equality and fraternity' as rights within the constitution, and the premise of the American constitution is 'life, liberty and the pursuit of happiness'. These two countries may be far from realising these objectives – liberty, equality, fraternity and the pursuit of happiness mean many things to many people – but their presence in the constitution affects the cultural parameters or values by which current practice is judged.

Whatever principles of government or notions of rights are produced within a national culture, if they are to be effective, leaders must be either willing or obliged to implement and respect them.

This tradition of democracy *claims* as its underlying principle the right of people to control the actions of government and hence their own lives and purposes and involves a notion of citizenship – a certain equality of status for all members of a society – and a recognition of the political, civil and social rights people need for status to be realised, a status which the British constitution does not however acknowledge.

The case for leaving the British constitution to 'evolve naturally' over the centuries has been unchallenged for too long. The arguments for a written constitution are widespread and have been accepted in most modern democracies, and have a special relevance today arising from the immense extension of state power and the danger of abuse. The present system in Britain, built upon the historical role of the monarchy, is geared to a strong executive, and its democratic elements are, as it were, accepted on sufferance by the governing class. A 'grace and favour' democracy is fragile, easily thrust aside while the legal precedents sustain a strong and unchallengeable executive.

Britain's peculiarly flexible, unwritten and obscure arrangements have allowed reform to be determined by the needs of the powerful, and not the needs of the people. This obscurity is evident in the total lack of entrenched rights, but also in the poorly defined relationship between Parliament and the courts. This results in some confusion over the basis on which the courts can choose to interpret existing law with the effect that, while the law remains on the statute book, such a creative interpretation can limit specific actions of government.

It is because of the peculiar historical development which led to Parliament itself being a high court, that there is an area of uncertain jurisdiction between Parliament and the courts, both of which are protected by their respective privileges. Thus judges, including magistrates, are appointed by the Lord Chancellor (using the Crown prerogative) but it takes drastic parliamentary action to remove them. And hence the occasional embarrassing paradox for governments that a judicial decision (for example, on government pit closures) will come up with a decision unfavourable to the government.

This mutual distancing between Parliament and the courts has long been accepted in practice, although the courts are required to uphold the laws passed by Parliament and the government is expected to obey the laws as interpreted by the courts, though it can change them.

Those in Britain who advocate a bill of rights often argue that they wish to transfer the power to uphold any entrenched rights from Parliament to the judiciary, specifically to limit the scope of action of a government.

Such a move would inevitably politicise judges, and if courts were given the last word on a bill of rights this would have the effect of limiting popular change. Instead it would entrench the status quo as the legitimate benchmark. And whereas mass political campaigns have forced the House of Commons to reverse some unpopular laws, few changes have come from the courts, which compared to the US Supreme Court have, with some notable exceptions, been conservative in their approach.

The interpretation of rights must, ultimately, remain in the hands of an elected assembly and be open to reform – simply because there will always be arguments about what 'rights' should be. Of course, democratic advances and rights are inevitably a compromise between that collective struggle, historical circumstance and the class politics existing at the time.

We do not have in Britain a single coherent set of organising principles. Instead in the past sixty years the notion of rights has developed piecemeal as a result of economic and political pressure on the state – a combination of progressive demands and capitalism's need for a healthy and basically educated workforce. William Beveridge, a Liberal, recognised this long before the Second World War.

In consequence, some social rights were recognised in the welfare state (though with questionable success), in the comprehensive school system, the health service and in public housing. Economic rights have been expanded from the protection of rights to private property, to include safeguards against unfair dismissal, to adequate redundancy pay, to statutory sick pay, to a maximum working week, to minimum pay and conditions, to statutory holidays and to collective provision of benefits for those out of work and pensions for the elderly.

There are many instances where the promise contained in the wording of rights has been denied or limited in practice. In particular the struggle between the right of labour to combine and the need for capitalism to be unfettered has moved backward and forward over the past 200 years as those with wealth and power have tried to protect their privileges in the path of pressure from below.

During the 1980s, Britain witnessed a reaction against many respected social, democratic and economic rights by a governing class confident of its ability to act beyond conventional constraints. This was Britain's flexible constitution in action.

The decade saw successive Conservative governments institute a wide range of undemocratic measures. The abolition of the Greater London Council was carried out 'in the best interests of London and Londoners'. Protection from unfair dismissal at work during the first two years of employment was removed. Many of the rights of trade unions were eroded. Strip searches against women at Greenham Common accused of a breach of the peace (for surrounding a nuclear base with enough atomic material in it to destroy the human race) were implemented. Members of CND, Liberty and trade unions were tapped and bugged by MI5.

Rights were extensively withdrawn in Northern Ireland, including the right to silence, and the right to broadcast interviews in support of the republican movement (such pressures including governmental efforts to ban interviews with Senator Ted Kennedy and Ken Livingstone on the subject of Ireland). The right to reinstatement after pregnancy was removed for women working for small businesses. Wages inspectors were cut by 60 per cent, currently allowing 30 per cent of firms to pay wages below the legal minimum set by the wages councils. Wages councils themselves were gradually removed, opening the way for employers to pay sweatshop wages. The right to equal pay for men and women failed to be implemented and differentials were higher than at any time since the Equal Pay Act of 1970.

Injunctions have been issued to prevent publication of sensitive and incriminating material such as appeared in *Spycatcher*. A senior civil servant, Clive Ponting, was taken to court for revealing secret documents embarrassing to the government about the sinking of the Argentinian ship the *Belgrano* during the Falklands War, even though he had made them available not to a foreign government, but to the British public.

And on top of this, 16 million people lost their right to legal aid – there may be a right to due process before the law, but there is no right of access to legal redress.

In reality, our constitution is an untidy and developing collection of compromises, the consequence of sullen responses to pressure; pressure which reflects the relative strength of wealth versus collective action at different periods of history. When powerful and undemocratic groups are forced to retreat, they wait for the time when they can regain their supremacy.

The superiority of our constitutional methods is illusory. Parliaments and legislatures in other democracies bear little resemblance to our own, often with different conceptions of rights and procedures resulting from different traditions of democracy. Those systems closest to our own were spawned in areas of the globe following periods of British colonial administrations, imposed without the consent of the indigenous populations.

The right to self-determination was never applied to the peoples of the British Empire. The 'Mother of Parliaments' was in existence throughout all of the years of colonial rule, responsible for the denial of rights. The Indian leader Gandhi, who had been arrested by the British colonial power, was ridiculed by Churchill who described him on his arrival at independence negotiations in New Delhi as the 'half-naked fakir loping up the steps of the Vice-regal lodge to parley on equal terms with the representative of the King Emperor'.

Gandhi, who had many friends in Britain, was asked on a visit to London in 1931, for the Round Table Conference on India, what he thought of civilisation in Britain, and responded, 'I think it would be a very good idea!'

What is needed is a radical reform of the British constitution establishing democratic accountability over those in power and democratic choice over the rights, principles and objectives which they will be obliged to protect and pursue. Throughout history objections have been raised to the simple principle of democracy on the grounds that 'the people' are incapable of taking important decisions, that government should be left to the elite, the experts, the technocrats.

The view that the best government must be government of the few has a long history and remains an important part of modern British psychology. The intellectual and cultural superiority of 'the higher classes' is used to justify the exclusion of the vast majority of people from influencing the hand of government. The rule of reason and principle, proven by tradition, should exclude the uneducated masses from power. The tradition of superiority based either on the virtues of the aristocracy or on special knowledge and expertise is recycled by academics and commentators.

For the aristocratic tradition, virtue stems supposedly from the disinterested nature of that class which is 'above politics'. This tradition is in contrast to the corruption and self-interest of business and 'trade' (or trade unionism). Thus the growth of a new commercial ethos has been seen as breaking with some rosy past.

The tension between the old and the new orders reveals how much British public life depended upon gentlemen's agreements: there were some things gentlemen just didn't do. The erosion of those values has strengthened the case for statutory edifices to protect basic freedoms like a bill of rights.

The aristocratic tradition – into which the rich and the clever are co-opted by peerages – with its interests protected by unity, continuity and stability, still conceives the workings of a modern democracy as factional, reforming and unstable.

The technocratic tradition by contrast is modern in outlook and offers a radical break with the past. Government can be operated through expertise, and society broken down into specialised functional units, governed by a system of rational management. The early Fabians Sidney and Beatrice Webb admired a technocratic administration of society along the lines developed in the Soviet state: not so much socialism as a sort of paternalism by civil servants and experts. The problems of government could, they believed, be solved by a rational discussion of ends among experts.

In its modern form, the tradition envisages a tidy separation of party politics and government from the specialised functions of the economy with an independent central bank, and management by industrialists, financiers and consultants.

Politics becomes a specialisation in its own right. Government becomes a process of administration, staffed by professionals, and though an element of popular accountability may be prudent, politicians are guided by advisers rather than their electorate. Political choices become the preserve of pundits, opinion researchers and think-tank reports. Economic choices are judged feasible or otherwise by consultation with self-appointed oracles in the City.

In both traditions, the people themselves are regarded as suspect – corrupt, ignorant or uninterested – and as the recipients or consumers of government policy rather than as citizens to whom government should be accountable.

The British people have acquiesced to many pronouncements from leading politicians and experts which were never true, and should never have been accepted. Leaders do not have a monopoly on competence, but they enjoy a substantial monopoly over the power to control the underlying nature of life in British society – to create security or insecurity, to protect the weakest or to liberate the fittest, to meet the needs of profit or the needs of people themselves. Choices such as these are of great importance.

In spite of declarations to the contrary that 'historical progress is dead', or that 'what we have is the best we can hope for', there is no reason why people should regard the society in which they live as the pinnacle of human achievement. If popular will is strong enough, important choices can still be made which will allow people to improve the condition of their lives. But they can only be made if the institutions of government are compelled to respond to democratic pressures.

Not only should people be free to campaign for enforceable rights which governments will then adhere to, but in addition the choice of rights, which includes the democratic rights established by the constitution, should be left to the people whom they will affect. This choice is not a final one. Rights need to be continually reassessed. New campaigns, new issues and new ideas will gather support while others decline. Furthermore, there has to be some guarantee that those empowered to implement or uphold any particular system of rights actually do so in practice. It is governments and the courts which implement rights and there must be some method for ensuring that they are held accountable to the people whom their power affects. If they are not, then there is no guarantee that rights which have formally been recognised will be effective or respected in practice.

Britain's government owes more to the aristocratic and technocratic traditions than to any other. We have inherited a hierarchical system of government dominated by the ethos of the Crown. Reforms over the years have left relatively untouched a number of constitutional devices which, originally designed to empower the monarch, can be used by the prime minister and senior Cabinet ministers to distance the actions of government from accountability to the electorate. The power of democracy is that it enforces accountability, and can replace those found wanting. An undemocratic political system has accountability too, but the governors are accountable to those *above* them and allegiance flows up the social hierarchy. It is this which distinguishes government in the spirit of the good king from government in the spirit of democracy.

But the chain of democratic accountability in Britain is very weak. The House of Commons is a very imperfect legislature. The government can dominate it with relative ease: individual MPs have inadequate resources to counter government power even if they wanted to, the hours are difficult, it is unrepresentative of the majority of the population, and the business is too great to allow proper scrutiny of the administration. The prime ministerial system

Democratic Rights or Ancient Traditions?

of government has been described as an 'elective dictatorship'. In reality, the power of government is severely limited, though not by the electorate: the House of Commons is only one of several groups or, for lack of a better term, institutions, whose support the prime minister will require to retain power and govern 'successfully'.

Members of Parliament and members of powerful institutions may believe they sustain a democracy. But the political system they inhabit embodies the idea of government by the wise expert. The nature of the British constitution not only isolates the executive powers under Crown prerogatives from control by the House of Commons, but also engenders conservatism and superiority within the governing classes.

This superiority is derived directly from the Crown, which is both the fountain of all honour and the source of much power and which provides a means for securing the loyalty of bureaucrats, the military and secret services as servants of the nation rather than the people. The Crown is the keystone in the arch of the state. The authority of tradition serves to strengthen the pillars of hierarchy and privilege on which the Crown rests and to divert attention from the absurdity of a hereditary head of state. Each part of the architecture must be preserved to protect the whole. Anyone bold enough to challenge the tradition of heredity in the Lords, for example, is accused of undermining the Crown. The Lords must remain intact because without it the monarchy would be threatened and that would threaten the British way of life itself. It is a symbiotic dependence – the Crown and the House of Lords protect each other.

Nevertheless, the strength of the Crown should not be underestimated. It holds in its power considerable rewards which reinforce a culture of subservience undermining and opposing a culture of democratic accountability under which we elect, support and maintain our representatives.

There is no greater illustration of the power of deference than when, after his abdication as Edward VIII, the Duke of Windsor, in an interview with the TUC-run *Labour Herald*, offered himself as president of a republic should a Labour government want to introduce one. The TUC, however, refused to print the story for fear that it would be thought to be republican.

Tradition has been used to block full-scale constitutional reform.

People speak of our unwritten constitution's flexibility and ability to survive through the centuries as a virtue but its continuity, which is the preservation of the powers of the Crown from democratic control, is precisely its weakness.

The British people are urged not to destroy a system which is said to have evolved to fit the needs of British society. According to John Patten, 'We turn against grand designs and build on what has worked; on what has been built up generation by generation by our people of all Parties in all Parliaments.' The constitution is the embodiment of the wisdom of parliaments throughout the ages which outweighs the impertinent claims of any one generation. Because the constitution has lasted, it is argued it has value.

But evolution of a constitution does not imply that it is the best, merely that the system which has evolved has best fitted its environment. An environment where power has been given to privilege and hierarchy will, over a period of time, have favoured certain outcomes over others, and will undoubtedly have protected those aspects of the constitution which favoured established or powerful interests. Sometimes the process of change will have worked in the interests of democracy, but will only have done so when popular pressure has combined with the willingness of established elites to allow reform.

Even so, the present system with all its faults, the traditionalists argue, should be preserved from change because it continues to enjoy the consent of the people. But passivity does not imply consent and never has done. An increasing number of people now harbour a deep and growing cynicism about politics and politicians. The government's complacency and lack of responsiveness has caused people to retreat reluctantly from political remedies, and to switch where they are wealthy enough to do so to individualistic ones – private health insurance, private housing, private education – with all the uncertainty and cost that involves, and with the outcome that a large number are far worse off.

This resignation and pessimism should not be mistaken for a welcoming endorsement of the status quo. People might accept things they never should, simply because they are encouraged to lack the confidence and hope that something can be done.

Collective solutions designed to meet society's needs failed to live up to expectations, but people must examine how far the blame rests with the political system which created local government, welfare services and nationalised industries in its own hierarchical, centralised and unresponsive image.

It is the nature of political institutions and not the nature of collective provision which has contributed to Britain's decline; what is needed is a new constitution which allows people to create their own solutions and define their own living conditions and removes the power from elites to do things for them.

3
The Common Ownership of Land

On the 900th anniversary of the Domesday Book, Benn explores the question of land ownership. It was one of the four main themes presented to the Labour National Executive Committee (NEC) by Benn and Eric Heffer, and it was rejected in 1986. In an age of privatisation, and the housing crisis in particular, the nationalisation of land remains a potent idea.

Nine hundred years ago this month, William the First, who was spending the winter near Gloucester, resolved to have a survey made of land ownership in the Kingdom of England, which he had conquered twenty years earlier after defeating Harold at the Battle of Hastings. Survey teams were dispatched everywhere, and recorded the names of all those who had owned the land before 1066.

King William understood the value of owning the land as a source of power and wealth, and so the Domesday Book records the names of his Norman friends to whom that land had been given, together with the number of slaves, serfs and workers there were on each farm, as well as the number of implements and animals. That is how the Domesday Book came to be compiled and it was a formidable achievement, the whole project being completed within a year.

Yet today, 900 years later, there is no proper land register, and we know that vast areas of the country are still owned by relatively few great landowners, including the dukes, and increasingly by major corporations, who are living well as a result of the escalating price of land.

Meanwhile spiralling land values are raising rents and costs in the big cities and helping to cause, or worsen, the inner-city poverty crisis; while, in the rural areas, the same increase in land prices is driving small farmers and smallholders off the land, causing depopulation and increasing the drift to the overcrowded towns.

Yet the money needed to develop both town and countryside is being withheld by rate-capping and the reduction of the rate support grant. Indeed, the government is now talking of replacing the rating system altogether with a flat-rate poll tax of £160 a year which would increase the burden on the poor while the richest people would continue to live, literally, off the fat of the land they own.

These are some of the reasons why the demand for the common ownership of the land is now being reopened – a demand that goes back over many centuries, and was taken up by the Liberals who happily sang Lloyd George's famous land song which said it all: 'The land, the land, the land on which we stand; why should we be paupers with the ballot in our hand? God gave the land to the people.'

In Scotland the memory of the highland clearances, which expelled so many crofters from their homesteads, is still alive. The abuse of power by Scottish landowners is still resented.

There is another factor too, which has given a fresh sense of urgency to this whole movement for common ownership, and that is the emergence of the environment as a major political issue. The Green movement especially has campaigned to prevent the despoliation of our countryside in the interests of profits, as is bound to happen under private ownership. Moreover, the huge giveaway of public assets, in the name of privatisation, has reminded people that a similar policy was used to steal our common lands in the Middle

Ages, by passing thousands of Enclosure Acts which handed our land to big landowners, some of whom are still in possession.

It has been estimated that if we did own our own land again, the gross revenue payable to the community could amount to £70 billion a year. Even allowing for some modest compensation, according to need, for those big landowners who had been required to give back our land, the new income might even replace the rating system altogether.

A few years ago, when oil and gas were first discovered off our coast, it was considered normal and natural to demand that the British people be allowed to own it, so that the revenues would come to us all. Some such action will have to be taken soon to find new sources of revenue to pay for community services, if we are not to end up with some poll tax plus further savage cuts in local community services.

We must now put the question of land ownership back at the top of the political agenda. And when better to begin than on the 900th anniversary of the Domesday Book of 1086?

4
The Disestablishment of the Church of England

Why does the Church of England remain a central plank of the British state with Lords spiritual in the House of Lords? In this article from the 1980s, Benn argues for rethinking the entire structure of the state – from the constitution to the established church.

I would like to take this opportunity to argue the case for the liberation of the Anglican Church from the British state by the disestablishment of the Church of England.

Though I was confirmed as an Anglican I have, over the years, become more and more interested in the relevance of the social message of Jesus the carpenter of Nazareth about peace, justice and the brotherhood and sisterhood of all humanity, from which so much of the socialist faith derives, and less and less concerned with matters of doctrine, mystery and mythology, though I deeply respect those whose beliefs centre on the creeds.

I was brought up to believe in 'the priesthood of all believers' and retain considerable scepticism about those bishops and clergy who might claim a prescriptive right to interpose their own interpretation of the Gospels, or the faith, between the people and the Creator – still more if those same bishops have been appointed by political patronage. In short, I regard myself as a serious student of the teachings of Jesus – no more and no less.

My argument is a simple one and can be briefly summarised. It is that the teachings of Jesus, about brotherhood and sisterhood and peace, and the need to preach them freely, have acquired a new urgency and importance in the crisis which now threatens to overwhelm the world, and must necessarily lead many Christians to challenge the role of the state as the instrument of government, and the status quo which it sustains, and hence should not be subject to state power.

The debate about the establishment of the Church of England goes far back into our history, and has, in the past, aroused great passions. The conflict which developed between the Pope and Henry VIII culminated in a complete break and the Acts of Supremacy of 1534, and those that followed it, required all subjects to recognise the Crown as head of the new Church of England, and to accept that church as the only legitimate church. This was a political and not a theological breach. It protected the state from criticism by the church, thus creating the very problem which now strengthens the state and weakens the church.

The real issue hinged on who should exercise ecclesiastical power in England, and the controversy over the king's marriage to Anne Boleyn in 1533, which the Pope would not allow, was the occasion rather than the cause of the dispute. But what emerged was a nationalised church, suppressing others, first subject to the king's personal authority; then, as the powers of the Crown came, over the centuries, to be shared with Parliament and people, the control of the church passed with it.

Theological arguments ebbed and flowed within the church, and Parliament insisted upon conformity with its decisions. The Blasphemy Act of 1697, which made it a criminal offence for Christians to 'deny any one of the persons in the Holy Trinity to be God', was only repealed in 1967. The Bible, long kept out of the hands of the laity for fear that it might undermine the authority of the priests, and encourage those who were campaigning for social justice, could only be printed by the authority of the king, as it had first been by Henry VIII. The Book of Common Prayer was a schedule to the 1662 Act of Uniformity and the original text, in the Houses of Parliament, still carries the jagged ribbons by which it was attached to that Act. These successive acts of uniformity were strictly enforced against all dissenters and independents.

The royal prerogative, by which archbishops, bishops, deans and others were appointed, was transferred to the de facto control of successive prime ministers who still today are free to exercise their discretion between candidates recommended by the church's Crown Appointments Commission, as Mrs Thatcher did in appointing Bishop Leonard to the diocese of London in 1981, though it is believed he was not the first choice of the church.

The two archbishops and the bishops of London, Durham and Winchester automatically sit in the House of Lords along with others who enter, in rotation by seniority, all exercising, as Lords spiritual, their rights to speak and vote as legislators. At the same time Anglican priests are held to be disqualified from election to the House of Commons on the grounds that they are represented by their bishops in the House of Lords – a disqualification criticised by the bishop of Bath and Wells in his 1982 Christmas message. The argument for this disqualification is not sustainable since the appointment of bishops precludes a democratic election from that clerical 'representation'. In addition, the church has its own assembly for handling its own internal affairs, which was made possible by the Enabling Act.

In practice, the Church of England has become a residual and comprehensive spiritual home for all who wish to use its services in the parishes in which they live, providing official support for the role of religion under the Crown as part of the social fabric of our society, now tolerant of all religions. Opposition to disestablishment would come from those who accept this system and fear that if its continuity was disturbed it might destabilise and secularise our whole way of life and diminish the influence of religion in all its manifestations.

We have grown so accustomed to these arrangements that their manifest absurdities and dangers are hardly noticed and rarely discussed in public.

How, for example, can we justify a situation where the monarch combines the functions of being, at one and the same time, supreme governor of the Church of England when in England, but who changes her denomination to preside over the Church of Scotland when in Scotland – even though in that capacity she enjoys no power of patronage nor can Parliament intervene in Scottish church affairs?

Suppose for a moment that the Church of England was not now established and imagine the public outcry there would be if a member of Parliament were to demand the nationalisation of that church to subject its leaders to political patronage and control of the order of its services. Or suppose it was argued that state control should now be extended to cover the Catholic, Nonconformist, Jewish, Buddhist, Hindu or Muslim communities.

These are all powerful arguments for disestablishment, but the case is stronger still if we examine the actual effects of having an established church in the current situation.

Take first the attitude of Christians to the issue of nuclear war. Many Christians who are not pacifists have now concluded that the old doctrine of a just war cannot apply to the production, ownership or use of nuclear weapons which would escalate armed conflict to the levels of genocide.

The bishop of Salisbury, who chaired the committee which wrote the report 'The Church and the Bomb', has raised this very issue and has won wide public support for its conclusions even though it was rejected by the synod. In 1982 the Assembly of the Church of Scotland voted by 255 votes to 143 in favour of unilateral nuclear disarmament.

But could the established Church of England take up a position on nuclear weapons that brought it into direct conflict with the government, while the Crown remained the titular head of both church and state? Mr Peter Blaker, the Minister of State for Defence, made this point on ITN on 6 August 1982, when he said: 'Obviously we would not be happy if the Church of England was to adopt a policy different from that of the government.'

Even the mild and reasonable arguments for the spirit of reconciliation, which the Archbishop of Canterbury introduced into his sermon at the service of thanksgiving at St Paul's Cathedral after the Falklands War, apparently incurred the displeasure of the prime minister, who seems to have wanted a more militaristic celebration of the victory. And why not, since she appoints both archbishops and bishops?

Given that power of patronage, what bishop or cleric, with hopes of moving into Lambeth Palace or Bishopthorpe, would now dare to mount a sustained campaign against the militarism and jingoism which are officially blessed from No. 10 Downing Street?

But even if all these problems could be resolved, a nationalised church could never take its proper place in the world ecumenical movement. Yet the teachings of Jesus have spread across the world and know no national boundaries. Like the ideas of socialism, they are international in outlook and perspective. That is another powerful reason for liberating the church from the control of any nation-state with its national, rather than its international, outlook. Religious conviction is also a very personal act and cannot be regimented by legislation or enforced by the state. So, both the international nature of Christianity and its reflection in personal faith point away from the idea of having a state religion.

I believe that the time has come to begin a national campaign for disestablishment. How it is to be done can be safely left for future discussion. It would certainly end all ministerial and parliamentary control over appointments, doctrine and worship, and end the automatic right of bishops to sit in the House of Lords. It would necessarily free the monarch of the day to worship in any way that he or she might wish, or not at all, as a member of any church or none.

The financial arrangements would need to be looked at separately, and if Parliament thought it right that any public money should be paid to the Church of England, for example for the upkeep of cathedrals or church buildings, the financial claims of other denominations would need to be considered on the basis of absolute equality.

All this could be settled once the principle of disestablishment had been agreed. There are of course clear precedents to guide us. The Church in Wales was disestablished in 1920 after the passage of the 1914 Welsh Church Act. Since then the Crown has not had the power to appoint bishops in Wales and such bishops do not sit in the House of Lords, and no significant body of opinion has been expressed in favour of re-establishing it as a state church.

There is certainly support within the Church of England for disestablishment and many in the Anglican community worldwide might welcome and approve the liberation of the Church of England to release it to work more effectively. Disestablishment might also appeal to the large Catholic community, to the free churches and even to the Church of Scotland, which is in a special position, established but not under direct state control. In addition, there are over a million Jews, Buddhists, Hindus, Muslims and Sikhs and, according to the Gallup polls, over a quarter of the whole population who would classify themselves as humanists, following no particular faith, who might favour a change that gave them equality of status.

The case for disestablishment thus rests on various grounds: historical and theological; practical and moral; constitutional and democratic; international and equitable. But the strongest case of all, as it would need to be argued within the Anglican community, would necessarily hinge on the argument for liberation. As the crisis of our society deepens, the moral basis that must underpin all political judgements is becoming clearer and clearer, and the church must be liberated from its subservience to the state.

Britain needs a liberation theology which has the courage to preach against the corruption of power by speaking for those who are its victims. Nowhere is that more necessary than in the inner cities where the poverty and deprivation are most acute, and where hard-pressed Anglican clergy feel themselves under the greatest pressure compared to their colleagues with more prosperous suburban or rural parishes. The church needs freedom, to challenge the decisions of government, Parliament and the whole Establishment, and the materialist values which have elevated the worship of money above all else – and the people need to know that these rotten values are not endorsed by a state religion.

If democracy is to reflect through its decisions the deeper needs of humanity, and its aspirations for international peace and justice, and for brotherhood and sisterhood in our relations with each other, we must now break the link between church and state.

5
Power, Parliament and the People

After the experience of the landslide victory of Thatcher in 1979, Benn questions the residual potency of the Establishment in the British state, and beyond. He asks what obstacles this hegemonic bloc would put in the way of a majority should Labour win an election.

The Labour movement's commitment to parliamentary democracy, from the days of the Chartists, stems from the belief that the industrial organisation of labour, plus the use of the ballot box, can become the agents that will alter the structure of society. This will be done peacefully by electing a government with a majority in the House of Commons, which can then use the statute book and the machinery of the state to bring about that transformation by consent.

But the assumption that Parliament and the machinery of government, once they are at the disposal of an elected Labour majority, can be free to achieve the objectives of that administration raises a number of questions for socialists.

Traditionally, many on the left have believed that the state machine in capitalist society existed primarily to uphold and reinforce that system, whichever party is in office. They sensed that it operated through its natural links with the Establishment, links that remain in existence whoever forms a government.

In recent years the continuity of the policy objectives of the mandarins in the Civil Service, and the power which they exercise, has come under close examination, and tends to confirm the left's analysis. The role of top officials in the Treasury, the Foreign Office, the Home Office and the Ministry of Defence in particular has been seen as having central significance in controlling economic policy, defence, the police, the intelligence services and Britain's relations with the rest of the world whoever is in power.

If Labour can win a majority, what then are the prospects for a Labour Cabinet, appointed personally by a Labour prime minister to form part of 'Her Majesty's Government' to take charge in a meaningful sense after they have received popular mandate?

There were important achievements during the years in power (1964–70; 1974–9), but none of those governments secured the central objective of bringing about 'a fundamental and irreversible shift in the balance of wealth and power in favour of working people and their families'. It is natural, in searching for an explanation for this failure and in regrouping to secure a better future, that the role of the state should have been studied. It is equally natural that this study should have led to a charge of hostility to parliamentary democracy, for any deep analysis of the true nature of our system of government has led many people to question just how democratic it really is.

Let us consider the situation that would be created by the election of a Labour government, with a working majority. Beneath the euphoria, all socialists will know that the real task of taking power will only just have begun.

True, a monetarist and militarist group of Tory ministers will have been swept into opposition. True, the new House of Commons will contain Labour MPs in sufficient numbers to repeal old legislation and enact new laws and budgets. True, there will be genuine good will among a majority of electors, or else we would not be there.

But in another sense nothing will have changed. Those who control the centres of financial, economic, military and administrative power, and those who own or run its mass media will be meeting to discuss urgently the best way of preventing the new government from carrying out policies to which they are bitterly opposed.

The House of Lords, determined to prevent its own abolition, will still have a huge Tory majority and will be planning how to use it to protect its own position and frustrate the wishes of the electors, perhaps with the help of the judges.

The senior ranks of the Civil Service, who have played a large part in shaping the policies of the outgoing government, will be in conclave to defend those policies and to deflect ministers from reversing them too far. The defence chiefs, fearing the removal of their nuclear weapons and a cutback of their budget to bring us in line with European levels of expenditure, will be discussing, probably with their NATO colleagues, how to obstruct the new Cabinet.

The Governor of the Bank of England will be considering how the City can be mobilised effectively to safeguard the profits it has been making from its global transactions. And big business, together with the bankers and financial houses, will be arranging discreet gatherings to discuss how to insulate themselves from the effects of the new policies they fear will be introduced.

The security services, whose files will contain full entries on all the new MPs, will be hoping to influence the allocation of portfolios to exclude certain people from key jobs and to prevent those whom they dislike but who do get appointed from having access to information that MI5, MI6 and Special Branch regard as especially sensitive.

The newspaper proprietors will permit a short honeymoon for the government in their editorials, partly because the public support for Labour, as expressed through the ballot box, will include some of their readers and cannot be ignored at the outset; partly to build up a wholly false reputation for their newspapers of having given the new government 'a fair chance'; and partly because they may cherish the hope that a highly selective diet of skilful praise and cynicism could be used to woo some Cabinet members away from their commitments.

In the Common Market Commission in Brussels and the NATO headquarters nearby, in the IMF and at the head offices of the multinationals, position papers will have been prepared of two kinds. The first will be for use in direct negotiations with the new Labour government, to show how far these organisations are prepared to go to accommodate the government's aspirations and how it would be impossibly dangerous to seek to go all the way with it. The second set of strictly confidential papers would consist of contingency plans to frustrate those policies in case it became clear that Labour really meant business and could not be shifted by persuasion.

Across the Atlantic in the White House, the Pentagon, the State Department and the Treasury, they would be studying more detailed plans, based on long-term appreciations, updated regularly and given added urgency as soon as the polls in Britain had begun to hint at the possibility that a Labour government might be elected. The options set before the president and the National Security Council would include every possibility, from an offer of extending special economic and defence aid to buy off unwelcome policies, to highly classified plans to discredit individuals in the Labour government or destabilise it completely.

The listing of this formidable array of opposition which the next Labour government will face is not intended to create a sense of despondency or to divert us from the tasks we have set ourselves.

Quite the reverse is the case. It is to encourage us to think through the consequences of what we have decided is necessary if we are to tackle the basic problems that beset society by methods that are both democratic and socialist.

The cruellest hoax we could play on the electorate would be to pretend that we could transform their prospects or realise their hopes without major reforms of the institutions that wield power in Britain, whoever sits in No. 10 or occupies the ministerial offices in Whitehall.

Those who say it will not be easy when Labour is returned to office are right, but not always for the reasons they believe. We must not deceive ourselves into believing that our opponents will accept fundamental change provided it is carried through democratically. They will not. Their interest lies in preserving the power and wealth that they have against all attempts to change it. It is we who are the advocates of democracy and they who only pay lip service to it.

When a Labour government with socialist policies, and the will to implement them, is elected we shall soon learn that they will fight it all the way and seek to undermine it. That is why democracy, even more than socialist rhetoric, is so much feared and hated by those whose power derives not from a parliamentary majority but from the ownership and control of land and money, and the occupancy of key power bases in the administration, the military or the media.

It is for all these reasons that the next Labour government's success or failure will depend critically on its readiness to adopt a major programme of institutional reform designed to widen and deepen the democratic influences in our society, at the same time as it implements economic and social reform.

The Crown prerogatives, most of which are exercised by ministers, confer immense powers which can, if abused, frustrate the wishes of the electorate and undermine democracy. The House of Lords still retains a crippling power of delay. The prime minister enjoys immense and unacceptable powers of personal patronage, working with a Civil Service elite in a highly secretive manner. They are outside the effective control of the House of Commons which has, in key respects, abandoned its responsibility to hold the government to account, to itself and to the electors.

The Labour Party and the trade union movement are still held at arm's length from the government, even when the party is in office and they suffer from serious defects in their own democracy, despite some improvements in recent years. Thus, that direct connection between the people who are governed and those who govern, which should characterise a democratic system, is far from being effective, leaving much real power where it has always rested, free from the reach of public accountability. Labour ministers may gain office from time to time, but Labour will never be in power and socialism will never be achieved however many electors vote for it.

It is against this background that the reforms we need can best be understood. They all involve practical action early in the lifetime of the government.

II. The Many Faces of Democracy

6
A Socialist Reconnaissance

In 1970, Labour having lost the election, Benn began his journey towards radical politics with this pamphlet, published by the Fabians. This truncated version of The New Politics: A Socialist Reconnaissance *is often seen as the foundational text for Bennism that would evolve over the next four decades.*

This pamphlet is a reconnaissance of some of the issues, arising from industrial and technical change, which may be moving into the centre of politics in the '70s; and it suggests ways in which a socialist party working within the limits of democratic consent might approach them. It does not seek to spell out detailed policies.

Parliamentary democracy and the party system have in recent years been criticised not only for their inability to solve some of our problems but also for their failure to reflect others adequately. The public have been assumed by the strategists on both sides to be moved by economic arguments above all others. Important as these issues are, and will continue to be, they are not the only ones that matter, and the public may have sensed this more quickly than the political parties.

Fewer people now really believe that the problems of our society can be solved simply by voting for a government every four or five years. More people want to do more for themselves, and believe they are capable of doing so, if the conditions could only be created that would make this possible.

If the Labour Party could see in this rising tide of opinion a new expression of grassroots socialism, then it might renew itself and move nearer to the time when it is seen as the natural government of a more fully self-governing society. Unless we succeed in doing this there is a danger that the Labour Party might get bogged down in stylised responses and fail to attract the support of those, especially among the young, who want to see more real choices in politics, and less of a personal contest between alternative management teams.

If we want to make the Labour Party more relevant, we must as socialists begin with an analysis of the underlying changes which are now taking place in our industrial system.

We live at a time in history when both the personal and collective material options open to us, and the expectations we have, are far greater than ever before. Yet a large number of people feel that they have progressively less say over the events that shape their lives, because the system, however it is defined, is too strong for them.

Many of the social tensions in Britain which we are now struggling to resolve actually derive from this feeling of waning influence. It is impossible to believe that the only liberation required can be achieved, as conservatives suggest, by freeing a few thousand entrepreneurs from some government interference and providing them with higher material incentives by cutting taxation. Nor can public ownership, economic planning and improved and more egalitarian social services, essential as all these are, providing the basis for further advance, alone provide the answer. There must be further fundamental changes to liberate people and allow them to lead fuller and more satisfying lives.

People today – these new citizens with this new power – have responded to the pressure of events by banding themselves together with others of like mind to campaign vigorously for what they want; and thousands of such pressure groups or action groups have come into existence: community associations, amenity groups, shop-stewards movements, consumer societies, educational campaigns, organisations to help the old, the homeless, the sick, the poor or underdeveloped societies, militant communal organisations, student power, noise-abatement societies and so on.

These, like the early trade unions or political groups during the first industrial revolution, derive their causes, their influence and their power in some way from industrial change. Some of these groups come into being for a specific purpose and then dissolve again; others emerge as continuing organisations with political objectives to press certain issues but usually not to nominate candidates for election locally or nationally. They are a most important expression of human activity based on issues, rather than traditional political loyalties, and are often seen as more attractive, relevant and effective by new citizens than working through the party system.

They also are producing a new set of political leadership committed to a cause rather than the search for elected authority. The relationship that develops between this new structure of issue politics and the political parties, especially the Labour Party, *is* of crucial importance. Some such groups will be working for causes hostile to our own objectives. But the majority, being the expression of human values against oppression by authority and the system of centralised power, would be natural allies if only we can discover the right sort of relationship with them.

We must not mistake their criticism for hostility, nor resent the fact that those who work in them have chosen such a role in preference to working exclusively within the party. Each side has its own part to play in the process of socialist construction, and *this* is, in practice, recognised by the fact that many individuals work both in the action groups and in the party. Their importance lies in the proof they offer, by their existence and their successes, that people do have more power than many of them realise in achieving change from below.

The new citizen, despite their fears and doubts and lack of self-confidence, is a far more formidable person than their forebears.

Increasingly they dislike being ordered around by anyone, especially if they suspect that those who exercise authority underestimate them.

A growing number of them – everywhere – are just not prepared to accept poverty, oppression, inequality, bureaucracy, secrecy in decision-making, or any other derogation from what they consider to be their basic rights – and are gradually acquiring the power to enforce that view upon the societies in which they live.

In sketching the changing relationship between democratic politics – the huge new organisations – on the one hand, and the new citizen on the other, both created by technology, there is a common thread of argument. It is this: authoritarianism in politics or industry just doesn't work anymore. Governments can no longer control either the organisations or the people by using the old methods.

The Labour Party is uniquely fitted to understand that modern democracy requires a revitalisation and reformulation on a more sophisticated basis, of the old communications philosophy of government enshrined in the idea of Parliament as a talking shop. Indeed, unless we can develop such a framework we will never succeed in reconciling the twin realities of the age in which we live – on the one hand the need for supremely good national and international management of complex systems and on the other hand the need to see to it that the new citizen, who is also a potential beneficiary of such new power, is able to direct and control more effectively the uses to which technology is put.

This theme of continuing responsibility by leaders to the people and by the people to each other runs throughout the twelve issues next identified for a further socialist reconnaissance.

1. Human Dignity through Development and Diversity

It does not follow automatically from man's incredible scientific discoveries that industrial development will come quickly enough to save us all from starvation, or that he will gain control over the new power that he has created, or that with higher living standards he can develop in real freedom. Indeed, the possibility that human dignity could be as easily suppressed by the new centres of power as it was by the old forces of authority certainly cannot be excluded. Poverty and destitution in the world are still widespread; discrimination by race and class and sex is still deeply entrenched, even in the richest countries, and people are still held down by force, by the exercise of military, political or financial power.

Traditional socialist concern, with money as a measure of inequality, remains of fundamental importance, but it must also be seen as a problem of power. Where ownership is, or can be, separated from the power of management in industry, that ownership loses its capacity to dominate; where through social action money can no longer purchase advantages in health and education it loses some of its capacity to maintain privilege at the expense of the many. In recent years socialists have concentrated so much on the financial aspects of politics that they have underestimated the problems of power, and have allowed themselves to be deflected from effective policies to control it directly by supposing that nothing could be done until ownership was communal, and that when it was communal nothing remained to be done.

If we are to make human dignity our first objective, not only have we got to eliminate poverty by using technology; secure the best possible management of our resources; eliminate old economic inequalities and guard against the creation of new ones; construct new safeguards against the abuse of new power; but we must also see that our new-found capabilities do in fact permit human dignity to express itself in diversity.

This aspiration is not a new one – but it happens that this generation has acquired the power to make it possible.

2. Towards a New View of World Affairs

Of all the semantic tyrannies that make serious analysis difficult the use of the phrase 'foreign affairs' is one of the most absurd. Technology started to abolish foreign affairs when the first real travellers conquered man's geographical imprisonment at the place of his birth. And by the time Marconi's radio messages first crossed the Atlantic and international aerial bombardment started in the First World War, foreign affairs had outgrown their old diplomatic definition. In a world where colour television pictures, carried by satellites, can reach us from anywhere in less than a second, and when missiles with nuclear warheads can be targeted to any city, from any place in the world, it is meaningless to regard the cliffs of Dover as being of anything but scenic, cultural and nostalgic significance to the British people, as a frontier against foreigners, and the rest of the world.

We shall never discover the full potential for the unity of mankind through foreign policy or diplomatic talks. Our best hope may well lie in trying to bypass our differences by opening up new areas of cooperation. Trade and technology, the transfer of knowledge and know-how, the freer movement of ideas, these are what we should seek to promote.

Across a world communications network, once it is established, we must also seek to pass accurate information about each other's problems and achievements and transfer more of the teachings of the world's greatest thinkers, so that we can all gradually come to share the same sources of human inspiration as we educate ourselves and our children to realise that we live in a world no bigger in real terms than the television screen on which we observe each other's doings every day.

3. An Intensive Study of Organisational Problems

The theme of institutional reform emerged more strongly in Britain in the 1960s than at any time for a hundred years, following developments of the same kind in other countries. Political revolutions, industrial change, schools of business studies and the evolution of control theory following the invention of computers, all in their own way gave an impetus to these worldwide developments. It is clear that unless the world as a whole can find better means of managing all its many organisations and unless more efficient means of creating and developing new resources can be devised, the technological revolution will take too long to realise its full potential, and will not deliver the goods necessary for the material improvement in living standards of millions of people, now living in poverty, within their own lifetime.

For a socialist in a non-socialist society to speak approvingly of the key role of management makes him, for some people, suspect, because management is associated automatically with private industry, authoritarianism or bureaucracy, or most likely all three. But this cannot blind us to the fact that management skills are of the greatest importance and are in critically short supply. In any case, ownership has long been becoming separated from management, at least in large corporations, and that process of disentanglement can be assisted by, among other things, vigorous action by the workers.

The old crude industrial authoritarianism of the past is now being attacked as directly by modern management thinkers as it is by the trade unions who are determined to change it. For management, like modern government, is simply not practicable on an authoritarian basis anymore. It just won't work without a high degree of real devolution and a most sophisticated information network that feeds back continuing reports on how the human as well as the mechanical and financial parts of the system are coping with their work. The problems of bureaucracy are not only being studied by Mao and students influenced by his thinking. Initiative, and even survival, can be threatened by it and these are of equal concern to management.

One of the most difficult problems in the evolution of institutional forms is the construction of a decision-making system that makes it possible to take decisions at the right level. If they are all made too high up the result will be authoritarian, bureaucratic and unworkable.

If they are all made too low down the result can be duplication, incompatibility and anarchy.

4. Towards Workers' Control

Here in Britain the demand for more popular power is building up most insistently in industry, and the pressure for industrial democracy has now reached such a point that a major change is now inevitable, at some stage. What is happening is not just a respectful request for consultation before management promulgates its decisions. Workers are not going to be fobbed off with a few shares – whether voting or non-voting.

The campaign is very gradually crystallising into a demand for real workers' control. However revolutionary the phrase may sound, however many Trotskyite bogeys it may conjure up, that is what is being demanded and that is what we had better start thinking about.

Workers now have, through interdependence, enormous negative power to dislocate the system. Workers' control – if it means the power to plan their own work and to hire and fire the immediate plant management just as MPs are now hired and fired by the voters – converts that existing negative power into positive and constructive power. It thus creates the basis of common interest with local managers struggling to make a success of the business and to get devolved authority from an over-centralised bureaucratic board of management now perhaps sitting on them from above. The gap between some of the best management thinking that is now leading to the devolution of power right down to the working level on the one hand, and the workers' demand from below for real power at the place of work, on the other, is now so narrow as to be capable of being bridged and indeed it constitutes a natural convergence of two streams of thinking towards a common solution to the problem of how human satisfaction can be found in work.

One could go further and see in workers' control of individual plants as natural and inevitable a development of the role of the new citizen as is the evolution of the international company itself; and also imagine multinationals whose plants all over the world were subject to local workers' control, constituting a sensible division of functions and working well.

5. Direct Action against Bureaucracy

But we cannot wait for the evolution of ideal organisational systems before we, as new citizens, begin to seek to realise our objectives at the working level. The overwhelming majority of us now work for, and in, large organisations; or some part of our lives is guided or controlled by them, and we thus all have some experience of how they work.

Bureaucracy is not necessarily, nor even mainly, motivated by malevolence. It survives because no one challenges it or worse still because most people do not even question it. Many people calmly accept it even when it classifies us, categorises us, divides us up, blocks off our opportunities and initiative and presumes to tell us to what heights we can aspire in life.

Better organisational techniques and good leadership can reduce it, but we really cannot all wait for that to happen. The quality of organisations will never be improved unless their defects are actively resisted. Change from below, the formulation of demands from the populace to end unacceptable injustice, supported by direct action, has played a far larger part in shaping British democracy than most constitutional lawyers, political commentators, historians or statesmen have ever cared to admit. Without direct pressure from below operating on and through the political system we should never have got state education, our social security system, the health service or any serious attention paid to the environment.

Direct action also welds people together and helps them to move on and tackle other problems effectively. It discovers talent that would otherwise have gone unrecognised, re-stocks the community with new leadership and creates new checks and balances against the abuse of power.

Direct action in a democratic society is fundamentally an educational exercise; and its victories can only be won when they achieve the conversion of those in power through winning a majority of people to the viewpoint of the activists. In other circumstances, and in other countries where the machinery of peaceful change does not exist, the use of real force from below is right and must be organised to succeed against everything that can be mustered against it, and it must be accepted and supported as legitimate in the battle to secure or enlarge human freedom. Here in Britain it is only justified – and effective – as a means of alerting the community to what is wrong, and of making it clear that a body of new citizens wants to see it put right.

6. A Frontal Assault on Secrecy in Decision-Making

If a mature and more self-regulating society is to have a real chance of success, people must know much more about why and how the decisions that affect them are actually made. Unless this information is made available people will never discover what the alternatives are, early enough, to have any influence on which of them to support and which to oppose.

As far as government is concerned this must mean a completely fresh look at all the many barriers that exist to ensure that ordinary people do not know what is going on in government. The practice of secrecy that has grown up over the years, in Britain and all their countries, goes back to the very distant past. Obviously there are matters of high national security, short-term diplomatic or other negotiating positions, commercial secrets and information about individuals that have to be dealt with by ministers and officials on a strict need-to-know basis which it would be a plain betrayal of trust to divulge – even to other ministers and officials who do not require the information, let alone the public. But beyond that most of the current business of government could easily be made more generally known to those who were interested in it.

The justification given for secrecy is usually based on a complete and deliberate confusion of the national interest with the political convenience of ministers, buttressed by the natural preference of civil servants for the full protection of their role as completely anonymous ministerial advisers.

A move towards much more open government would not need amending legislation. A clear policy decision in favour of a progressive relaxation of secrecy, in practice, would be quite sufficient to deal with the problem. It would constitute a real gain for the community and would also be good for government, in that ministers and officials would be in a position to receive more relevant comments and advice from those outside, who would know more accurately what was at issue and when the matter concerned was due for decision.

7. The Democratisation of the Mass Media

Today the freedom of debate and discussion remains central to the control of power. But unless this freedom is amplified by high-speed printing presses or powerful transmitters it need not amount to very much more than the right to set up a rostrum at Speakers' Corner in Hyde Park. Regular access to the public at large is virtually the prerogative of publishers, newspaper proprietors, the massive BBC, commercial TV production companies and those business organisations that use the mass media to advertise their products – and their values. That about sums up the list of those with *effective* power to publish, apart from organisations which issue their own material.

The democratisation, and accountability, of the mass media will be a major issue for the '70s and the debates on it are now beginning. The press and broadcasting authorities have a responsibility for providing enough accurate information, at the time when it really matters, to allow people to acquire greater influence. The people, for their part, have the right to demand a greater ease of access to the community through the mass media and some more effective redress by a body with power to examine complaints, especially against the broadcasting authorities. What is wanted is more diversity of expression and not, repeat not, the centralisation of power in the hands of government or a bureaucratic monopoly.

8. New Priorities in Education

Education, like information and communications, is moving into the centre of political controversy. Indeed it has already become the focal point of debate and political controversy.

The denial of access for the many, by an elite, has proved to be a most powerful instrument for long-term popular subjugation. The majority of children have been – and still are being – branded as failures at eleven, then told they do not merit real secondary education; only to discover later that, as a result, they cannot qualify for higher education. Then, for the rest of their lives, they are kept out of many positions of responsibility, which are reserved for graduates.

The battle for comprehensive education is only half-way won at the secondary level, and is only just beginning at the level of higher and further education, where the massed ranks of the elitists are already in position to repel the expected assault by the many, with the familiar cry of 'more means worse'. It will be just as hard, but just as necessary, to win that battle and the sooner it is won the better.

At the moment we still accept a wastage of human ability which is so massive that if we could only tap a small proportion of the reserves of talent that exist we could raise both our standard of life, and the quality of it much more rapidly than now seems possible. But we can only achieve this if we concentrate far more attention on raising the level of the average in both people and performance rather than continuing to focus so much of our effort on the so-called best; and if we are also prepared to see the potential of education in helping us to overcome the hard-core problems of the poor, the sick and the deprived.

9. Beyond Parliamentary Democracy

The British Parliament cannot expect to be exempted from this general demand for greater participation from both within and without. The welcome erosion of the power of the whips has gone much further than most people outside politics realise in restoring to MPs the power to limit the automatic exercise of executive power by Cabinets.

The next stage in public participation in government is bound to come from the first serious reconsideration of the possibility of adding some direct decision-making, or at any rate comprehensive opinion-testing mechanism, to that of the ballot box, on specific issues.

The most discussed form of direct decision-making has been the idea of holding nationwide referenda on specific issues – either those which transcended party loyalties and were of supreme importance, or those on moral questions which are now by general consent left to a free vote of the House.

The idea of a national institute of public opinion which acted as the independent agent for assessing and reporting the national view *before* Parliament reached its final decision on some issues is another possibility. This would lack the mandatory nature of formal referenda which would present certain difficulties, while at the same time furnishing a significant focus for debate that would encourage the protagonists on either side to release far more facts than are now made available, and compel them to campaign on the issue up for decision instead of, as now, always on the far less precise issue of their own qualifications for office.

The establishment of machinery for testing the strength of certain views under official but independent auspices, comprehensively and not by sampling, might also be a constructive way of diverting the energy now put into street protest into educational campaigns in support of a certain view before the formal consultation was allowed to take place.

It does not follow that organised comprehensive consultations would have to be limited to matters requiring an immediate decision. Indeed, given the time lag between decision and full execution and the case that has been argued for, real consultations with the public are closed. It might well be possible to allow people to express a view about broad priorities for the future – what has been called anticipatory decision-sharing – that would be helpful to government and reassuring for the public.

Nor should it be thought that direct participation of this kind need be limited to national issues. It might be appropriate for, or indeed the only instrument of consent capable of being used to guide decisions on a local level or as part of a campaign to gain more effective participation in non-governmental organisations, the professions, trade unions or any other body where the members wished for a much larger say in their own affairs.

It would, however, be wrong to end a section on popular power without reminding ourselves that if change from below is to be – as seems likely – a growing force in politics and industry, the most effective pressures will come from those who band themselves together to win support from their fellows and then present their demands for change or improvement with the weight that comes from articulating a real requirement in a representative capacity. That way lies the do-it-yourself society that is now being born.

10. Redefining the Role of National Government

If government has now got to accept that many of its functions are being taken over by international institutions beyond its shores or are to be devolved, or hived off, or shared with the people below who are claiming greater rights as new citizens, we shall have to consider afresh exactly what the role of national government is to be.

National government must retain the supreme responsibility for the nation's fortunes in the broadest sense of the term and be the custodian of its national culture and identity. It must concern itself with security, now redefined to include the provision of a degree of protection for the individual against many of the new hazards of life that goes far beyond the provision of defence against invasion and civil disorder.

It must legislate the framework structure of rights within which people can confidently live and work, including the provision of new safeguards against the abuse of information it has gathered for its own purposes or which has been gathered by non-governmental organisations or firms.

It must allocate the nation's resources, not only of money raised by taxation, but perhaps even more importantly of qualified and skilled manpower, and apply them to meet needs that are most pressing. It must present the alternative strategies for public discussion, *before* the final and irreversible decisions are made. It must secure the accountability of all power centres operating within the frontiers of the state, and may find that control on behalf of the people is best secured by organic consultation.

It must also develop a consultancy function to help people to do things for themselves by the provision of technical or other information or advisory services, and it must actively discourage the idea that the government can, or should itself, seek to solve all the problems confronting everyone.

In short, government should concern itself mainly with the big decisions within the state, concentrating its attention on its major objectives; adjusting the system and the organisation structures to allow their realisation at various levels; and interacting intelligently and professionally with all those parts of other systems that touch upon government's own broad range of responsibilities for promoting the human welfare and dignity of its citizens.

11. A New Role for Political Leaders

They will have to be leaders, rather more in the Moses tradition, drawing their power less from the executive authority they have acquired by election and more from influence, helping people to see what they can achieve for themselves, and acting as a consultant, equipped with all the necessary support and facilities, to allow them to do it. This is not a charter for anarchism, nor a dream of creating a wholly self-regulating economic and political system. Leadership there must be, but not all from the top. Leadership is inseparable from responsibility and responsibility is inseparable from power, and if, as I have argued, power is now being disseminated more widely, leadership will have to be more widely shared too. Indeed, in a world bulging with new power, the sheer volume of work for leaders to do is so great that unless far more men and women take their share of the load of leadership and management, and become responsible, the whole system will break down through sheer unmanageability. No one could possibly be wise enough, or knowledgeable enough, or have the time and skill to run the world today even if they had all the authority and all the expert advice they asked for to do the job. Individual people have got to do it themselves and argue it out as they go along.

More than 500 years before the birth of Christ, Lao-Tzu, the Chinese philosopher, had this to say about leadership:

> As for the best leaders, the people do not notice their existence. The next best the people honour and praise. The next the people fear, and the next the people hate. But when the best leader's work is done the people say, 'We did it ourselves.'

To create the conditions that will allow the people to do it themselves is the central task of leadership today.

12. Rethinking the Role of the Labour Party

If any of the territory reconnoitred in this pamphlet proves, on closer study, to be suitable for a further advance towards democratic socialism, the only party in Britain capable of guiding people towards it is the Labour Party. But it must necessarily follow that the way in which it approaches its task, the nature of its own organisation and its own leadership role could also be altered if some of the arguments spelled out here have got any validity.

As a political party concerned to acquire power under the present system it cannot afford to preoccupy itself too much with the philosophical considerations or mid-distance forecasting that underlie much of what has been argued here. But it cannot present itself again as the champion of democratic socialist development without paying some attention to what this could mean for its own structure, nature and role. The debates that must necessarily take place on just these very matters could release a great deal of creative energy within the party and the movement. Only if we can learn how to do that to ourselves can we really be confident of our ability to do the very same thing on the much larger national scale which will certainly be necessary if any of our visions of the future of Britain are ever to be realised, by us all, as people, rediscovering the fact that this is our country and its future is what we want to make it – nothing less and nothing more.

7
Developing a Participating Democracy

Within days of the 1968 events in Paris and London, Benn was thinking how to redraft popular democracy. This speech, given at the Annual Conference of the Welsh Council of Labour, on 25 May, is particularly prescient in its calls for reacting to technological change and the demands of devolution.

Just as technology is revolutionising industry, so it is outdating our political institutions as well. Our educational system, our system of local government, the Civil Service and the legal system are all now under critical examination because technology has made them obsolescent. But what about Parliament itself? Can we assume that it will go on, in exactly the same form as we now have it, forever and ever? I very much doubt it.

Much of the present wave of anxiety, disenchantment and discontent is actually directed at the present parliamentary structure. Many people do not think that it is responding quickly enough to the mounting pressure of events or the individual or collective aspirations of the community.

It would be foolish to assume that people will be satisfied, for much longer, with a system which confines their national political role to the marking of a ballot paper with a single cross once every five years. People want a much greater say. That certainly explains some of the student protests against the authoritarian hierarchies in some of our universities and their sense of isolation from the problems of real life. Much of the industrial unrest – especially in unofficial strikes – stems from worker resentment and their sense of exclusion from the decision-making process, whether by their employers or, sometimes, by their union leaders.

Frustration too provides much of the driving force for nationalism in Wales and Scotland among those who want to participate more fully in policymaking. Even the Black Power movement is an indication that immigrants are not prepared to rely entirely on white liberals to champion their cause and are determined to assume a more direct responsibility for securing their rights.

All these tendencies are indicative of a general – and inevitable – trend away from authoritarianism and towards personal responsibility. Even relatively benign and temporary authoritarianism that rests upon elected power is being challenged.

We are moving rapidly towards a situation where the pressure for the redistribution of political power will have to be faced as a major political issue. The implications of this for our system of parliamentary democracy, and for the Labour Party which works within it, are far reaching.

The redistribution of political power does not mean that it will all be decentralised. Indeed, in some military, industrial and technical areas, centralisation is inevitable. The existence of international organisations, large international corporations, and the acceptance of international standards of measurement and performance all remind us of our interdependence. To dream of living in splendid isolation grouped together according to historical culture is to follow a completely romantic illusion.

The redistribution of power by decentralising it is of great importance. But it is much more complicated than an exercise in geographical fragmentation. It means finding the right level for each decision and seeing that it can be taken at that level. It also means transferring much more power right back to the individual. Our parliamentary system has changed radically over the centuries. At first it was little more than a means by which feudal landowners tamed the power of kings. In the nineteenth century the landowners and industrialists were forced to share their power by the emergence of the middle and working classes. But these people were not content to be represented by anyone other than themselves. That is how the Labour Party came to be formed.

Looking ahead we must expect equally radical changes to be made in our system of government to meet the requirements of a new generation. I am not dealing here with the demand for the ownership or control of growing sections of the economy. I am thinking of the demand for more political responsibility and power for the individual than the present system of parliamentary democracy provides.

I am thinking of a participating democracy under which more and more people will have an opportunity to make their influence felt on decisions that affect them. If that is our objective, as I believe it must be, what special characteristics would a popular democracy have that is now lacking in the parliamentary democracy? It seems to me that there are six areas in which change will have to be made.

The first requirement for a participating democracy involves giving people the right to know more about government and what it is doing. Nothing buttresses the established order so effectively as secrecy.

The searchlight of publicity shone on the decision-making processes of government would be the best thing that could possibly happen. For centuries this was the only power the House of Commons had. The new ombudsman, the probing of the specialist committees and the partial lifting of the old fifty-year clamp on public records are all moves in the right direction. Opening the Commons chamber to the television cameras would help too.

But I would be surprised if the process stopped there. In Sweden departmental and even cabinet papers are, unless they involve national security, named individuals or commercial secrets, available for public inspection. In this country there is already considerable pressure to reveal exactly how the intricate structure of inter-departmental and Cabinet committees actually works.

The more light we throw on the workings of government the less we shall have of the obsession with personalities. While the public and the press are denied the right to know what is being discussed and how decisions are being arrived at we are bound to have columns and columns of personal tittle-tattle masquerading as serious political comment.

The second requirement for a participating democracy is that government should be allowed to know a great deal more than it does know about the community it was elected to serve.

This requirement is essential if we want to see decisions made on the basis of accurate fact. You cannot manage an advanced society, which is a vast complex interconnecting system, unless the facts are available. That is one reason why we are now strengthening the statistical services and encouraging the publication of much more data of all kinds. No economic policy can work unless its effects can be forecast accurately, or its consequences be simultaneously monitored to provide for rapid feedback.

In the '70s computers will be widely used for managing the economy by means of a sophisticated process-control system not dissimilar from that now used in large automated plants. The value judgements will all be human and political but we shall have a reasonable chance of doing what we want to do and achieving what we set out to achieve. All this depends on having information available to program the system.

If we had this information available to guide us in social policy the present arguments about selectivity would fade away. The day will come, not long hence, when taxation and social security systems will be capable of complete integration. Then we shall be able to decide politically what to do about means and needs on a personal basis, entirely free from anomalies. Each individual will then be in a position to settle his cash account with the community in an orderly way paying tax or receiving benefit according to his circumstances.

The possibilities that are opening up are not without serious dangers. Processed information about individuals could be the basis for a police state and a mass of new safeguards would be required. But on the positive side this information could and should compel government to take account of every single individual in the development of its policy. Just to exist will be to participate. We are a long way from that now.

The third requirement in a participating democracy will certainly involve the direct sharing of decision-making with the electorate as a whole. The five-yearly cross on the ballot paper is just not going to be enough. Inevitably we shall have to look again at the objections to the holding of referenda and see if they are still valid. Public opinion polls – now studied under a microscope by every serious politician – are no substitute. The samples interviewed are only a tiny percentage of the population and even those who are questioned share no responsibility for the answers they give.

If some real issues – perhaps for a start of the kind that are now decided by private members' bills – were actually put out for a decision in principle by referendum the situation would be transformed. This would involve real responsibility. We might not all like the result. But at any rate by sharing responsibility an interest in public policy would be stirred in every household.

Here too technology may ultimately help us. Electronic referenda will be feasible within a generation and with it could come a considerable uprating of the responsibility and understanding of ordinary people.

The fourth prerequisite for a participating democracy involves a radical re-examination of the way in which our mass communications are handled.

Considering the power the mass media now exercise it is surprising how little thought has been given to the inter-relationship between them and democracy.

A prime minister can address the whole nation, if necessary at an hour's notice. A press tycoon can print his own article on the front pages of his own newspapers and have it read by millions.

But for ordinary people, or even for extraordinary people with minority views, the only way of answering back is to walk about with a placard and hope the press or television cameras will take a picture. Compared with the technology available to the mass media the public is still stuck with a communications system that has hardly changed since the Stone Age.

Perhaps this is one explanation for the fact that protest is edging ever closer to violence. Those with minority views – strikers, those who dislike immigrants or are immigrants, oppose the war in Vietnam or want self-government for Cornwall – have precious little access to the community through the mass media.

Minority opinions do find an outlet in books and through relatively small-circulation papers and magazines. But access to the microphone or TV camera is very strictly limited – by both the BBC and the commercial TV companies.

What broadcasting now lacks is any equivalent to the publishing function. At the moment it is controlled by editors with slots to fill and a few selected minority views get in some of the slots. But three minutes of cross-examination while you are roughed up by a folk-hero TV interviewer, or a clip of film showing a protest march on the 10 o'clock news, is no substitute for the right to speak.

The day may well come when independent groups of publishers would be allocated so many hours of broadcasting a month and told to help those who have something to say, to say it clearly and well, to national audiences. Unless we make a move in that direction we shall simply be denying ourselves access to a whole range of ideas – good, bad and indifferent – which we ought, as responsible citizens, to be allowed to know about through the mass media.

The fifth requirement in a participating democracy will be to build up the strength of representative organisations of all kinds so that they can be consulted and as far as possible become self-regulating.

The obvious model here is the professions which have been consulted and have regulated themselves for centuries. In the nineteenth century the trade unions emerged to represent working people and they too have been consulted and are being asked to take on new functions. The stronger the trade unions are the more functions they can assume and the more effective they will be. The government has been pouring money into private industry to rationalise and strengthen it. Now it is being suggested that public money might be put into the trade unions to help them to rationalise and become more efficient and effective.

We shall also have to look again at the role of the pressure group. This phrase still has an unpleasant ring about it. But modern democracy is now largely dependent on the pressure groups who represent real interests and are often a valuable source of ideas for future policy.

The function of government is to spot trouble before it becomes explosive, pick the brains of those who have thought the problems out and evolve from these ideas a series of practical remedies.

The more representative and professional pressure groups can be, the more government can work with them and the more responsibility can be devolved. This is one way in which power can be redistributed.

The sixth requirement for a participating democracy involves the devolution of much more responsibility to regions and localities.

This does not involve the fragmentation of society into mere geographical areas. It means identifying those decisions which ought to be taken in and by an area most affected by those decisions.

It will be an agonising and difficult task to wrench away from Whitehall powers that have been exercised there for centuries. But this sort of surgery is inevitable and the machine that will be left will be all the more efficient for being free of detail it cannot manage, leaving it to concentrate on the immensely complicated job of reaching more scientific decisions on national matters.

The pressures for changes along these lines are as inevitable as was the incoming tide that ultimately engulfed King Canute. These are among the main political issues that will be argued about in the '70s and beyond. However unwelcome this pressure may be to those who now believe that the parliamentary system of government is, as now constituted, the finest expression of man's constitutional genius, adjustments will have to be made. If they are not, discontent, expressing itself in despairing apathy or violent protest, could engulf us all in bloodshed. It is no good saying that it could never happen here. It could.

Since the Labour Party now works through the parliamentary system, changes in that system will have profound implications for us too. Moreover, like Parliament, the Labour Party is just another political institution. And like Parliament it could become just as obsolete, just as quickly.

The widening gulf between the Labour Party and those who supported it last time could well be an index of the party's own obsolescence. Party reform now is just as important as the evolution of the parliamentary system. A participating Labour Party will involve just as many changes.

This year we elect a new general secretary and, working with the national executive, he will have about two years to reorganise the party machine at Transport House and throughout the country. It will be a tremendous task. Indeed the whole function and role and character of the party will inevitably have to change. The keynote here too will need to be participation and involvement exactly as in the case of the parliamentary system itself. For the evolution of the Labour Party is very closely bound up with the evolution of parliamentary democracy. In a world where authoritarianism of the left or right is a very real possibility, the question of whether ordinary people can govern themselves by consent is still on trial – as it always has been and always will be. Beyond parliamentary democracy as we know it we shall have to find a new popular democracy to replace it.

8

The Politician Today

From a speech made to an international conference of political consultants in December 1970, Benn repositions the politician within a media age which has become less enamoured by politicians and seeks a way for Labour to reimagine itself.

The new citizen of today is not prepared to leave it to them – in government – any more than he is in the church, in industry, in the trade unions, in the universities or in local communities. Strange as it may seem, responsibility can only be exercised by those who are given responsibility, and the only discipline that people will accept is the discipline which they impose upon themselves. They see politics more and more in terms of issues and less and less in terms of selecting a 'hero-king' who will lead them out of the wilderness and into the promised land.

I do not, therefore, believe that any amount of public relations effort, designed to package a modern political hero to be presented to the public as a saviour, will really greatly help. Instead of seeing politics as a perpetual climb up the ladder of power, culminating in the exercise of ministerial authority, I see the role of a politician in quite a new scenario.

First, he must be a representative, maintaining contact not just with his party colleagues but with the thousands of organisations that have come into being as an expression of the human response to the pressures on us all from technical and industrial change.

Second, he must be an adviser, helping people to realise their full potential and analysing and connecting the issues which concern them so that society does not fragment and disintegrate into the pushing and shoving of rival interests.

Third, he must be an educator who explains what is happening – and why – so that people are not frightened because they do not understand and thus fall into protest or apathy or demand that others be disciplined to protect their own interests.

Fourth, a politician is a legislator and an administrator – working in partnership to lubricate the processes of change by altering the ground rules and controlling the bureaucracies and humanising the actual business of running a modern state.

Fifth, a politician must recognise that the only real instrument that he has for changing a society is the instrument of persuasion and that winning the hearts and minds of his fellow countrymen matters even more than winning elections or winning votes in Parliament or staging, and then winning, confrontations between 'goodies' and 'baddies' at home or abroad.

Looking back over a hundred years of British parliamentary democracy and seeing why great changes occur, I have become convinced that these were not the products of enlightened leaders but of the pressure of people from below, who have worked through the agency of political leaders, whose greatest quality may well have been their realism.

We would never have had the vote in Britain for men – and certainly not for women – if it had not been demanded and conceded. We should never have had state education, the welfare state, the National Health Service or many of the other civilised developments of which we are proud if the demands for these things had not bubbled up from below. And the present vigorous campaigns against pollution, for a better quality of life and for a greater respect for ecology, were not thought up by inspired ministers or far-sighted civil servants. They came from the people and we are now conceding what they want.

The danger of parliamentary democracy – if it is presented as if it were nothing more than the achievement of an elected monarchy – is that it retains the arrogance of the benevolent despot and seeks to cloak the elected MP with something of the divine right once reserved for royal personages. At its worst, it still keeps the citizen at arm's length from the business of decision-making and bullies him into believing that the ballot box is the last word in participation.

However attractive this idea may be, it won't do because it won't work anymore. The game is up and we have to think the whole thing out again.

I have certainly not come here with a crystal ball with which to help me peer into the future of democratic politics. Certainly the crystal balls which were used in the last election were well and truly smashed when the results were announced.

But if, as I believe, the policies of the present government fail to solve the problems which confront us, people will not turn back to Labour unless we have thought through this change which I have been trying to describe, and set the political process into a wider perspective that takes account of the bigger role which the people themselves want to play.

We shall have to extend our representative function so as to bring ourselves into a more creative relationship with many organisations that stand outside our membership but are working for objectives that are compatible with our own.

We shall have to offer ourselves in our new consultant role showing people how it can be done rather than seeking to convince them that if they vote for us their problems are over.

We shall have to accelerate the processes of change so that we are not encumbered by the institutional baggage carried from the past, and we shall have to recognise the role of persuasion as the main instrument of change.

The future of democracy is sometimes thought to be in the balance with some pessimists predicting either a return to authoritarianism or a soft squishy slide into anarchy or perhaps both, in either order, the one succeeding the other.

No democrat can be other than a statutory optimist, believing that it is possible for people to govern themselves and survive the stresses that now mount so dangerously. But if this statutory optimism is not to be mere daydreaming, it must involve reconnecting the political system to the immensely powerful new centres of human energy that now exist. The future will not be made by the scientists, the ambitious politicians – with or without the help of political consultants – or by the introduction of modern managerial methods into the great departments of state.

It will be made by the people themselves and shaped by the structure of values to which they subscribe. Anyone who wishes to contribute to that future has therefore got to get into that dialogue and listen and learn and argue and convert. There is no short cut.

All these things were happening, just under the surface, while the last Labour government was at work. But we were so busy with the business of government that we somehow disconnected ourselves, pulled the plugs out and then were a little surprised to find that our batteries weren't being recharged.

We didn't lose because people didn't know what we had done, but because we seemed to have crossed to the other side of the we/they frontier and we didn't find time to explain what was happening. People did get frightened.

They were frightened of long-haired students and immigrants and workers on strike and foreigners and decimalisation and metrication and they looked for the nice, safe, familiar traditional characteristics that were so skilfully offered to them by Mr Heath and his colleagues.

But we would be foolish to suppose that people will be forever satisfied with that particular brand of pendulum politics, swinging alternative teams in and out of office. More people want to get in on the act and I see it as our business so to reconstruct the Labour Party that a Labour government will never rule again but will try to create the conditions under which it is able to act as the natural partner of a people, who really mean something more than we thought they did, when they ask for self-government.

9
How Democratic Is Britain?

This is an abridged version of Benn's pamphlet The Speaker, the Commons and Democracy, *published in 2012, which builds on Benn's argument for constitutional reform with a particular look at parliamentary institutions.*

We are told that power has moved over time from the throne to the Lords, from the Lords to the Commons and from the Commons to the people. But in practice power has now moved to the prime minister who then, exercising powers of the Crown without explicit consent from Parliament, dominates the whole system.

A prime minister with these constitutional powers is in theory accountable to Parliament, whose support any prime minister requires to stay in office. But the prime minister is in practice able to use the fact that he or she is leader of a normally disciplined majority party, and in addition controls access to a range of governmental posts and state honours with which to provide a cushion of loyal and generally reliable support in Parliament.

The House of Commons is the only elected part of Parliament and democratic principles should require that all prerogative powers be controlled by that House.

At present any prime minister must depend upon the support of powerful ministers or interest groups both inside and outside Parliament, but reliance on the consent of the governed is minimal. A modern prime minister controls government like a feudal monarch, exercising Crown powers but dependent on key interests to support the regime.

Powers of patronage are one weapon at the disposal of the prime minister granted by the Crown. The problem of patronage begins long before any honour or government position has been awarded. The influence of patronage extends far beyond the number of people who actually receive an honour or appointment, to those who expect or desire one. For a very large number of people, their position, promotion or honour depends upon the favour of senior ministers, and civil servants who have the ear of the prime minister. They would be less than human if this did not in some way affect their conduct. The threat of dismissal and the ability to reallocate important portfolios ensures that those within government remain loyal to the prime minister.

Government ministers have to agree to abide by rules of conduct which the prime minister issues personally. These rules are laid down in a minute entitled 'Questions of Procedure for Ministers' drawn up by the Cabinet secretariat and issued by each prime minister when he or she takes office. Procedural minutes have never been submitted to Cabinet for approval, but contain regulations governing everything from a minister's exposure in the media to the use of official cars.

The most important of these rules is the convention of collective responsibility, originally established when the monarch still presided over Cabinet, in order to strengthen ministers against the Crown. When the franchise was extended, collective responsibility became an instrument for sustaining the Cabinet against Parliament and the electorate. If collective responsibility is to protect individual members of government from being picked off one by one, the government must present a united face, take collective responsibility for actions, and then stand or fall together.

If Parliament were to defeat the legislation of one minister, it could be held to be a defeat for the Cabinet as a whole. If the government were then forced to resign it could cause the dissolution of the Commons, ending the life of the Parliament and jeopardising MPs' seats. The intertwining of the interests of the Cabinet with the interests of the legislature gives the government considerable power – the Commons will only use its ability to defeat the government as a last resort. 'Either the executive legislates and acts, or else it can dissolve.' Either the government and its majority in the Commons stand together or they fall together.

The outcome is that government backbenchers, who will generally want to see their party continue in power rather than risk losing all at a general election, can usually be relied upon to fall into line. Backbench rebellion against governments has therefore been limited. The 1950s and '60s saw very few outbreaks of cross-party voting against a government due to the strict enforcement of party whips. Dissent has increased since the 1970s partly because it has been shown that a government can stand a number of minor defeats and resignations without falling. But it probably remains the case that on an issue that might be a threat to the government, or which might precipitate a vote of confidence, party discipline will be severe and when it really matters backbenchers will support the government, such as was evidenced in the Conservative government decision to close large numbers of coal mines and its backbench rebels fell into line.

Collective responsibility not only galvanises backbench support for government, but disciplines rebels and dissenters within government. 'Difficult' ministers can be blocked or moved to the sidelines by threats of dismissal by the prime minister, the removal of responsibility for a specific policy or by letting it be known to the senior civil servants in that department that the minister is out of favour with the prime minister. In this situation, civil servants withdraw active cooperation from the minister.

The power to threaten the collective dissolution of Parliament through a prime minister's own resignation and a call for an election has in fact never been tested in practice. John Major was forced to retreat on one motion in Parliament on Maastricht, and when Wilson threatened in 1969 to resign unless the parliamentary party accepted the White Paper on trade unions, 'In Place of Strife', he was advised that if he tried to dissolve Parliament the then chairman of the Parliamentary Labour Party would follow him to Buckingham Palace to request that James Callaghan take over. Wilson capitulated and the White Paper was dropped.

However, in certain circumstances the threat of resignation can be effective and votes of confidence within Cabinet can succeed where hours of persuasion have failed. An alternative sanction for a prime minister will be to threaten the sack, potentially destroying a ministerial career.

In these ways the prime minister is able to make personal decisions, in consultation with a few key colleagues, binding on the whole government so that decisions which are not collectively taken must be collectively supported in Parliament and in the press. In Callaghan's 'Questions of Procedure' it had already been established that 'decisions reached by the Cabinet or Cabinet Committees are binding on all members of the government'.

Wilson had previously required that those members had a duty 'not merely to support the Government but to refrain from making any speech or doing any act which may appear to implicate the Government'.

In spite of the assumption that collective Cabinet responsibility is a convention of the constitution, it was waived by Wilson in 1975 over the issue of the referendum on European membership. Later Callaghan, in a parliamentary answer, made it clear that collective Cabinet responsibility applied when he said it did.

When it is in force, collective responsibility does not simply bind Cabinet ministers, but applies to all members of the government including ministers of state, law officers, undersecretaries of state and the whips, who will be expected to support the decisions of the

Cabinet, both in Parliament and elsewhere in public. It will also be expected to apply to MPs who serve as parliamentary private secretaries to ministers. In consequence the prime minister can expect up to half of his or her parliamentary majority to be guaranteed by virtue of these MPs being members of government. However, this is sometimes dependent on what has been dubbed 'the pay-roll vote', which increases in keeping with the appointment of more ministers and their parliamentary private secretaries.

A large amount of government business passes through a system of Cabinet committees, staffed by ministers appointed by the prime minister. At any one time there are likely to be over a hundred ad hoc and standing committees. Through this system difficult ministers can be bypassed and problematic issues can be removed from the agenda of full Cabinet, a system used extensively by Margaret Thatcher. According to the 1992 'Questions of Procedure' they buttress

> the principle of collective responsibility by ensuring that, even though an important question may never reach the Cabinet itself ... the final judgment will be sufficiently authoritative to ensure that the Government as a whole can be properly expected to accept responsibility for it.

In other words decisions made by a prime minister and his or her appointees in Cabinet committee have the force of a Cabinet decision, even though the issues may never come to Cabinet or be discussed with interested ministers. The prime minister can even keep the minutes of committees secret from Cabinet ministers not present.

Harold Wilson wrote in 1974:

> The fact that no Minister is in practice able to participate in the decision-taking process over the whole range of Government policy does not alter the position. The obligations of collective responsibility are binding on all members of the Government, in the sense that it is unacceptable for any Minister publicly to dissociate himself [sic]

from the policies and actions of the Government of which he is a member. If he feels impelled by reasons of conscience so to dissociate himself, he must resign in order to do so. This applies to all Ministers; it applies especially to members of the Cabinet.

Prime ministers have a position in Cabinet which is very much more than first among equals, and they can ensure that policy is made in highly personalised and secretive form under their own direction. But in spite of the personal character of many of the decisions, all members of the government will be expected to support the decisions made in committee.

The Civil Service and Accountability

A further element of personal control of government is given to the prime minister by his or her position as head of the Civil Service. The relationship is not one-way. The senior ranks of the Civil Service have their own particular agenda and the fact that they hold the key to substantial control of the Whitehall machine gives them a great deal of influence over the prime minister.

In parallel with each Cabinet committee is an official committee sharing the same title as its ministerial counterpart, but with the suffix (0). The most important of these is the Committee of Permanent Secretaries known informally in Whitehall as the Cabinet (0). Taken together, this network of Civil Service committees forms the permanent government, and plays an important part in coordinating – and shaping – government policy.

The prime minister, as head of the Civil Service, controls a substantial executive machine. His or her control is exercised quite simply: the prime minister appoints and confirms permanent secretaries and has some control over their status and operational conduct. The result is that permanent secretaries within each government department are likely to have greater loyalty to No. 10 than to their own minister. Indeed, civil servants have been known to keep prime ministers informed of the activities of ministers who act against their implied wishes. In addition the Cabinet Office has its own extensive research facilities and will prepare briefings and papers for use in Cabinet, which support the prime minister's position on any matter, including those which are the specific concern of a Cabinet minister.

But while the prime minister as head of the Civil Service commands great power, senior civil servants tend to view governments as visitors to the royal suite at the Grand Hotel and they themselves comprise the real permanent government, loyal to a sense of national interest embodied in the Crown. Despite attempts by Margaret Thatcher as prime minister to break this inherent resistance to radical policies, through a series of fundamental reforms, the power of the permanent secretaries remains strong. Because of the high degree of centralisation, civil servants are able to maintain a broad continuity in policy between different governments in line with their own judgement of what is best.

Former head of the Civil Service Department (subsequently Cabinet Secretary) Robert Armstrong spoke frankly when he wrote in 1974 that 'it would have been enormously difficult for any minister to change the framework [of policy], so to that extent we had great power', adding 'I don't think we used it maliciously or malignly, I think we chose that framework because we thought it the best one going'.

A similar attitude was held by George Young, deputy head of MI6, in 1979. He says quite openly that

> the higher reaches of the Civil Service undoubtedly make most of the decisions for Ministers and put them in front of them and say 'Minister do you agree?' The ethos of the higher reaches of the Civil Service is not one of stirring up hornets' nests, particularly if some of your best friends are hornets, but in my experience of dealing with Ministers ... they don't hear what you say; you tell them something, it goes in one ear and it's out of the other and they're busy thinking up the next Parliamentary answer to the next Parliamentary question.

The present constitutional arrangements are such that elected governments may not be able to pursue policy on which they are elected and which they believe is in the public interest since they may be obstructed by the guardians of the interests of the Crown. According to Ian Bancroft, a former permanent secretary of the Civil Service Department, 'the Service belongs neither to politicians nor to officials but to the Crown and to the nation'. The Crown becomes a device with which civil servants can defend the 'nation' from what Ferdinand Mount, a former policy adviser to Mrs Thatcher, calls

> the instantaneous, immediate, hot-and-strong breath of public opinion. The civil service is a self-regulating, self-selecting, self-perpetuating, self-disciplining corps which regards loyalty to the Crown in its capacity as the embodiment of the nation as a great deal more than a mere shibboleth.

The Civil Service – and experts in general – can at best only reflect *their own perception* of the public good and at worst a prejudicial view of people as unable to decide what is in their own interest. Such perceptions will almost always favour continuity against reform, since the bureaucrat will be part of a hierarchy, and his or her activity will be weighted with one eye on promotion, and so will favour the known preferences of superiors. In this way new ideas, challenging ideas and the ideas of the elected government can be filtered out by the power of the dominant institutional ethos.

In addition, membership of the European Union has greatly increased the dependence of ministers upon Civil Service expertise. Senior civil servants from all European Union countries meet in a body called the Committee of Permanent Representatives or COREPER. Most decisions reached in the Council of Ministers will have been agreed in advance by COREPER. These pre-negotiations between civil servants are of substantial importance, and can be used by EU civil servants to press a common agenda on the various governments. Civil servants are in a key position where they are trading information on their government's bargaining position and intentions. In negotiation they will aim to reach agreement on an agenda of 'feasible' policy options. Government objectives filter down from Cabinet and ministers but the decisions are taken in a whole network of EU committees, panels and organisations.

This may be the case with any large bureaucratic structure, but the European Union remains a special case because of the policymaking role it gives to twenty appointed commissioners. Substantial areas of government are under the control of the Commission, which is charged with both the initiation and execution of EU policy. The Council of Ministers in the European Union is a lawmaking body and the Commission serves as its 'government'. The structure is far from democratic. Yet more and more power is being poured into the EU. Member governments will have to concede to majority voting in the EU on a range of issues and if they fail to do so the EU can use British courts to overturn the policies of British governments.

Loyal but Not an Opposition

The most significant of the democratic constraints on prime-ministerial power is the timing of a general election. But when a large amount of power is vested in one person, and a vote has to be cast across a multiplicity of issues determined over the previous parliament, the outcome cannot be a continuous democratic accountability for government. In addition, at just the time when the prime minister is most vulnerable, party loyalty will be at its strongest.

The opposition is assumed to be the most significant of the controls on government. An effective opposition can embarrass the government and cause it to spend time answering questions away from its chosen agenda, but the effect is limited in important respects, not the least of which is that in recent times the opposition parties have come to share many of the policies of the party in power. That the opposition party represents a prime minister government-in-waiting poses a permanent threat to the security of the present incumbents. But for an opposition's attacks to have any force, its alternative programme must have support and in fact the opposition's desire to be seen as a government-in-waiting can hinder its function as critic of government policy and principle.

The outcome is not effective opposition, but effective consensus – a situation not unlike that existing between the Whigs and the Tories 140 years ago.

All parties now agree on membership of the EU, on the role of NATO, on the maintenance of nuclear weapons and on the primacy of free markets. Her Majesty's Loyal Opposition seems almost to have become persuaded that its loyalty supersedes its opposition.

Government by consensus has been helped by the extension of the select committee system under reforms implemented in 1979. It was intended that these would give backbenchers an opportunity to prise information from civil servants and ministers. In reality party whips have come to control the appointment of individual MPs to committees and their membership reflects the balance of the parties within the House. The select committees have become effectively a network of coalitions, knitting government and opposition backbenchers together through a common desire to reach unanimous conclusions. They are able to extract information from civil servants and ministers on the minutiae of policy, but may not explore alternatives to policies which the government undertakes. The permanent secretaries, having initially viewed the committees with some trepidation, have realised that they provide an additional route by which controlled information can be officially disseminated.

This consensus is strengthened by the magic circle of the Privy Council, whose members are supposed to consult together confidentially, without risk of information 'leaking' outside. In the parliamentary context this is an important system which maintains close relations between the government of the day and the opposition leaders. Backbenchers as a whole are excluded from the deliberations.

This club lubricates 'the usual channels' – which are the inter-party talks that go on all the time between the main frontbenches about the conduct of business in the House – and in a war situation, such as the Falklands in 1982, provides an opportunity for highly confidential briefings to be undertaken to win the opposition over to the acceptance of the government line. There is in the system an element of the conspiracy by the governing class against the governed which has serious implications for freedom of information and makes for an unhealthy consensus on some issues. In this sense the Privy Council is an undemocratic feudal club.

This process is reinforced by attempts to co-opt those who propose radical change to the system of consensus government.

Radical politicians are vulnerable to being co-opted – it is very flattering for a shadow minister to be called in and told in confidential Privy Council terms about, say, Northern Ireland affairs. Even in the Labour Party the accountability of the parliamentary party to the national party has been to some extent undermined by a parallel system of centralised power which is buttressed by patronage.

Such temptations are used in Britain to sustain a status quo which is unfavourable to the interests of the majority of the British people.

Assaults on Democracy

Britain is like a motorbike with four-wheel braking. It is amazing, given the existing constitutional and cultural constraints, that we make any progress at all. There was a flourishing renaissance of appointed public and semi-public posts under recent Conservative governments, to the real detriment of more representative bodies. Health authorities have been restructured to reduce the number of elected representatives and to replace them with appointees; budgets have been given to the training and enterprise councils (TECs), consisting of appointed businessmen and -women who now control substantial public funds; urban development corporations (UDCs) have been appointed and given control of massive budgets of upwards of £200 million, such as the London Docklands Development Corporation. With wide planning and development powers previously under the control of local elected councils and accountable to their electorates, the UDCs have applied criteria for which they are accountable to no one save the minister.

Britain's problems are intimately connected with the continuance of such aristocratic and technocratic hierarchies. Some industrialists would apparently rather be made peers, put on quangos and made governors of the BBC, before finishing on the Arts Council, than try to be successful businessmen or -women. Individuals, including many Labour leaders, are seduced by ribbons and ermine, and bemused by ritual and privilege. All hierarchies want to preserve rather than change institutions as each person looks upwards to please the person above, rather than downwards to provide what people below need.

The House of Lords, now reformed, can still present a substantial obstacle to a government, particularly one which might attempt what a Conservative MP called 'any stupid or revolutionary law if the Commons were so minded to do such a thing'. Governments must be subject to checks and balances, but these should be democratic, not imposed by appointed and hereditary elites. Under the 1949 Parliament Act the House of Lords can delay legislation, passed by the House of Commons, for one year, unless the legislation is a money bill. Therefore, because there is still an in-built Conservative majority in the Lords, a Labour government theoretically has a life of only four years, while a Conservative government, with a majority in both houses, has a full five-year term within which to pass legislation. Although the House of Lords will usually favour a Conservative government, its natural preference for the status quo will provide a brake on radical legislation from right or left, as the Lords' defeat of the War Crimes Bill in 1991 illustrated.

But neither the 1911 nor the 1949 Act has removed a Lords veto on subordinate legislation, that is, legislation made on the authority of powers delegated under statutes passed in the Commons. As the volume of government business increases, substantial legislation is made by ministers and local authorities under delegated powers without debate in Parliament. The Lords retain the right to strike down all legislation of this type, and could put a serious brake on a government whose policies they considered 'stupid and revolutionary'.

Democratic checks and balances were provided at local level in the early years of elected local government. But today local government has been reduced to little more than a tier of administration. When local government is squeezed from the centre, central government is not just restricting political opposition but restricting the system of democratic checks and balances. If the party of government objects to what local government is doing, it should campaign locally to defeat it: local councils should come under no form of control other than by the police station in the event of corruption, and the polling station in the event of unpopularity.

But Conservative governments of the 1980s crushed the challenge that local government posed to their power by constraining and, in the case of the GLC and the other metropolitan boroughs, eliminating local councils. Those councils that remain are forced to operate within severe financial restrictions set by central government.

By law now if local councillors vote for policies for which they have been elected which exceed centrally imposed spending limits, they can be made personally liable for any overspending judged to have taken place. Councillors may be made bankrupt or disqualified from office. No such punishment was imposed on government ministers after the financial debacle of Black Wednesday when £10 billion of public funds were lost. Nor was there provision to hold ministers or their appointees personally to account for the millions spent on developing Canary Wharf in the Docklands fiasco.

Local government has been reduced so that unwilling councils now have a role similar to that performed by the magistrates and the lord-lieutenants in the early nineteenth century, offering very little challenge to the power of the executive.

Official Secrecy

Nowhere has lack of accountability to the democratic process been more apparent than in our security services, trusted with substantial powers which leave them free from any effective democratic control. The extraordinary complacency with which the allegations in *Spycatcher* were received was the end result of monotonous propaganda over the years that such incidents were in the interests of the Crown and the defence of national security.

A major part of the work of the security services, traditionally closely connected with the military, has been for domestic purposes. The army has intermittently put down colonial and domestic revolts, as in Northern Ireland, and the security services have been used in the surveillance of domestic activity including that of trade unionists, members of CND and workers of the National Council of Civil Liberties. That there is a role for the security services is itself an issue for the people to decide, but such a service should certainly be democratically accountable for its actions. Parliament does not have to be told what the security services are planning to do in advance, only that people should know, after the event, on what grounds phones have been tapped, on whose authority individuals have been placed under surveillance or had their homes searched, which foreign governments have been undermined, which supported and why.

But instead, ex-members of the security services have explicitly rejected democratic control.

On a Channel 4 programme, *After Dark*, Lord Dacre, himself an ex-employee of MI6, and former master of Peterhouse College, Cambridge, was asked whether the secret service should be democratically accountable. He replied:

> I would like to see it accountable indirectly by having the ultimate authority outside party politics, and if there were a body which consisted of respectable people, respected by all sides, then it wouldn't be dependent on the government of the day ... It wouldn't be subject

to a particular party which happened to be in power and it would be subject to the state, not to the government.

Currently the security services are free to choose their own enemy under loose definitions given at different times. In the 1970s the Labour Home Office minister, John Harris, defined subversives as 'those who try to undermine the government of the state by violent or other means'. If you argue for constitutional reform you may be a subversive. Earlier, the Home Secretary, Maxwell Fyfe, gave a directive that the security services were free to act at a distance from ministerial control. Individual ministers, even senior members of government, have little access to security material even when it is of direct concern to them. Gerald Gardiner, Labour Lord Chancellor in 1964, one of the most senior privy counsellors, asked to see his own security file and was denied access. The security services do remain formally accountable to the prime minister, but, as Peter Wright demonstrated, members will flout that accountability if it conflicts with their own perception of the interests of the nation or state.

There is a complex intertwining of British and American security interests. American influence over British security was accepted during the 1950s and '60s under the royal prerogative of treaty-making as part of a deal to share American nuclear secrets and maintain a British nuclear force, notionally independent but under American control. It was because of this link that, according to some considerable evidence, James Angleton of the CIA was able to instruct MI5 agents to place Harold Wilson, when prime minister, under surveillance as a suspected Soviet agent. 'The accusation was totally incredible but given the fact that Angleton was head of the CIA's Counterintelligence Division we had no choice but to take it seriously,' Wright wrote.

Wilson was not the only target of these activities, which extended to Edward Heath, who was apparently considered by some in the security services to be too weak to be trusted with the premiership.

All these activities conducted against politicians and others were undertaken by a small group or groups who nonetheless had convinced themselves that their duty was to the Crown. Empowered to act by the royal prerogatives, they were also excluded from accountability by a duty of lifelong confidentiality owed to the Crown.

The whole *Spycatcher* affair, whatever the culpability of the individuals concerned, highlights a constitutional process, a structure of government, which permits state powers to be exercised against elected government and in secret.

Secrecy provides probably the most significant constraint upon effective opposition and accountable government. The new Official Secrets Act, introduced in 1988, eased some controls and allowed the disclosure of mundane matters, but extended other controls over information necessary for proper accountability. In particular the Act extended official secrecy to cover all matters concerning international affairs. The increasing integration of British policy into a European Union framework means that more and more aspects of government policy can be protected by official secrecy, if the prime minister so chooses.

The prime minister's control of information, in particular that related to the national interest, has led to Parliament being deliberately misled on several occasions. The invasion of Egypt in 1956, for example, was claimed to be in response to an Israeli attack. In reality, it was part of a pact between the Israelis, the French and the British to invade Egypt and topple Nasser. Indeed Peter Wright seems to confirm what others have claimed that 'at the beginning of the Suez crisis, MI6 developed a plan, through the London Station, to assassinate Nasser using nerve gas'.

It was also on the grounds of national security that the prerogative was used to establish the 130 permanent American bases in Britain after the Second World War. Parliament was told that these were for training missions, although it soon became clear that they were fully operational military bases. Similar Crown powers were used to commit substantial public funds to the development of nuclear weapons in the 1940s and, more recently, to the Chevaline and Zircon projects without the knowledge or approval of Parliament.

Whereas Britain has a thirty-year rule covering the release of secret information, the vast majority of US government activity is open to public scrutiny. The cases of Oliver North and Peter Wright provide a very interesting comparison. Colonel North was brought before Congress for his part in the illegal selling of arms to fund right-wing political activities in Nicaragua. Peter Wright, by contrast, confessed that he took part in the destabilisation of an elected government and yet, rather than trying to establish the truth or falsity of his allegations, the government tried to silence him.

The British state is a leaky ship. Civil servants who have access to sensitive material are in a position to make damaging disclosures to the opposition frontbench and can cause substantial embarrassment to the government.

The prime minister can of course leak anything he or she pleases through lobby briefings of the press, but at the same time can initiate a leak enquiry into any disclosure of information which has not been approved by him or her (such as occurred in the Clive Ponting case, not because he was passing sensitive information to the enemy, but because he had leaked information to the British people which discredited the government). In fact the new Official Secrets Act has been reformed to plug the gaps by which civil servants could justify leaks as being in the public interest. It has also brought much tighter restrictions to bear upon ex-members of the security services to prevent repetitions of the *Spycatcher* affair.

There is some role for official secrecy, but not to keep the activity of government and the process of decision-making under wraps, or to limit the ability of Parliament to enforce effective accountability. Unless the Commons can claim, on behalf of the electorate, a greater knowledge of what is happening, its role will slowly shrink back to that of *ex post facto* and ineffective auditor of decisions already taken, leaving government MPs as lobby fodder, merely rubber-stamping government decisions.

The European Union and Parliamentary Government

A development of potentially extraordinary significance has breathed new life into the authority of the royal prerogatives, adding greatly to their strength and to the government freedom to implement them against the wishes of Parliament. This change came with British membership of the European Union. Membership of the EU has increased the power of government and reduced the lawmaking role of Parliament, transferring lawmaking to the executive in a manner which uses the prerogatives on a scale not seen since 1649.

Until 1972 the prerogatives could only be used with binding legal force by the prime minister or executive in areas that were consistent with law made in Parliament. The House of Commons could set the boundaries within which Crown powers had their freedom. Britain's entry to the European Union removed control of laws, made under the Crown prerogatives in the EU, from direct control by Parliament.

The European Union is sustained by treaties, and therefore legislation made in the EU has effect in United Kingdom law under the prerogative. The 1972 Act, which is an enabling Act, allows EU law to become binding in United Kingdom courts without any requirement for further parliamentary approval.

Section 2(1) of the Act states:

> All such rights, powers, liabilities, obligations and restrictions from time to time created or arising by or under the Treaties, and all such remedies and procedures from time to time provided for by or under the Treaties, as in accordance with the Treaties are without further enactment to be given legal effect or used in the United Kingdom shall be recognised and available in law, and be enforced, allowed and followed accordingly.

This means that law is able to be made using Crown powers which then have immediate and direct effect in British courts.

As a result there are now two lawmaking authorities in operation in Britain. Under the present treaty arrangements EU legislation will override any law passed in the House of Commons.

A ruling of the European Court of Justice in 1978 made this point clearly. It instructed any national court to give primacy to the provisions of EU law:

> If necessary refusing of its own motion to apply any conflicting provision of national legislation, even if adopted subsequently ... it [would not be] necessary for the [national] court to request or even await the prior setting aside of such provisions by legislative or other constitutional means.

In consequence, legislation passed in the House of Commons will only become law if it does not conflict with legislation made in Brussels. Even so it will only remain law as long as the EU does not legislate to supersede it. The constitutional irony of this position is that whereas, before entry to the European Union, Crown powers could only be exercised in the legislative space left by Parliament, the position has to some degree been reversed: Parliament now only has lawmaking power in the space left for it by Crown prerogatives exercised by British ministers in Brussels.

The Crown now sets the boundaries within which the House of Commons has legislative freedom. The legal implications of this position were demonstrated on 10 March 1989, when the British High Court granted an interim injunction suspending the 1988 Merchant Shipping Act. The Act was referred to the European Court which overturned it on 26 July 1991, on the grounds that it was in breach of European Community law. In his judgement in the High Court, Lord Justice Neill made the point clearly: 'One cannot over-emphasize that, where applicable, Community law is part of the laws of England.'

Taken together, the treaties have acquired a quasi-constitutional status in British law, giving courts the power to decide which policies are legitimate on criteria determined under the Crown prerogatives. British governments are therefore bound by a large volume of legislation in the form of regulations and directives made in Brussels. This has placed very real legal obstructions in the way of any British government's free choice of policy and the right of the electors.

Entrenched in the Treaty of Rome and the Single European Act is a commitment to the free movement of labour and capital. Any policy that would seek to intervene significantly in the operation of free markets in Britain is formally against the treaty commitments and could be enforced as such by the British courts.

The Treaty of Rome explicitly prohibits any support to industry which might distort competition between member states, and the Maastricht Treaty imposed a strict budgetary discipline upon member states, forcing the Public Sector Borrowing Requirement to fall and establishing an independent European Central Bank, so effectively removing constitutional control of monetary policy from the governments of member states inside the eurozone.

Every British government is obliged to inform the European Commission if it plans to give financial support to industry, and if the Commission decides that the aid is against EU rules it will outlaw it. The 1974 Labour government was forced to give way on several policies, including regional employment premiums, temporary employment subsidies and government aid to offshore drilling supplies, which were judged contrary to the laws of the then Common Market.

Even if short-term market interests dictate that a factory has to close – even in circumstances where it was decided by the government that it be in the long-term interest of the country to keep it open – the obligations imposed by the treaty might outlaw any government assistance, even if it had been a major policy in that government's manifesto to provide such assistance.

This severely limits the freedom of government and the electors to decide on policies of their own choosing. A similar situation would never be accepted in America: California cannot ban imports of goods from New Mexico or Texas, but it is quite free to subsidise its own industry. Under the American constitution a socialist government would at least be constitutionally legal and could be elected with the freedom to carry out interventionist policies. But a government with a similar programme in Britain would be ruled to be in breach of our European treaty commitments. The Treaty of Rome has effectively put us in handcuffs, binding us to a constitution drawn up under Crown powers, which, to a significant degree, entrenches free market capitalism.

Much of the European Union debate has become, quite wrongly, entangled with the idea of sovereignty. Various commentators and critics of Europe lament the inability of Parliament to have sovereign control of its own territory. But no government – or monarch for that matter – has ever enjoyed complete independence or freedom from external circumstance. As is often said, it is peculiar to speak of a reduction in the sovereignty of the British Parliament by closer membership of Europe when, in or out, Britain's economic policy is influenced by interest rates in the Bundesbank and foreign policy by resolutions in the UN and decisions within NATO. Absolute sovereignty, in this sense – especially of Parliament which is a false notion anyway – has never been possessed by anyone. There have always been important external constraints on the freedom of governments to act. It has never been true that government could do what it liked.

But it is a severe limitation of democratic government and the electors when they are to lose control of their own legal order or the laws placed on the statute book, and government is not able to choose how to respond to external pressures or events.

Even were the government fully accountable to the British people, the people are clearly not in a position to control the basic rules governing society and their lives if laws made in Brussels can overrule domestic law made in Parliament. Against the striking impact which membership of the European Union has on the British system of government, it is argued in Europe's favour that it can provide Britain with far more progressive legislation and rights than will come from domestic government. Cynicism with British government encourages people to look to Brussels to save them from the mess. Many people have lost faith in the British political system to recognise their claims. The incorporation of the EU Social Chapter by the current government is yet another expression of the British tendency to look elsewhere in order to solve domestic problems. While the previous government was able to negotiate an 'opt out' from legislation to limit the working week, claiming this to be a victory for workers' rights, and was able to exclude itself from the Social Chapter and to campaign for Britain's right to be a low-wage economy, governments of all colours have used EU law to entrench market forces which allow companies to close factories and remove their investments from Britain without any check by British law.

People should be asking why Britain cannot have a social chapter of its own, why we don't have progressive legislation to protect the environment and why governments have so drastically reduced the power of local democracy. The answer to these questions is not to be found in Brussels, and the cost of trying to find it there is immense, in terms of our capacity for democratic self-government.

Conclusion

The position described by Bagehot in 1867 in *The English Constitution* has effectively been reversed. Bagehot described the monarch as the dignified element of the constitution, providing legitimacy to the disguised 'efficient' exercise of power by Parliament. Today it would be more accurate to describe the House of Commons as the dignified part of the constitution, which is there to 'excite and preserve the reverence of the population' while the powers of the Crown, controlled by the prime minister, are the efficient part 'by which [government], in fact, works and rules'.

But the crux of the matter is not that the prime minister has unlimited power – the prime minister is quite clearly not a dictator – but that the structures which determine what is politically feasible are generally undemocratic. The prime minister is able to use the prerogatives, and in particular the powers of patronage, to create a distance between his or her own executive actions and the controlling influence of the Cabinet, and in particular the control of the House of Commons. Here the party and MPs, particularly in the case of the Labour Party, can quite properly constrain the prime minister's freedom of action. Once isolated from the source of democratic authority the prime minister will be open to extra-parliamentary action from powerful interest groups and elites, not the least of which are the City, big business, the European Union, the Civil Service, the military, the media and, in the case of a Labour government, the unions, not to mention international pressures from foreign agencies and governments.

The prime minister will make compromises in order to retain the support of these groups and remain in power. As a result the semi-elected Parliament is reduced to one of a number of centres of influence which collectively determine the exercise of the prerogatives.

10
Democracy under Capitalism

In this extract from the 1993 book Common Sense: A New Constitution for Britain, *written with Andrew Hood, Benn looks at the rise of neoliberalism and its impact on democracy and rights.*

Capitalism has survived because it is powerful, not because it offers people the best or most worthwhile lifestyle or supports the rights of consumers, citizens or workers. In many countries market forces inflict immense hardship. Low prices for harvests whose markets are flooded by Western surpluses help keep African countries in famine, and when grain prices are favourable, the money earned is used either to repay loans to Western banks or to buy arms from Western firms, to continue civil wars, many of which are the product of national boundaries and Cold War politics inflicted on ex-colonial peoples. The new world order that is needed is one which could prevent half the world starving while the other half has food to burn, can have economies which succeed without having to export arms, and which recognises the rights of other cultures to organise their own economic systems.

Many of the problems facing the British, if not the world, economy stem from market forces having too much influence and there being too little intervention and planning in defence of human values protected by the state. No one calls for market forces to regulate everything. The armed forces and the judiciary will always be maintained by the state. Indeed markets cannot survive without a system of law enforcement to protect rights to private property. Without some institution to enforce contracts and private property, the capitalist market system would crumble, and without regulation to control the activities of large firms and protect consumers and workers, the outcomes would be unacceptable. But for many so-called new liberals the sole function of the state should be a minimal one.

Groups like the Institute for Economic Affairs and individuals like Professor Hayek, Milton Friedman and many 'Thatcherite' conservatives favour the 'rolling back of the state' to expose everything to market power. The Oxford fellow John Gray makes the point clearly: 'No system of government', he says, 'in which property rights and basic liberties are open to revision by temporary political majorities can be regarded as satisfying liberal requirements. For this reason, an authoritarian type of government may sometimes do better from a liberal standpoint than a democratic regime': classic repudiation of human rights and their role in shaping democracy.

The political right has in tandem with the liberation of market forces been justifying economic policy in which government has no responsibility for economic effects, and establishing a new consensus behind market forces and capitalism. What matters in this new consensus is the level of income tax, the size of state spending, and the smooth operation of the market untrammelled by financial deficits. Economic objectives are now determined by the needs of capitalist markets. Policy is to be geared to profit maximisation and economic growth, and this is achieved by letting market forces reduce wage levels without interference from trade unions. The rendering of market forces as non-political has been endorsed by the European Single Market, and through moves towards closer European monetary union, and has been the basis of calls for the Bank of England to be made independent of government control, either in its own right, or as part of a European network of independent national banks.

The removal of regulatory mechanisms has led to an absurd level of uncertainty and pessimism in the economy attributed by the people to a sense of neglect of their interests. Not so many years ago, high unemployment was what was meant by a recession. Now a recession has become something for economists to declare to have begun or ended, regardless of unemployment. For most people the recession will not be over when the City regains confidence and the FT index climbs a hundred points. Recession means business closure, job losses and low incomes.

The judgements of financiers and City bankers on economic issues are being adopted as an established orthodoxy rather than as reflecting a particular interest, to the exclusion usually of small businesses or trade unions. This bias is a mirror image of government economic policy of the kind which has left the economy vulnerable to speculative gambling; £10 billion of treasury funds were lost on 'Black Wednesday', September 1992, when the pound was unceremoniously expelled from the ERM.

The result of the unleashing of market forces and credit was the consumer boom, rising inflation, four years of interest rates over 10 per cent, and disastrous increase in imports and a recession which has destroyed jobs, put many people in hock to their banks, created tremendous insecurity and led to over 3 million people unable to earn a living. Utilities were sold short, giving shareholders quick returns. Collectively these policies fuelled a boom in financial markets while manufacturing was struggling to recover the level of output it had achieved in 1979. The financial speculation finally fell over its own feet in the October 1987 stock market crash. It is precisely the flexibility and volatility of markets – in particular of financial markets – which make them poor environments in which to create the certainty needed by producers and which eliminate the hopes which a charter of rights seeks to revive.

Yet, despite this abject failure, there is still the refrain that there is no alternative. Planning and industrial intervention are anathema. Businesses are trusted to instigate strategies in the public interest but local authorities are assumed incapable even of policies to create jobs and rebuild local communities. Government policy in the 1980s was specifically designed to distance local government from intervening in industrial regeneration. The urban development corporations set up to rebuild areas like the East End docks, and the government's enterprise zones, created areas of the country attractive to business because of substantial tax breaks, and because almost all local planning restrictions were removed.

These more recent examples of the dismantling of democratic bodies in the interests of profit were part and parcel of the abandonment of the economy to free markets which left people undefended against market forces. As a result, economic inequality has got far worse. According to the low-pay unit, inequalities in pay are larger now than at any time in the past century. Inequalities of wealth generally are also extreme. The poorest 50 per cent of the population in 1989 had only 6 per cent of the nation's personal wealth, a fall of 9 per cent from 1980.

The majority of people rely on selling their labour to survive. This is the unique feature of the economic system we have created. Under feudalism, a serf had to work to survive, but had access to *common* land, possessing, collectively with others, the means to a livelihood. Capitalism transforms everything but sea and air into private property and private wealth, allowing them to be owned indefinitely, and protecting them from future seizure by a powerful legal system defending private-property rights. Feudal peasants had private property too, but they also had recourse to a community-owned means of livelihood separate from the vagaries of market transactions.

Capitalism, by appropriating all land and all machinery and factories as private property, removes from the vast majority the right to work outside a system of market regulation and market discipline and hence any real control over their lives. Instead people's labour is transformed into a commodity like any other, and workers are their productivity, marketable attributes, flexibility, scarcity and the fact that they offer an employer value for money. But while the vast majority who are compelled to work to earn a living also have to depend on public provision for the education of their children, the health of their family and their pension when they retire, a minority derive sufficient income from investments to do without the assistance of the state. Despite all protestations that we are a society of classless consumers, bar a minority described as the underclass, the real division is still between those who subsist on their earnings, be they doctor, artist, bus driver, barrister, and those who subsist on income from someone else's labour.

The labour market works like any other respecting the laws of supply and demand with the consequence that it places different values on different backgrounds, education, skills and gender. Some skills are flexible and relatively plentiful. Many people have the skills to be a cleaner and the pay is low. Many people could learn bus driving and therefore in spite of a high demand for bus drivers in London pay is relatively low. But fewer people can qualify or pay for training as a barrister. The demand is less, but the supply is even lower. Barristers don't necessarily work harder than bus drivers – the vast difference in pay reflects the relative scarcity of barristers as a result of the imposition of artificial barriers.

In addition, a deliberate policy of high unemployment has kept pay claims low by the permanent threat of a pool of labour. The high supply of unemployed labour, artificially created and sustained by government policy, has led to the income of the poorest fifth of the population falling between 1979 and 1989 while the income of the richest fifth has risen by over a third. So much for the free market.

Restricted entry to the bar, and other occupations, begins at school. Low achievers leave school by the age of sixteen. Those with good GCSE results win access to A-level education, and the 'best' go on to university. And Oxford and Cambridge graduates, despite all assumptions in the 1960s and 1970s about the decline of elitism, have recolonised, or remained in control of, the BBC, the Civil Service and the judiciary, in absurdly disproportionate numbers.

Capitalism leaves people no choice but to take their chances selling their labour in this highly rigged market which tilts the balance against the powerless – the majority – and towards the powerful. Market forces do not have power and efficiency in excess of all other economic systems. Free market capitalism is not as fixed and immutable as the sunrise. It is a changing and evolving system sustained by human institutions and human ingenuity and often not free at all. The price mechanism supposedly coordinates and determines the production of goods in capitalism but is so imperfect a way of communicating information that businesses rely upon extensive market research, product testing and mass advertising. The resources spent by companies and governments researching the peculiarities of capitalism and trying to forecast its outcomes are immense.

There is no inevitability about current inequalities arising out of so-called free market capitalism just as there was no inevitability about the West African slave trade of the seventeenth century, although no doubt black slaves were told it was bad luck they were born black.

Decent income and wealth are as important a means to the equality of status which is citizenship as any of the other entitlements provided for in a bill of rights. The process needs to be continued to extend the idea of equal status into the economic relationship between employer and employee, and to the more fundamental relationship between those who own wealth and who are given freedom to act to increase it, and those without substantial wealth who are only given freedom to choose between a range of jobs and wages for which they are qualified.

Fairness should be extended to the treatment of labour and finance or capital. While companies have been given extensive freedom to move capital around the world, the free movement of labour is heavily managed by immigration controls which are biased towards those with investment capital. A factory can close with no period of notice, but workers must have a ballot before they close a company for a day.

There is no reason why flows of capital should not be managed in the same way as flows of people. Movements of capital have a major effect on the economy of a country, and provide those who control it with extensive political influence.

Rules over ownership of capital, like ownership of a car, should limit its detrimental use in society. Constraints on capital could make its use accountable to the needs of society rather than to the desire for profit.

Extending democratic accountability over capital might start with the removal of its control of the workplace. Currently, the governance of firms lies in the hands of managers who are technically responsible to majority shareholders. While the property qualification of the franchise for electing governments was finally removed at the beginning of the century, property rights still define who has control of the place of work. Industrial democracy would go some way to restoring the balance of power in the workplace. In particular it might provide one way of limiting the immense influence given to the small number of wealthy people who continue to own and control the British media by giving the power to appoint and dismiss management and editorial staff to the printers and journalists rather than to the shareholders.

The impact such a change might have highlights the extent to which economic power is inevitably political. It is as important that people control the choice of underlying principles for the economy as it is that they control the choice of procedural rights which support democracy. People should be free to decide for themselves how to organise their workplace, their local community and the national economy for the country as a whole. The social and economic rights established by the Commonwealth of Britain Bill would go some way towards building this broader concept of democracy and citizenship, re-establishing the control of democracy over the productive forces in a way which could allow people to have the economy work for them and for their needs, rather than for people to have to continue to spend their lives working for the needs of the economy.

11
Democracy and Marxism

In this speech, Benn explores his relationship with Marxism, and why it receives such a bitter reaction in Britain. He goes on to show how the labour movement should not abandon the right to take popular action.

The intellectual contribution made by Marx to the development of socialism was and remains absolutely unique. But Marx was much more than a philosopher. His influence in moving people all over the world to social action ranks him with the founders of the world's greatest faiths. And, like the founders of other faiths, what Marx and others inspired has given millions of people hope, as well as the courage to face persecution and imprisonment. Since 1917, when the Bolsheviks came to power in the Soviet Union, we have had a great deal of experience of national power structures created in the name of Marxism, and of the achievements and failures of those systems. Some of the sternest critics of Soviet society also based themselves upon Marx, including Leon Trotsky, Mao Zedong, Tito and a range of libertarian Marxist dissidents in Eastern Europe and Eurocommunists in the West.

Before I begin, let me make my own convictions clear.

I believe that no mature tradition of political democracy today can survive if it does not open itself to the influence of Marx and Marxism.

1. I believe that communist societies cannot survive if they do not accept the demands of the people for democratic rights upon which a secure foundation of consent for socialism must ultimately rest.
2. I believe that world peace can be maintained only if the peoples of the world are discouraged from holding to the false notion that a holy war is necessary between Marxists and non-Marxists.
3. I believe that the moral values upon which social justice must rest require us to accept that Marxism is now a world faith and must be allowed to enter into a continuing dialogue with other world faiths, including religious faiths.
4. I believe that socialism can only prosper if socialists can develop a framework for discussing the full richness of their own traditions and be ready to study the now-considerable history of their own successes and failures.

If an understanding of socialism begins – as it must – with a scientific study of our own experience, each country can best begin by examining its own history and the struggles of its people for social, economic and political progress.

British socialists can identify many sources from which our ideas have been drawn. The teachings of Jesus, calling upon us to 'love our neighbour as ourselves', acquired a revolutionary character when preached as a guide to social action. For example, when, in the Peasants' Revolt of 1381, the Reverend John Ball, with his liberation theology, allied himself to a popular uprising, both he, the preacher, and Wat Tyler, the peasant leader, were killed and their followers scattered and crushed by the king.

The message of social justice, equality and democracy is a very old one, and has been carried like a torch from generation to generation by a succession of popular and religious movements, by writers, philosophers, preachers and poets, and has remained a focus of hope, that an alternative society could be constructed. The national political influence of these ideas was seen in the seventeenth, eighteenth, nineteenth and twentieth centuries, and in the revolutions in England, America, France and Russia, each of which provided an important impetus to these hopes. But it was the Industrial Revolution, and the emergence of modern trade unionism in the nineteenth century, which provided a solid foundation of common interest upon which these utopian dreams could be based, that gave the campaigns for political democracy and social advance their first real chance of success.

If British experience is unique — as it is — in the history of the working-class movement, it lies in the fact that the Industrial Revolution began here, and gave birth to the three main economic philosophies which now dominate the thinking of the world.

The first was capitalism. Adam Smith, in his *Wealth of Nations*, developed the concept of modern capitalism as the best way to release the forces of technology from the dead hand of a declining and corrupted feudalism, substituting the invisible hand of the market and paving the way for industrial expansion and, later, imperialism. The Manchester School of liberal economists and the liberal view of an extended franchise combined to create a power structure which still commands wide support among the Establishment today.

The second was socialism. Robert Owen, the first man specifically identified as a socialist, also developed his ideas of socialism, cooperation and industrial trade unionism out of his experience of the workings of British capitalism.

And the third was Marxism. Marx and Engels also evolved many of their views of scientific socialism from a detailed examination of the nature of British capitalism and the conditions of the working-class movement within it.

Yet, despite the fact that capitalism, socialism and Marxism all first developed in this country, only one of these schools of thought is now accepted by the Establishment as being legitimate. Capitalism, its mechanisms, values and institutions are now being preached with renewed vigour by the British Establishment under the influence of Milton Friedman. Socialism is attacked as being, at best, romantic or, at worst, destructive. And Marxism is identified as the Antichrist, against which the full weight of official opinion is continually pitted in the propaganda war of ideas.

Why then is Marxism so widely abused? In seeking the answer to that question we shall find the nature of the Marxist challenge in the capitalist democracies. The danger of Marxism is seen by the Establishment to lie in the following characteristics.

First, Marxism is feared because it contains an analysis of an inherent, ineradicable conflict between capital and labour – the theory of the class struggle. Until this theory was first propounded the idea of social class was widely understood and openly discussed by the upper and middle classes, as in England until Victorian times and later.

But when Marx launched the idea of working-class solidarity, as a key to the mobilisation of the forces of social change and the inevitability of victory that that would secure, the term 'class' was conveniently dropped in favour of the idea of national unity, around which there existed a supposed common interest in economic and social advance within our system of society, whether that common interest is real or not. Anyone today who speaks of class in the context of politics runs the risk of excommunication and outlawry. In short, they themselves become casualties in the class war which those who have fired on them claim does not exist.

Second, Marxism is feared because Marx's analysis of capitalism led him to a study of the role of state power as offering a supportive structure of administration, justice and law enforcement, which, far from being objective and impartial in its dealings with the people, was, he argued, in fact an expression of the interests of the established order and the means by which it sustains itself. One recent example of this was Lord Denning's 1980 Dimbleby Lecture. It unintentionally confirmed that interpretation in respect of the judiciary and is interesting mainly because few twentieth-century judges have been foolish enough to let that cat out of the bag, where it has been quietly hiding for so many years.

Third, Marxism is feared because it provides the trade union and labour movement with an analysis of society that inevitably arouses political consciousness, taking it beyond wage militancy within capitalism. The impotence of much American trade unionism and the weakness of past non-political trade unionism in Britain have borne witness to the strength of the argument for a labour movement with a conscious political perspective that campaigns for the reshaping of society, and does not just compete with its own people for a larger part of a fixed share of money allocated as wages by those who own capital, and who continue to decide what that share will be.

Fourth, Marxism is feared because it is international in outlook, appeals widely to working people everywhere, and contains within its internationalism a potential that is strong enough to defeat imperialism, neo-colonialism and multinational business and finance, which have always organised internationally. But international capital has fended off the power of international labour by resorting to cynical appeals to nationalism by stirring up suspicion and hatred against outside enemies. This fear of Marxism has been intensified since 1917 by the claim that all international Marxism stems from the Kremlin, whose interests all Marxists are alleged to serve slavishly, thus making them, according to capitalist Establishment propaganda, the witting or unwitting agents of the national interest of the USSR.

Fifth, Marxism is feared because it is seen as a threat to the older organised religions, as expressed through their hierarchies and temporal power structures, and their close alliance with other manifestations of state and economic power. The political establishments of the West, which for centuries have openly worshipped money and profit and ignored the fundamental teachings of Jesus, do, in fact, sense in Marxism a moral challenge to their shallow and corrupted values and it makes them very uncomfortable. Ritualised and mystical religious teachings, which offer advice to the rich to be good and the poor to be patient, each seeking personal salvation in this world and eternal life in the next, are also liable to be unsuccessful in the face of such a strong moral challenge as socialism makes. There have, over the centuries, always been some Christians who, remembering the teachings of Jesus, have espoused these ideas, and today there are many radical Christians who have joined hands with working people in their struggles. The liberation theology of Latin America proves this, and thus deepens the anxieties of church and state in the West.

Sixth, Marxism is feared in Britain precisely because it is believed by many in the Establishment to be capable of winning consent for radical change through its influence in the trade union movement, and then in the election of socialist candidates through the ballot box. It is indeed therefore because the Establishment believes in the real possibility of an advance of Marxist ideas by fully democratic means that they have had to devote so much time and effort to the misrepresentation of Marxism as a philosophy of violence and destruction, to scare people away from listening to what Marxists have to say.

These six fears, which are both expressed and fanned by those who defend a particular social order, actually pinpoint the wide appeal of Marxism, its durability and its strength more accurately than many advocates of Marxism may appreciate.

The Communist Manifesto, and many other works of Marxist philosophy, has always profoundly influenced the British labour movement and the British Labour Party, and has strengthened our understanding and enriched our thinking.

It would be as unthinkable to try to construct the Labour Party without Marx as it would be to establish university faculties of astronomy, anthropology or psychology without permitting the study of Copernicus, Darwin or Freud, and still expect such faculties to be taken seriously. There is also a practical reason for emphasising this point now. The attacks upon the so-called hard left of the Labour

Party by its opponents in the Conservative, Liberal and Social Democratic parties and by the Establishment are not motivated by fear of the influence of Marxists alone. These attacks are really directed at all socialists and derive from the knowledge that democratic socialism in all its aspects does reflect the true interest of a majority of people in this country, and that what democratic socialists are saying is getting through to more and more people, despite the round-the-clock efforts of the media to fill the newspapers and the airwaves with a cacophony of distortion.

If the Labour Party could be bullied or persuaded to denounce its Marxists, the media – having tasted blood – would demand next that it expelled all its socialists and reunited the remaining Labour Party with the SDP to form a harmless alternative to the Conservatives, which could then be allowed to take office now and again when the Conservatives fell out of favour with the public. Thus British capitalism, it is argued, would be made safe forever, and socialism would be squeezed off the national agenda. But if such a strategy were to succeed – which it will not – it would in fact profoundly endanger British society. For it would open up the danger of a swing to the far right, as we have seen in Europe over the last fifty years.

But having said all that about the importance of the Marxist critique, let me turn to the Marxist remedies for the ills that Marx so accurately diagnosed. There are schools of thought within the Marxist tradition and it would be as foolish to lump them all together as to every Christian denomination into one and then seek to generalise about the faith. Nevertheless, there are aspects of the central Marxist analysis which it is necessary to subject to special scrutiny if the relationship between Marxism and democracy is to be explored.

Marx seemed to identify all social and personal morality as being a product of economic forces, thus denying to that morality any objective existence over and above the inter-relationship of social and economic forces at that moment in history. I cannot accept that analysis.

Of course the laws, customs, administration, armed forces and received wisdom in any society will tend to reflect the interests and values of the dominant class, and if class relationships change by technology, evolution or revolution, this will be reflected in a change of the social and cultural superstructure. But to go beyond that and deny the inherent rights of men and women to live, to think, to act, to argue or to obey or resist in pursuit of some inner call of conscience – as pacifists do – or to codify their relationships with each other in terms of moral responsibility seems to me to be throwing away the child of moral teaching with the dirty bathwater of feudalism, capitalism or clericalism.

In saying this, I am consciously seeking to re-establish the relevance and legitimacy of the moral teachings of Jesus, while accepting that many manifestations of episcopal authority and ritualistic escapism have blanked out that essential message of human brotherhood and sisterhood. I say this for many reasons.

It is very important for many reasons that religion and politics should not be separated into watertight compartments, forever at war with each other. For centuries the central social arguments and battles which we now see as political or economic were conducted under the heading of religion. Many of the most important popular struggles were conceived by those who participated in them as being waged in pursuit of religious convictions. Similarly, some of the most oppressive political establishments exercised their power in the name of God.

Unless we are prepared to translate the religious vocabulary which served as a vehicle for political ideas for so many centuries into a modern vocabulary that recognises the validity of a scientific analysis of nature, society and its economic interests, we shall cut ourselves off from all those centuries of human struggle and experience and deny ourselves the richness of our own inheritance.

Marx and Marxist historians have, of course, consciously reinterpreted ancient history in the light of their own analysis, but no real dictionary can be restricted to a one-way translation based upon hindsight. We need a two-way translation to enable us to understand and utilise, if we wish to do so, the wisdom of earlier years to criticise contemporary society. It is in this context that I find some other aspects of Marxism unsatisfactory.

Marx made much of the difference between scientific socialism and utopian socialism, which he believed suffered from its failure to root itself in a vigorous study of the economic and political relationships between the social classes. The painstaking scholarship which he and Engels brought to bear upon capitalism has left us with a formidable set of analytical tools, without which socialists today would have a much poorer theoretical understanding of the tasks which they are undertaking.

But, having recognised that priceless analytic legacy that we owe to Marx, in one sense Marx himself was a utopian, in that he appeared to believe that when capitalism had been replaced by socialism, and socialism by communism, a classless society, liberated by the final withering away of the state, would establish some sort of heaven on earth. Human experience does not, unfortunately, give us many grounds for sharing that optimism. For humanity cannot organise itself without some power structure of the state, and Marx seems to have underestimated the importance of Lord Acton's warning that power tends to corrupt: mistakenly believing this danger would disappear under communism.

It is here that both the moral argument referred to above, and the issue of democratic accountability, which have both played so large a part in the pre-Marxist and non-Marxist traditions of the British labour movement, can be seen to have such relevance.

For allowing for the weaknesses of labourism, economism and the anti-theoretical pragmatism which have characterised the British working-class movement at its worst, two of the beliefs to which our movement has clung most doggedly were the idea that some actions were 'right' and others were 'wrong'; and the obstinate determination to force those exercising political or economic power over us to accept the ultimate discipline of accountability, up to now seen mainly through the regular use of the ballot box, through which all adults would have their say in a universal suffrage to elect or dismiss governments. The British working-class movement has over the years clung passionately to these twin ideas of morality and accountability in politics and they constitute the backbone of our faith. Some Marxists might argue that these objectives are too limited, are not specifically socialist and constitute little more than a cover for collaborationist strategies which underpin bourgeois capitalist liberal democracy, complete with its soothing religious tranquillisers. I readily admit that a humanitarian morality and accountability are not enough, in themselves, to establish socialism, but they are essential if socialism is to be established, and if socialism is to be worth having at all. A socialist economic transformation may be achieved by force, but if so, it then cannot be sustained by agreement, and socialism may degenerate into the imposition of a regime administered by those whose attempts to maintain it can actually undermine it rather than develop it.

How, then, on this analysis, should we approach the arguments between the Marxist and some non-Marxist socialists, which have in the past centred around their different assessment of the importance that should be attached to the role of parliamentary democracy?

Before we can do that we have to examine, in some detail, what is meant by the phrase 'parliamentary democracy', for it lends itself to many definitions. Seen from the viewpoint of the Establishment, Britain has enjoyed parliamentary government since 1295. All that has happened in the intervening period is that the Queen-in-Parliament has agreed to exercise the Crown's powers constitutionally.

This means accepting legislation passed 'by and with the advice and consent of the Lords Spiritual and Temporal in Parliament assembled', and accepting that an elected majority in the House of Commons is entitled to expect that its leader will be asked to form an administration by the Crown; and that that administration will be composed of Her Majesty's ministers, who in their capacity as Crown advisers will be free to use the royal prerogatives to administer and control the civil and military services of the Crown.

It can be seen that in a formal sense Britain is far less democratic in its form of government than those countries whose peoples may elect a president, both houses of their legislature and have entrenched their rights in written constitutional safeguards. Why then does the British labour movement appear to be so satisfied with our democratic institutions?

In one sense, of course, it is not. The abolition of the House of Lords and the abrogation of British accession to the Treaty of Rome are among the items likely to feature high on the agenda for the next Labour manifesto.

But if, as I believe, the real strength of parliamentary democracy lies in the fact that the power to remove governments without violent revolution is now vested in the people, that is a very significant gain, which should not be dismissed as being of little account, a fraud to be exposed, bypassed and replaced.

One of the reasons why the British Labour Party and the British people are so suspicious of certain supposedly revolutionary schools of Marxist thought is that they believe that insufficient attention is paid by them to the importance of our democratic institutions, thus defined; and fear that if they were to be dismantled, we should lose what we struggled so hard and so long to achieve. We would then be set back, perhaps with no gains to show for it. Parliamentary democracy is an evolving system, not yet fully developed, which enjoys wide support for what it has achieved so far.

Those that call themselves revolutionary socialists and denounce the rest of us as nothing more than left-talking reformists are not, in my judgement, the real revolutionaries at all. They are nothing more than left-talking revolutionists who, while pointing to the deficiencies in our parliamentary democracy, offer themselves as candidates for Parliament, and none of them are planning an armed revolution or a general strike to secure power by a *coup d'état*. If such people do exist, I have not met them, heard of them or become aware of any influence they have in any known political party of grouping of the left.

Nor for that matter is there much hard evidence to suggest that there should be wide public support for a counter-revolution to topple an elected Labour government by force, on the Chilean model.

Though these may seem to be highly theoretical matter, it is necessary to complete the analysis, to refer briefly to the varying circumstances in which popular action is legitimate.

There is clearly an inherent right to take up arms against tyranny or dictatorship, to establish or uphold democracy, on exactly the same basis, and for the same reasons, that the nation will respond to a call to arms to defeat a foreign invasion or repel those who have successfully occupied a part of our territory.

In a different context, we accept certain more limited rights to defy the law on grounds of conscience, or to resist laws that threaten basic and long-established liberties, as for example if Parliament were to prolong its life and remove the electoral rights of its citizens. The defence of ancient and inherent rights, as for example the rights of women, or of trade unionists, or of minority communities, could legitimately lead to some limited civil disobedience, accompanied by an assertion that the responsibility for it rested upon those who had removed these rights in the first place. And, at the very opposite end of this scale of legitimate opposition, lies the undoubted right to act directly to bring public pressure, from outside Parliament, to bear upon Parliament to secure a redress of legitimate grievances. Such extra-parliamentary activity has played a long and honourable part in the endless struggle to win basic rights.

To assert that extra-parliamentary activity is synonymous with anti-parliamentary conspiracies is to blur a distinction that it is essential to draw with scientific precision, if we are to understand what is happening and not mistake a democratic demonstration for an undemocratic riot; a democratic protest for an undemocratic uprising; or a democratic reformer for an undemocratic revolutionary.

The labour movement in Britain, egged on by a hostile media, is now engaged in a microscopic examination of its own attitude to the role of extra-parliamentary activity. Such an examination can only help to advance socialism. Perhaps the simplest way to understand these issues is to examine the attitude of the Conservative Party to the same issues. The Tory Party and its historical predecessors have never wasted a moment's valuable time upon such constitutional niceties. Throughout our whole history, the owners of land, the banks and our industries, have been well aware that their power lay almost entirely outside Parliament, and their interest in Parliament was confined to a determination to maintain a majority there, to safeguard their interests by legislating to protect them. Extra-parliamentary activity has been a way of life for the ruling classes, from the Restoration, through to the overthrow of the 1931 Labour government and the election in 1979 of Mrs Thatcher.

In power they use Parliament to protect their class interests and reward their friends. In opposition they use the Lords, where they always have a majority, to frustrate the Labour majority in the Commons, and supplement this with a sustained campaign of extra-parliamentary activity to undermine the power of Labour governments by investment strikes, attacks upon the pound sterling, granting or withholding business confidence – all using, when necessary, the power of the IMF, the multinationals and the media.

Labour has real power outside Parliament, and the people we represent can only look to an advance of their interests and of the prospects of socialism if Labour MPs harness themselves to the movement outside and develop a strong partnership, which alone can infuse fresh life into Parliament as an agent of democratic change.

These matters and the associated issues of party democracy have received a great deal of attention within the labour movement over the last few years and it is not hard to see why. We want the Labour Party to practise the accountability it preaches. Seen in that light, the adherence of the labour movement to parliamentary democracy, our determination to expand it, becomes a great deal more than a romantic attachment to liberal capitalist bourgeois institutions. By contrast, it can be seen to have a crucial role to play in achieving greater equality and economic democracy.

III. Industry

12
The Case for Workers' Control

After Labour lost the election in 1970, Benn was made head of the NEC of the party, but he was becoming increasingly vocal in his radicalism. A speech made in 1971 at the Amalgamated Engineering Union (AEU) conference called for workers' control.

One of the mistakes of the Labour Party has been its tendency to think that economic management and budgetary policy alone could get us the growth we want, or that legislation could solve the immensely complicated human relations that really determine the atmosphere in industry.

I feel this particularly strongly as a result of my experience as Minister of Technology over the four years that I spent there. We did a great deal that was useful in encouraging the reorganisation of industry, in shipbuilding and engineering, and by assisting the spread of new techniques that would help us to earn our living with less sweat and unnecessary effort.

But in one sense I became convinced that operating at ministerial level on problems of industrial organisation could be a sort of technocratic dead end. There is a limit to what you can do by mergers and public money and encouraging better management, even when you are dealing as humanely, as we tried to do, with the problems, say, of Upper Clyde shipbuilding.

What we are really looking for surely is a new approach to industrial policy that takes account of the human factor and makes our policy fit the people it is intended to help, instead of doing it the other way round. The old idea of management from the top has got to be looked at again.

It isn't only the old family business where the grandson of the founder has inherited power that he is quite unfitted to wield. The new grey-flannel brigade with their degrees in business studies, familiar with the language of accountancy and computers, and their shiny offices away from the dirt and noise of the factory floor are still often too remote, and claim too much power that they haven't the experience or knowledge to exercise properly.

I am strongly in favour of educating people in the complicated problems of organisation that have to be dealt with by upper management. There are plans to be made and long-term investment decisions that have to be got right, and big marketing operations to be mounted and a host of administrative problems to be sorted out. Without expertise in these areas a firm can easily run into difficulties or even go bankrupt.

But it is also true that the man who actually has to do a job of work on the factory floor, or in a foundry, or in a shop or office, is the best person to know how his or her work should be organised. There is nothing that creates more ill will in industry than when people are denied the elementary authority they need to plan and guide the work they are qualified to do.

One of the most horrifying experiences of my ministerial life was to walk round factories with management that obviously didn't know what was going on, or who was doing what, and yet quite happily assumed that the right to manage on behalf of the shareholders included the right to tell everybody what to do, and when things went wrong to try to find a remedy without consulting the men and women on whose work and effort the whole future of the firm depended.

I believe that there is more seething discontent in industry as a result of this situation than anyone is ready to admit. Indeed I think that many of the industrial disputes which we read about in the papers are merely triggered off by wage claims, and really reflect the deep feelings of workers who are fed up with being treated as if they were halfwits only fit to be told what to do and never asked for their advice or given the power to do things for themselves. They are consistently underestimated and their intelligence is insulted because the structure of power in industry has failed to take account of the vastly improved educational advances of recent years; and because of the fact that the mass media – with all their faults, on which I have strong views – have created a far more intelligent community than any country ever had in the whole of its history.

If we are going to talk about industrial policy let's start with the people. Let's forget about legislation for a moment and start talking about industrial democracy. And I mean industrial democracy and not just better communications, or more personnel managers, or consultations, or participation or company news sheets. Least of all am I talking about putting one 'tame' worker on the board of a company, or trying to pretend that a few shares for the workers will make them all into little capitalists and iron out real conflicts of interest.

I am talking about democracy. And democracy means that the people ultimately control their managers. Just that, no less and no more. It's time we asked ourselves some fundamental questions about the management of industry.

For example, why should the people who own a firm control it? We abandoned that principle years ago in the political arena. For centuries the people who owned the land in Britain ran Parliament. It took a hundred years of struggle to give the people the power to choose and remove their political managers – MPs and ministers. If we can trust the country to democracy, why on earth can't we trust individual firms to the people who work in them? This is not a particularly revolutionary doctrine in all conscience. No one is suggesting – at least I am not – that you do it by throwing petrol bombs or starting a guerrilla movement in Morecambe. You could just as easily do it by peaceful industrial bargaining and by removing the obstacles to it by legislation.

I have always thought it was a great pity that working people in Britain set their sights so low. A wage claim to offset rising prices and improve real living standards is very important for workers and their families. But if the employer passes it on by raising his prices, which the workers have to pay back to him through the shops, the gain is not always as good as it looks. Worse still, it doesn't alter the power relationship between the worker and his employer at all. Indeed, if the higher prices lead to higher profits and higher dividends, it can actually widen the gap between rich and poor and thus prop up the very system that we ought now deliberately to be trying to replace. The trade union movement – in both the private and public sectors – ought now to develop a conscious long-term policy of negotiating itself into a position of real power in industry. Nobody can doubt the negotiating strength of the trade union movement in a modern industrial society. Indeed, the government is now underlining that power by attacking management for giving way so easily to wage claims. But why do management give way? Because they have no option. The dislocation that a prolonged strike will cause can sometimes be far more costly to the firm than paying the claim in full.

If the trade union movement were to bargain as strongly for industrial power as it does for higher wages, the management would also be ready to concede. Because then the alternative would be the high financial cost of a strike or the relatively low cost of sharing their power with the workers in their own firm.

No one could expect to achieve everything in the first year. But if the trade union movement set itself the target of negotiating for the workers' power in each firm to acquire greater control of that firm, by agreement with the present management, over a five-year period – in my opinion it would succeed.

Moreover this could be done even with the present government in power since no legislation would be needed. It might be that later a Labour government would have to legislate to make it possible to finish the job by giving the workers the explicit right to do this.

After all, the present Industrial Relations Bill provides the most elaborate system of ballots to enforce the Tory view of trade union democracy and provide for the recognition of agency shops and the like. What could be easier than for a Labour government to legislate, to carry it a stage further, so that the boards of directors of all companies were subjected to the same procedures for ballots when they were nominated by the shareholders and could be recalled, or replaced, if they did not measure up to the job?

If we did that, many of the problems of communication in industry would settle themselves. A board of directors who depended for their continuation in office on the consent of their workforce would bend over backwards to communicate with them and consult them and let them participate and allow them to run their own work. They would have to.

Of course such a solution would not be without difficulties. A firm managed by consent would not find any of its problems solved by magic. It would still have to attract investment by getting a return on its capital. It would still have to find markets for its goods and produce the right products for those markets. It would still be liable to price itself out of the market by paying those who worked in it more than the market could bear. It would still need the best management it could possibly get, including the graduates in business studies. But with this one difference. They would be working, as workers, for the other workers and not for the shareholders alone.

Some trade unionists of the old school might object to this for another reason. They might fear that it would impose too great a responsibility on them and weaken their power to bargain for higher wages. But it would certainly not affect their bargaining role. They would still have to bargain about wages and conditions with the management the workers had chosen, just as they now have to bargain with the managers that the shareholders have imposed on them. After all, the electors still bargain with a government even when they have elected it.

But it is true that this bargaining would be done under conditions in which the workers had to share the responsibility for the consequences of the increased wages they were asking for and everything else they did.

Indeed, one of the most powerful arguments for adopting the policies that I am discussing is exactly that responsibility would be placed upon workers in industry who already have massive power but are now denied the responsibility that should go with it. The third industrial revolution has transferred this bargaining power to the workshop, but the legal structure of our companies has not been adapted in such a way as to allow this responsibility to go with this new power.

For the community as a whole, a policy for industrial democracy could help to combat inflation and increase productivity. Wage claims that might really bankrupt the firm would obviously not be pressed in a firm where self-management had placed the ultimate responsibility on the workers. And if the workers in a firm could be given the power to plan their own work, to take account of their own skills, productivity might increase more rapidly than could ever be achieved by hiring hordes of management consultants, to tell the managers to tell the workers what to do in the interests of the shareholders.

But this alone would not be enough. It might – and I believe it would – provide the outline of a practicable sensible alternative to the short-sighted and reactionary Industrial Relations Bill now before Parliament.

But what it would not do would be to solve another equally difficult problem of the unacceptable differential between the highest-paid directors in any company and the really low-paid workers whose incomes are an affront to a society that pretends to be civilised.

It is true that the problems of differentials would certainly be discussed in any firm that had adopted self-management. But the percentage system by definition continually increases differentials again. Ten per cent of £15 a week is very different from 10 per cent of £20,000 a year and nothing that we have yet thought up, by way of national machinery, or ministerial intervention, offers us an answer to that problem.

It may well be that we have been looking at the problem from the wrong angle. It might be better to re-examine it from the point of view of the firm itself, since it is the firm which earns the income for everybody who draws his salaries or wages from that common pool. It is clear that if those at the top draw too much out of that pool there will be less for those at the bottom. The moral responsibility for seeing that those at the bottom get an adequate income must surely rest squarely and fairly on those others who draw a bigger income from the same pool.

If this is so, then it is the ratio between the top salaries and the bottom wages in each firm that ought to interest us. Suppose, just for example, we set this ratio at 10:1. To take one case: suppose we laid it down that if the lowest wages in a firm were £15 a week – or £750 a year – then the highest salary paid should not exceed £7,500 a year. Ten to one is a very wide ratio, but there are thousands of firms – if not the overwhelming majority – where the lowest-paid do get £15 a week and the directors get £10,000, £20,000 or more, which is not ten times as much, but twenty or thirty times as much.

So far I have not dealt with public enterprise. It is a sad reflection on the way in which we have set up our nationalised industries that, even in those industries, we have got nowhere near real industrial democracy, nor achieved any fairer distribution of incomes between the board members and the lowest paid. So if the policies which I have been discussing were only applied in the public sector, it would do more to change their social purposes and working environment than the act of nationalisation itself. But there is no reason why we should not get exactly the same benefits even in firms that are privately owned. The shareholders could be contained into their more limited role, as investors, free to move their money in and out, but deprived of their present insupportable and unenforceable claim to be the sole arbiter of the fate of the workers in the firms they own, or the sole authority to whom the management should be responsible.

What then is the case for the extension of public ownership? Clearly if by industrial democracy, and an egalitarian incomes policy, we could drive capitalism back into a more limited role, as a form of investment deprived of the power that has historically gone with it, the argument about public ownership changes its character. But that is not to say it loses its force.

Quite the reverse. One thing should certainly be clear from our experience of the last Labour government – and perhaps nobody is better qualified to say it than I am, because I was responsible for administering the policy. Never again should a Labour government pour money into private industry without claiming, and acquiring, the same rights as any other private investor in exactly the same proportion as the total public investment stands to the private investment.

If we had done that in the last Labour government, many of the firms that we helped – certainly in shipbuilding and in the aircraft industry – would have automatically moved into the public sector simply by virtue of the grants and loans we made available. It would have been better to have done it that way. Next time we should see this as a conscious and constructive approach to the extension of public ownership.

After the Tories have first bankrupted, and then nationalised, and then subsidised Rolls-Royce, we would certainly have nothing to fear from their opposition to such a policy in a general election campaign. Indeed, I think the whole public attitude to public ownership has undergone a fundamental change and there is far more widespread support for it than there was even a few years ago.

And if nationalised industries were seen to be democratically run, and to be distributing incomes more fairly as well as being accountable to the public for the major decisions they make, we could take a massive step towards democratic socialism. And we could do it by the traditional means of common sense and public consent which lie at the hearts of the traditions of parliamentary democracy and the British labour movement.

13
A Ten-Year Industrial Strategy for Britain

Composed by Benn, Frances Morrell and Francis Cripps and presented to the Labour Party Industrial Policy Sub-committee in 1975, their industrial strategy was intended for the party conference that autumn, but it was rejected. It was later published as a pamphlet.

This memorandum proposes a ten-year industrial strategy designed to halt the process of de-industrialisation and restore Britain's manufacturing capacity.

1. The heart of the problem is that British manufacturing industry, the primary source of our national income, is trapped in a spiral of decline, and after thirty years of low investment is contracting under its own momentum. Britain's economic and industrial crisis springs directly from this devastating trend to contraction whose symptoms are inflation and unemployment. And this problem must be completely distinguished from the present world recession although it is likely to be accelerated by it.
2. We must therefore now aim to double the annual rate of new investment in manufacturing industry using the NEB and the Planning Agreements so that within ten years we will be spending £6 billion a year, at today's prices.

3. Government must meanwhile provide systematic support for firms in financial difficulty so that they can maintain jobs and make their contribution to our national income during the first phase of re-equipment.
4. Additional investment on the scale required must necessarily draw heavily on money from taxation and pension and insurance funds which in future will need to invest a higher and agreed proportion of their new funds in manufacturing industry every year.
5. The government contribution to this programme will necessarily require the evolution of an economic strategy which will ensure a return to full employment and will help industry to gain new markets and regain those lost to foreign competitors.
6. The government and public agencies must accept responsibility for planning the funding, manpower policy, location of jobs and provision of public utilities and services which would accompany such an investment drive. Since democratic planning is essential, guidelines should be openly discussed and agreed, and should require government planners to disclose information, including their own criteria for decision-making, and agree to plan with trade unions and management and other interested parties at the appropriate level before taking a major decision. This democratic planning concept will provide a new and broader framework within which full industrial democracy can develop along the lines to which we are committed.
7. The party should seek to reach a new agreement with the trade union movement on the basis of this strategy and in the light of our desperately difficult economic circumstances.
8. This crisis in our present economic system is deep and real and our socialist analysis helps us to understand that the problems it has thrown up cannot be blamed, as the Tories would have it, on working people who are now expected to pay the price for Britain's industrial failure.

Britain's industrial future, whatever the verdict of the British people on the Common Market, depends upon the adoption of such a policy which combines sustained new investment on an unprecedented scale with determined support for our existing industrial base.

The only alternative open to us is the acceptance of the continuing shutdown of British industry that has accelerated since 1970, and the low wages, rising unemployment and emigration of our skilled workers which has historically accompanied these circumstances in the past.

The Spiral of Decline

The trend to contraction of British manufacturing industry has gathered force in the last four years. If this trend is allowed to continue, we will have closed down 15 per cent of our entire manufacturing capacity and nearly 2 million industrial workers will have been made redundant between 1970 and 1980.

The shift of workers into low-paid service jobs in this country is a symptom of depression and not, as in the United States where per capita income is twice as high, a manifestation of prosperity. The suggestion often made that as a country we might live by exporting services such as tourism and banking is wildly unrealistic. Our service exports last year were £6 billion; our earnings from the export of manufactures were £14 billion and this excludes the saving of imports represented by production for the home market.

Industrial depression is beginning to turn Britain into a branch economy controlled by multinational corporations whose policy is more and more to produce elsewhere and sell here. In this way the decline of our manufacturing base is reinforced by multinational pessimism about our future. The trend nature of our industrial contraction is confirmed by examining the performance of British industry in the boom of 1973. Compared with the last peak in 1969, one-quarter of manufacturing industry showed an absolute fall in output and 90 per cent showed a fall in employment.

Overall, the increase in manufacturing output was about 7 per cent below that required to secure full employment and a strong balance of payments. The 7 per cent shortfall of industrial capacity was matched by a 7 per cent fall in manufacturing employment. During the period 1970–4 the average number of manufacturing jobs lost through redundancy was about 160,000 a year. Less than one in three of the jobs lost was effectively replaced by creation of a new job in the manufacturing sector.

The growing shortage of industrial capacity is reflected by worsening balance of trade in industrial products. Over the four years 1970–4 the volume of imports of manufactures to Britain rose 67 per cent, twice as much as British exports of manufactures which rose only 35 per cent. The trend nature of the contraction of industry, spread across almost all sectors, is confirmed by the geographical spread of industrial dereliction within Britain and by the fact that the trade balance has worsened in almost every category of industrial product.

The lack of capacity, loss of markets to foreign competitors and contraction of jobs from which we now suffer follow years of low investment in British industry. Over the decade 1963–72 the value of investment per worker in manufacturing industry in Britain was lower in every year than in every other competitor country for which we have figures – and in general it was only about one-half the average level in those countries.

Past failure to invest is not the only cause of our economic and industrial decline. Different schools of thought attach different weights to the influence of government management of the economy, the activities of large multinational companies, the stalemate in management–labour relationships, and the destructiveness of the class organisation of British society. But our low investment can be measured, it can be remedied and we know that higher investment is a prerequisite for industrial recovery. For this reason we argue that the direct answer to the accelerating collapse of British industry must lie in the provision of an adequate level of investment to provide the successful industry on which our future national income depends. But new investment is not immediate in its effect, and during the next few years the government must also be willing systematically to support firms and enterprises in trouble, and offer assistance to companies and workers to enable them to continue to operate. This two-fold recovery programme will provide the basis for an industrial strategy for a decade.

Doubling the Annual Rate of Investment

Within the next decade Britain must increase the rate of investment in manufacturing industry from the present £3 billion a year to double this level – roughly £6 billion a year at today's prices. Investment on this scale will be needed to expand the growth of productive capacity at an adequate rate, to provide a sufficient flow of new jobs and to re-equip workers by modernising low-wage, low-productivity jobs throughout industry.

This investment must be determined by long-term needs and must not be deferred on account of temporary manifestations of excess capacity during the world recession.

To carry through such a large expansion of investment will be an unprecedented task. Over the last decade investment in manufacturing industry rose by one-third, an average of 3 per cent a year. In the next decade Britain needs to increase manufacturing investment by at least 10 per cent a year – more than three times as fast. We shall need to increase the rate of new job creation to some 150,000–200,000 a year – three or four times as high a rate as in the past – if we are to ensure adequate opportunities for redeployment. In addition it will be necessary at least to double the rate of expenditure on re-equipment and modernisation of existing jobs.

The National Enterprise Board and Planning Agreements are the instruments of this investment policy. The Industry Bill sets out the functions of the board as follows:

(a) establishing, maintaining or developing, or promoting or assisting the establishment, maintenance or development of any industrial enterprise;
(b) promoting or assisting the reorganisation or development of an industry or any undertaking in an industry;
(c) extending public ownership into profitable areas of manufacturing industry;
(d) promoting industrial democracy in undertakings which the board controls; and
(e) taking over publicly owned securities and other publicly owned property, and holding and managing securities and property which are taken over.

If the instruments the labour movement devised are to satisfy the objectives we have proposed, we must fund them on a scale which matches the magnitude of the problem.

The Economic Framework

The industrial programme can only succeed in an economic environment which ensures a return to full employment and helps industry to regain markets lost to foreign competitors. Without such a prospect, investment to modernise and expand British industry will result in excess capacity and redundancy of industrial labour.

A high level of demand and employment is also essential to protect living standards and to provide resources for increased investment. The main argument against maintaining full employment has been its impact on sterling. Reflation of demand therefore depends on an effective programme to strengthen the UK balance of payments. Such a programme must include measures to help British producers to compete in the home market and in world markets, strict limits on public and private spending overseas, and the monitoring through planning agreements of the international transactions of large multinational companies.

It is only by using these measures to secure a full use of resources and by reversing the process of de-industrialisation that the spiral of inflation can be broken and Britain restored to solvency.

Guidelines for Democratic Planning

The machinery for planning already exists, in companies, public enterprises and the government. The problem we face is how to ensure that the planning machinery operates in accordance with policies agreed by the labour movement and in the interest of working people.

The Industry Bill already provides for disclosure, consultation and industrial democracy as applied to the plans of companies and public enterprises in order to secure for working people the right, through trade union representatives, to influence the plans of the enterprises in which they work, and to move towards joint control.

It is essential that we should now also apply the same principles of consultation and planning within government.

Conclusion

We argue that the spiral of inflation and industrial collapse must be broken by a return to full employment, massive investment and systematic support for firms in trouble. The alternative approach recommended by big business and the Tories is to allow unemployment to rise, unprofitable plants to close, and excess labour to be made redundant until the power of working people to defend their jobs and having standards is finally broken.

This policy of wage cuts and shake-outs is intended to restore the efficient working of the market economy. But in this it cannot possibly succeed. High unemployment and closure of unprofitable firms would cripple industry, perpetuate low investment and encourage practices of job protection which lead to overmanning. In circumstances of deflation and unemployment, the market economy cannot function to shift resources into the expansion of industry. The process of redeployment following closures and redundancies does not take place. Redundancies are no longer a factional problem which can be solved in advance-notification retraining and compensation for hardship. Instead redundancy and closure reinforce the vicious circles of low profits, low investment, high taxation and inflation. Even though workers may be induced to trade their jobs for high redundancy payments, the nation cannot be compensated for the loss of production and tax revenue and will incur a rising burden of social security payments.

For all these reasons it is essential that the labour movement should now adopt a strategy which meets the needs of working people by securing an extension of public ownership, industrial democracy in the organisation of work and the planning for industrial recovery so that government, managements and union representatives can jointly devise means of safeguarding existing production and plan new investment needed to restore Britain's economy as a manufacturing nation.

14
The Miners' Strike

In March 1984, Benn won the by-election for Chesterfield, a mining constituency in Derbyshire. In May, the Miners' Strike started in earnest. Benn was unwavering in his support for the miners and saw in the conflict a deeper political battle, as this article in September 1984 shows.

When the Home Secretary said three days ago that miners convicted of picket offences might well serve life sentences, that was an indication of the desperation that the government felt and they knew when they said that that they could never beat the National Union of Mineworkers.

We now know, not that Arthur Scargill ever doubted it, that the government has planned this strike. Mr Lawson who was Energy Secretary said in the House of Commons in answer to a question of mine in July, 'I was Energy Secretary in 1981. I could have had a strike then.' Why didn't they have a strike in 1981? Because they were not ready in 1981. They had other things they wanted to do first.

They had to get the law changed so that they could starve the miners when the strike came. They had to recruit more police, and they had to pay the police more for the work the police would do when the strike came. They had to make allowance in their public expenditure for the cost of the strike, and Lawson, who is now

Chancellor of the Exchequer, said in the House of Commons two months ago, 'The investment in this strike has been well worthwhile.'

I say all this because it must be obvious to everybody that this is a struggle between 'them' and 'us'. Nobody can separate themselves from this struggle. The miners are in the forefront now, just as a year or two ago, and still today NUPE is in the struggle in defence of the public services and the low-paid; just as Ray Buckton was in the struggle in the ASLEF strike to resist flexible rostering in the railway industry; just as the NGA was in the forefront of the struggle when Eddie Shah tried to break the trade union agreements in the printing industry; and just as the GCHQ workers at Cheltenham were in the forefront of the struggle earlier this year when trade unionism was banned from that particular communications centre. It is one big struggle.

Everything hinges now upon the support that the labour movement, every trade unionist, every single member of the Labour Party and millions of others give to the miners now, because this struggle has been brought forward and made possible by the enormous courage and sacrifices of the mining community, and of young miners who are the finest there have ever been in the history of the NUM. The determination of the women's support groups has proved that women are capable of a contribution that many members of the trade union movement never dreamed possible, even six months ago.

One of the most remarkable things, to me at any rate as a former Energy Secretary, is how little truth has been told about the real issues in the mining dispute. After all, the arguments about uneconomic pits are fraudulent arguments. It is wrong to close any pit while old people die of hypothermia in the winter because they cannot afford to keep warm. It is wrong to close down pits and disperse the most skilled mining community in the world in order to build up nuclear power when you and I know very well that nuclear power is primarily to build nuclear weapons and it is quite unsuitable for the long-term energy needs of the country.

The Miners' Strike

We know now that the government has been practising in Northern Ireland for years the police tactics that they are now preparing to use against the mining community. The Home Office has admitted that they have issued plastic bullets to some of the police forces in Britain. We have seen the cavalry charges by the police, banging the truncheons on the riot shields like a lot of Zulu warriors, trying to frighten people and intimidate them. We have witnessed the way the magistrates have been manipulated, the way the judges have become tools in the hands of a Home Secretary who tells them that they have got to give life sentences to miners engaged in picketing pits.

It is one big struggle. And the reason we are going to win it is because so many people in Britain have now put their hopes behind the NUM. They know that if the miners were ever to be defeated, and they will never be defeated, that it would be giving a green light to Mrs Thatcher to ride over us with her jackboots and her tanks and millions of people would suffer. Therefore they are behind the NUM and they must express that support in positive action, as the railwaymen have done, and as the seamen have done and as we expect the steelworkers and others to do who can give practical industrial backing to the NUM cause.

When the history of the Miners' Strike of 1984 comes to be written I believe it will be seen to have been much more than an ordinary dispute. You can tell that when you go on the big demonstrations and you see housewives and youngsters and old people and people who would never come out on an ordinary miners' demonstration. They are coming out because they focus their hopes on your victory. In 1381, they called it the Peasants' Revolt, and I believe in 1984 this is a miners' revolt on behalf of everybody in Britain who is trying to build a decent society.

Let's look beyond this dispute. Let's look at what it is we want for Britain. We are a very rich country and one of the reasons we are rich is because we have got so much coal, 1,000 years of coal. Why can't we build with our skill and our resources a society that is a socialist society worthy of our own people?

There are demands we have got to take up now and carry forward with the same determination that the NUM has shown in fighting for the mining industry. We want useful work for all. There is no justification for unemployment when you think of all the needs there are to be met. They tell us the microchip will mean permanent unemployment. If you have earlier retirement and a three-day working week, if you expand the public services that Rodney Bickerstaffe represents, if you provide twenty-four-hour-a-day care for old people, there is work for all. And we should demand work for all and devote the resources to it.

We are an internationalist movement: we are at one with the German metalworkers who were on strike for months for the thirty-five-hour week; we are at one with the black miners in South Africa under Mr Botha, Mrs Thatcher's friend, who are not allowed to organise proper trade unions; we are at one with the peace movement in America and the civil rights movement in America; we are at one with the Third World where millions die of starvation because we exploit them and then spend the profits on weapons of war.

These are enormous objectives. Because what they are saying is what generations of working-class people have said throughout our history, that we want a society in which the people who create the wealth determine how it is used, in which we go back to the basic values of brotherhood and sisterhood, against the idea of profit and loss, that we believe in solidarity because an injury to one is an injury to all.

You have taken up a historic cause. It is the most important political event in my lifetime, superseding the General Strike, superseding anything that has happened before, and the main weight and burden of it falls upon miners, their wives and families, and the communities in which they live. But the whole labour movement has a moral obligation to support your struggle in every possible way. And we believe that victory for the miners will be victory for working people here and all over the world.

15
Argument for Full Employment

In a speech in the Commons on industry and employment, 12 November 1985, Benn argues that the current unemployment rate at over 10 per cent was a government decision in order to control workers. Full employment had been achieved before and could be again.

It is not a government objective and no minister has ever spoken about the restoration of full employment. The problem of unemployment is a wide one and goes well beyond an economic debate. There is the tragedy of young people in Liverpool who have not worked since they left school and have no prospect of work, and the women who are doing part-time low-paid jobs and who will be affected for the worse by the change in Sunday trading.

Unemployment has an impact on the amount of money available for the public services and on the amount of money available for local government. There is also the effect of unemployment on the ethnic communities. But there is another aspect of unemployment, and that is the cost. It is very simply costed, because the government spend £7.5 billion a year on unemployment pay. The loss of taxation and National Insurance as a result of 4 million unemployed is another £12.5 billion. That is £20 billion basic, but then there is a loss of production by the people who are unemployed.

If we take it as a reasonable assumption that people in work could have at least 80 per cent of their production matched by those out of work, we are talking about another £52 billion of production, if we had full employment. With so much suffering and so much cost, why have this government abandoned the objective of full employment? When I first came into the House thirty-five years ago this month, the idea of maintaining full employment was a consensus point. Harold Macmillan has now appeared in the House of Lords commenting again, but of course all Conservative leaders – Churchill, Eden, right through to the noble lord – accepted that the maintenance of full employment was one of the central points of policy. It is fair to say that the policies pursued by the consensus governments that followed one another did not succeed. That is why I do not listen with enthusiasm to Harold Macmillan, while others do.

That was the objective, and now that objective has been dropped. The fact that it has been dropped is not an accident. I have never accepted the idea of what is sometimes called Thatcherism. I do not believe that it is about monetarism, and I do not believe that political decisions are taken by going into a room with a cold towel round one's head and looking at a calculator to find out what the Public Sector Borrowing Requirement (PSBR) will be. After looking at the experience of the consensus years, the government decided that they needed the dole to discipline the workforce. That is what it is about.

The Hon. Member for Bury North [Mr Burt] said how happy people are and that they are all at one. What has happened is that the fear of unemployment has given management a power that it has not had since the 1920s or Victorian times.

Unemployment performs vital economic functions. It keeps wages down. If a worker goes to his employer and says, 'I cannot live on the money', the employer will say that there are 4 million people on the dole who will be happy to do the job. For the same reason, unemployment weakens the unions. It undermines the public services, which are costly. The government do not want to finance them.

Unemployment justifies rate-capping and, of course, it boosts profits. If wages are kept down, marvellous profit figures can be produced, and it is the profit figures that make the Cabinet confident, because they do not intend to go back to full employment and do not believe in doing so. To restore full employment, it would be necessary, with 4 million unemployed and a five-year parliament, to create 1 million new jobs a year. That is what it would take to get back to what was the consensus of all parties in Parliament for forty years.

I take up the point made by my Hon. friend the Member for Newham North-East [Mr Leighton]. Twice in my lifetime we have created 1 million new jobs a year, all funded by public expenditure. The first time was from 1938 to 1942. It was public expenditure on rearmament at the end of the 1930s that gave us 1 million new jobs a year. That was when the PSBR was 27 per cent of the national output – ten times what it is today. If people are taken off the dole, put into armaments factories and taxed on their earnings, the project finances itself. It was done by very strong central direction and by public expenditure.

I do not need to stress to the House that rearmament was not done by private expenditure. Granny did not buy a Bren gun, Mother did not have a tank, and Father did not buy a Spitfire with an A-registration. It was all done by the government. People say that government cannot create jobs. Of course they can, if they wish to do so.

The second example was from 1945 to 1948, when we brought 3 million servicemen out of the armed forces and put them back to work. It was the biggest example of defence conversion that there has ever been. Compared with it, the problems of defence conversion that an incoming Labour government would face would be simple. In Bristol, my old constituency, the Bristol Aeroplane Company, as it used to be, stopped sending out trucks with Blenheim bombers and a few months later it was producing prefabricated houses. That was done by having a central control over the economy. The powers were there and the objective was clear. The powers were used. If we want to restore full employment, it will not be done by tinkering about with the PSBR.

I did not hear the whole of the speech of the Right Hon. Member for Glasgow Hillhead [Mr Jenkins], but anyone who thinks that joining the European monetary system and going back to an incomes policy will get us back to full employment is absolutely wrong, because those actions are simply tinkering on the margin. If we want to get back to full employment – the objective that we should set ourselves in Britain, for a range of social, political and economic reasons – we shall have to do more than that. We must re-equip and re-establish British manufacturing industry by direct methods. It is no good speaking about industry as if it is an optional extra, assuming that if it loses it can be closed down, as if manufacturing is like white side-walled tyres – one has it if one can afford it. We have got to have industry.

Any sensible planning of a modern society would include the planning of investment in high-technology industries and in the maintenance of what are now called the smokestack industries, mainly to justify closing them.

Next, we would have to refurbish and develop the infrastructure. I am often amazed when I see industrialists, whose whole market depends on public expenditure, calling for cuts in public expenditure. Hon. members will know the old joke in the construction industry that sewage is their bread and butter. When sewers are renewed and when bridges are built, there are jobs for the construction industry, and we need a modern infrastructure, but that would involve public expenditure.

Next, we would have to expand the public services. If it is said that now that we have the microchip there is no demand, I could take any member of this House, as other hon. members could, to hundreds of houses where there are old people. In the modern jargon, they are now called the psycho-geriatrics. They are simply a bit old and confused. They need homes to live in; they need twenty-four-hour-a-day care. To meet their needs would create jobs. We need

Argument for Full Employment

day centres. We need creches so that women can be released to go to work or to college. No one can persuade me that Britain is not full of things that need to be done. Just as rearmament brought us back to full employment, so the expansion of the public services can bring us back to full employment.

If technology allows us to achieve the necessary national output without seven days a week of back-breaking work, let us have earlier retirement and a shorter working week. Let us raise the school-leaving age, and enable adults to go in and out of education. If we wish to do those things, we shall have to plan our trade, for if we reflate the economy when we have not a manufacturing base, we shall be flooded not with imports of the raw materials or engineering products which will be needed, but with consumer products.

If people had to wait a little longer for a Honda, but could get a hip operation a bit sooner, what would be wrong with that? That is the sort of priority we would have to set. Unemployment is a form of import control. An unemployed person cannot afford a Japanese video, French wine or American tobacco. The government have import controls, but they apply only to the unemployed, the low-paid and the people living on supplementary benefits.

We would have to stop the export of capital. Since the government came to power, for every family of four, £4,300 has left Britain. The Chancellor of the Exchequer says that we must tighten our belts because that is the way to solve the problem. But if a worker tightens his belt, the employer sends the money to South Africa, where the wages are lower still, because Botha's police will not allow the unions to organise. The export of capital could not continue if we wished to solve the unemployment problem.

We would also have to ease the arms burden. I have already mentioned Japan, but people do not often talk openly of the fact that the Japanese spend only 1 per cent of a much bigger national income on defence. We spend 6 per cent. Why are the shops in Britain full of Japanese videos, cameras and motorcycles? It is because that is what the Japanese produce. Our government's hopes are based on tourism and selling battlefield communications systems to the Americans. We have abandoned the serious intent of being a major manufacturing nation. That policy would have to change.

The Secretary of State for Defence comes to every household every week and takes £24 off a family of four to finance the defence burden. We would have to deal with the Treaty of Rome. We could not solve any of the problems under a constitution which makes it illegal to intervene with market forces. We would have to have a major expansion of public responsibility and control over our economy.

I do not believe that anything less than the measures I have outlined would bring us anywhere near to the achievement of full employment. The government do not want it. The wets could not get it, although they tried. The SDP–Liberal Alliance thinks that if we squeeze the wages in Whitehall, join the European monetary system and have a federal Europe, full employment will come automatically. The Mitterrand dash for growth came a cropper because he did not really deal with the power structure. His economy zoomed up and fell flat. Mitterrand's policy failed because, apart from anything else, he could not escape from the Treaty of Rome. The Treaty of Rome and the way in which it operated brought down the French economy.

To achieve full employment we need fundamental changes in our policy and in our thinking. If this House is to be a forum for the nation, one of its functions is to tell the people outside that we cannot have full employment simply by tinkering with the economy. If we want full employment again, we have to set the objective and take the powers to bring it about. We must have the courage to implement it. That is what the choice will be when the general election comes. It will not be much influenced by whether there are a few tax cuts, purchased by selling off public assets. The choice will be a basic one. I have a feeling that, after their experience with this government, the British people will be ready to take it.

16
On 'Outsourcing'

In 2001, after retirement, Benn started a weekly column for the Morning Star. *In this article he goes up against the prevalence of management consultants, and the invidious practice of outsourcing.*

One of the most powerful weapons now used by business against labour is the management consultant, brought in, we are always assured, only to recommend ways of improving efficiency and productivity. However, the real purpose of the consultant is often to downsize, outsource work to others and invent reasons to lay off those who are employed by the company that has taken them on. This practice of bringing in consultants has grown steadily over the years and is now spreading to the public sector as well, being used as an excuse to break down and privatise operations that have been controlled by democratically elected local authorities, public agencies and even government departments.

A consultant's report can always be presented as being completely objective, since it comes from those who bring special expertise to the job and, being independent, can be trusted to give advice that is not available inside the organisation. In practice, many firms bring in consultants to provide them with arguments for doing what they want to do anyway, and the consultants know this very well and make sure, before they start, of exactly what is required of them. They will carefully check their recommendations with the management that has engaged them before they submit them to the directors, who will then be able to endorse them to their own workforce, who are expected to go along with what is proposed. The outsourcing of jobs previously done by staff employed in-house can, on the advice of consultants, be steered towards companies with which the consultant already enjoys a special relationship. Where the consultants are asked to follow up their own recommendations with the company, they have power without real responsibility in the organisation.

The main gain of outsourcing to those who suggest it is, of course, that the threat of putting work out to tender can be used to worsen conditions for existing staff. If work is actually put out, then those employed to do it may have lower wages, poorer working conditions and be less protected from redundancy. This was the case when hospital cleaning contracts went out, often lowering the standard of cleanliness for staff and patients alike.

It is high time that the trade union movement challenged this whole philosophy and rediscovered the case for industrial democracy, which would give those who actually do the work the chance to get the information they require, discuss and decide for themselves how the work that they do could be more efficient, and what they need – and expect – from their own management.

The British labour movement has a fine tradition of arguing for greater industrial democracy, as for example in 1910, when Thomas Straker, the secretary of the Northumberland miners, in evidence recommending public ownership of the pits to the Sankey Commission, said:

> Any administration of the mines, under nationalisation, must not leave the mineworker in the position of a mere wage-earner, whose sole energies are directed by the will of another ... He must have a

share in the management of the industry ... He must feel that the industry is run by him in order to produce coal for the use of the community, instead of profit for a few people.

The Union of Post Office Workers, now a part of the CWU, had the same commitment. With the far higher level of education, technical knowledge and understanding that there is today, it must be obvious that the knowledge and skills required in-house far exceed those which can be imported by this new breed of management consultant, who seem to hover like vultures above us and tell us what to do, entrapping us all in a nightmare of bureaucracy that is both inefficient and destructive of our own powers of imagination and capacity to innovate.

Nor would this in any way threaten the genuine management expertise that exists in-house, for most workers respect good managers and want to support them. In any case, managers are themselves under threat from the consultants, who may well be undermining their own authority and their jobs, too.

New Labour is collapsing around us in a flurry of gimmicks and mutual recrimination. However, all those of us who are looking beyond the present impasse must necessarily be coming up with positive and practical solutions that can also win widespread support; and we must re-establish faith in the contribution the labour movement can make to benefit those who use the services that are provided, as well as those who actually provide them.

Privatisation is the life-blood of the consultants. We should turn our back on both and believe in ourselves again.

17
The IT Generation

In a letter to his grandchildren in 2010, Benn shows that he is still thinking about the future of work, and how technology was changing social relations, and potentially offering a new internationalist horizon.

All of my grandchildren, like everyone of their generation, take the Internet and its social possibilities for granted. The technicalities of using it are hard for parents and grandparents to master, but it has helped to create the best-informed generation in history and gives them freedom to exchange information and compare interests across the world.

This very fact has made it a deadly threat to the powerful. Throughout history control of communication and information has been crucial to political control. Dictators use that power over information to dominate their people, even if there is no provision for democracy.

The church in the early days maintained its power because it was run by clerks who were literate; the Heresy Act of 1401 made it a criminal offence for a lay person to read the Bible. If anybody had an opportunity to study it, they could challenge the authority of the Pope.

Bishop Tyndale, the dissident Christian, lost his life, and Mercator, the revolutionary map-maker, was imprisoned because they gave ordinary people the opportunity to challenge the information propagated by the powerful.

The power of the priesthood eventually came up against the secular power of the king and so Henry VIII nationalised the church; the Anglican Church then exercised its new power by telling the faithful that God wanted the king to be king and, as church attendance was compulsory, this was a powerful instrument of control.

The Royal Mail was established in 1660 by Charles II, motivated in part, it is believed, by his desire to open his subjects' letters to find out if they were doing anything that might threaten his authority.

Luke Hansard, who gave his name to the reporting of Parliament, was initially imprisoned for publishing its proceedings. Some courageous advocates for civil liberties and the freedom of the press have campaigned against restrictions – such as the Official Secrets Act – which prevent the public from knowing what governments are doing, while governments want to know what everyone else is doing. With the growth of radio, the Conservative government of the day made broadcasting a public industry for the same reason that Henry VIII had taken over the church.

The United States recognised the potential and importance of controlling information globally. When Bill Clinton was in the White House, the Pentagon issued a document called 'Full Spectrum Dominance', which stated that the US intended to establish control in space, land, sea, air and information, of which information was the most important.

The Internet has potentially transformed all that, and my grandchildren's generation is already experiencing the results. Newspapers are losing circulation to the electronic media; half of all Britons read a daily paper now, compared to three-quarters thirty years ago. It is possible to organise international events such as the Stop the War demonstrations and the G20 protests – on the same day in fifty or sixty countries. And information and opinion can be disseminated instantaneously without the intermediate role of an editor or censor.

This is already seen as a threat to established power, which is why China insisted that Google monitor the information it provided in China, and why an electronic intifada is being fought by the Palestinians in their struggle for justice; and why, it has been alleged, the CIA plants damaging information on Wikipedia about people whom it does not like.

I believe that the Internet offers us the best hope ever of getting through to each other and challenging abuses of power, and I am absolutely confident that this generation will use technology – blogging, Facebook, YouTube and Twitter, together with mobile phones and digital cameras – more effectively than has ever been possible before in the eternal struggle for peace and justice.

The global village can be experienced on every London bus. People from all corners of the earth are momentarily brought together in one small community. Globalisation is a fact of life. There is no reversing the change that it has brought about. But I prefer the word 'internationalism' to describe what is happening rather than 'globalisation', which has tended to be used to justify the reach of the international corporations worldwide. For in the global village there are many religions, races and common problems that now receive attention.

A hundred years ago news of a famine in some far-off corner of the globe would probably have never reached you; if it did, it would be the result of a dispatch sent by sea, of interest only to the Foreign Office. I remember when I was a little boy on holiday at Stansgate, Essex, my father was on the telephone, shouting. I asked my mother and she said, 'Father is talking to the Viceroy of India, in Delhi': so I wasn't surprised that he had to shout. It was only later that I realised that he, as Secretary of State for India, was responsible to Parliament for the government of India, including what is now Pakistan, Bangladesh and Burma. We once had a visitor from India – the Maharajah of Alwar – who gave me a turban and prince's outfit. He was later murdered.

Today a famine in Somalia or Ethiopia is a famine in your village.

You hear about it at once, on television, through the net and on the phone. Over half the global population now uses mobile phones, and it is impossible to escape responsibility for helping to deal with famine, even if only because it and associated instability are a threat to the security of everyone. Globalisation has changed the world forever. My generation must come to terms with it or be outdated and irrelevant.

But global power is not new at all, for the history of empires from the beginning of time has been about rule across the world by the strongest nations over the weakest in order to acquire resources, cheap labour and markets. This applied to the Greek and Roman empires, to Tamerlane's conquests stretching from Central Asia to the Mediterranean, to the Ottoman, the British and now the American empires; and the arguments in favour of imperialism were identical to those put forward in support of globalisation.

Indeed, when the war in Iraq is recognised – even by the then chief American banker Alan Greenspan – as having been about oil, the question arises: why not buy the oil from Iraq, instead of invading it in order to get control by force? The answer is that globalisation today manifests itself, as did the old empires of the past, in military-industrial might, which is quite prepared to resort to violence if it thinks it necessary for the preservation of its interests.

China has already become a superpower, India is close on its heels, Brazil is big enough to qualify. This will fundamentally alter the balance of power in the world. In my lifetime I have seen the British Empire disappear and its replacement, the American empire, begin its relative decline. American supremacy may soon be replaced by Chinese or Indian.

Neoliberal globalisation is often presented, quite falsely, as the means by which the rich and powerful can help the poor; any suggestion that it is immoral or self-interested is rejected as crude propaganda. But the price is paid by the exploited workers, and often the environment, through degradation of the land. It benefits a very limited range of people, for there is no suggestion that the free movement of capital carries with it a requirement for the free movement of people. That would lead to social disruption and would be completely unacceptable politically.

Thus a company – feeling under threat and stretched by international competition – can close its factories in Britain and transfer them to India or Thailand or Malaysia, where overheads and wages are much lower, conferring a benefit on the shareholders and the directors.

But if workers in India, Thailand or Malaysia seek entry to Britain, where the wages are higher, they will be stopped by the immigration authorities and sent straight home, denying them the right to maximise their income. Internationalism has always been at the core of Labour Party thinking, and socialists have seen their responsibilities to working people in all countries – very often against the interests of their employers in the home country.

In the First World War, opposition came from German socialists as well as British socialists and, although overwhelmed by the bellicose propaganda, their solidarity was paralleled by the alliances that united people against the rise of the Nazis in the 1930s.

Similarly, the anti-colonial struggles waged by Indians against the British Empire and by Africans against the European colonialists and apartheid were supported wholeheartedly by the labour and trade union movement in Britain.

In the 1950s the Movement for Colonial Freedom (now called Liberation) was the great campaigning organisation, much as the Stop the War movement is now. I was active in MCF, which supported the African National Congress against the apartheid regime in South Africa, and there were French, Belgian and other European socialists who gave similar support to their liberation campaigns, for example during the Algerian War.

I think therefore that globalisation needs to be redefined as modern internationalism, and modern internationalism forces us to see the world as a little spaceship in which all the occupants have a common interest in survival and that that survival requires cooperation.

Not only is cooperation morally right and necessary, but an attempt to prevent it is neither possible long-term, nor acceptable even to the powerful, because they know that they cannot control the poor indefinitely. If they try, bloodshed will inevitably follow.

Communication has been transformed in a generation, whether by air or by airwave. The world is closer to our living rooms than Edinburgh or Penzance or Belfast were when I was born in 1925. Internationalism in practice does more to weld these disparate communities together at home than you perhaps may realise. Muslims who have been isolated as a result of propaganda in Britain now find themselves befriended, supported and encouraged by socialists who live here alongside them, and this is the building, at home, of the foundations of what will be needed all over the world.

IV. Britain in the World

18
For Sanctions against South Africa

In an article for the Guardian *in 1964, Benn calls for international sanctions against the apartheid regime. He remained a leading figure in the struggle for the next three decades.*

Of all the weaknesses that beset those in authority, blindness to reality is always the most crippling and usually the most inexcusable. Historians are merciless with 'blind' politicians – the men who base their decisions on a grave misreading of the times in which they live and who never see the great issues which are being fought out right under their noses. Historians are helped by hindsight, and hindsight is easier than foresight. So much so that some statesmen are too busy studying the lessons of the past to read the writing on the wall.

But foresight is not as difficult as it seems. The exact pattern of future events may be unpredictable, but the factors which will interact to produce these events are almost always clearly visible in the contemporary scene. Anyone who now seriously attempts to forecast world developments over the next decade can easily find all the evidence on which to base a sound estimate. And of all the developments looming up at us from the mists ahead, the outline of the coming crisis in South Africa is already the most clearly discernible.

The South African crisis has got everything. There is no great issue that is not reflected in it. It may be seen as the last stand of colonialism in the African continent. It may be seen as the nation which has most firmly entrenched human inequality and indignity into its constitution. It may be described as the most systematic police state in the world. It may be analysed as revealing the most acute class struggle since Karl Marx wrote *Das Kapital*. It may be studied as the focus of racial discrimination.

Any single one of these characteristics is full of revolutionary potential. Taken together they represent an explosive force of multi-megaton proportions capable of being triggered off by another Sharpeville or one more death sentence on a Mandela or a Sisulu. And when it starts the whole continent will be drawn in. Like Lincoln's America, Africa 'cannot endure permanently half slave and half free'. The blood that was shed in defence of that proposition a century ago will run as freely in Africa before the '60s are out. Nor can we hope to confine the struggle to Africa alone. The world will polarise into two camps and the political fallout will drift across the oceans to poison the atmosphere wherever mixed communities are struggling to live together – even in Smethwick and Notting Hill.

What greater folly can be imagined in this situation than to fail to see it, or to see it and try not to notice it? Yet that is what this present government is doing, voting against apartheid at the UN and simultaneously supplying arms that will maintain it in force. It is just this sort of hypocrisy that reduces Britain's influence in the world. At least those who openly support Verwoerd on the basis of 'kith and kin' are honest. At least City financiers who draw an income from the diamond mines of Kimberley do not speak at Conservative rallies about liberty.

But Britain cannot stand aside or live forever off the profits of apartheid. It is wrong and it won't work. There is no conflict here between lofty idealism and hard-headed realism. Both demand the abandonment of the shoddy acts of state that pass for a policy, and

For Sanctions against South Africa

a firm national commitment to support action against the tyranny of the South African regime.

If the international law that we sought to establish at San Francisco means anything, action must be taken. This has to be said plainly if we are to understand the case for international sanctions that has been so earnestly discussed by such a distinguished international conference in London this week. It is no good dismissing its work by saying that 'sanctions are an act of war' as if that settled the argument. Sanctions may help us to avert war. But they are an act of force that amounts to a declaration of war and that is why they are right. Of course Britain cannot act alone. Nobody is suggesting that she should. In fact Britain is now acting almost alone – but on the wrong side.

It should be our job to join now with other countries to plan international action soon enough to avert the inevitable uprising. In fact, this week's conference on sanctions should be elevated to a governmental level. The earliest opportunity may come when the International Court of Justice reaches its judicial decision on the status of South West Africa. This judgement should be enforced by an ultimatum to Pretoria backed by the threat of a total economic blockade. We must all hope that this ultimatum will be effective without the use of military force. If it is not, a UN combined operation may have to be mounted for a landing in Walvis Bay and a march on Windhoek. And, when that has been completed, a second ultimatum may well be necessary demanding the abandonment of apartheid throughout the union and the adoption of a new constitution.

If this is what we mean to do, the sooner the South African government can be made to realise it, the better. There will certainly be no progress until it understands that we mean business. And if we are to bring ourselves to mean business we have got to face the fact that stern action is the only alternative to disaster. If we do not see it in time, the historians will see it and wonder why we did not.

19
European Unity: A New Perspective

Throughout his career Benn was a critic of the EEC and European economic unity. However, in this article from March 1981 he is concerned with the position of Europe within the Cold War divisions between the US and the USSR, in particular the role of NATO.

I want to examine Europe, divided between East and West, and then look much further ahead to new possibilities of cooperation that may exist for the future of our continent. In brief, can we unite the whole of Europe in the next generation?

If Europe is to survive, and humanity is to be spared a nuclear holocaust, we *must* attempt that task. There must be fresh thinking, and a new agenda. The present division is symbolised by the Berlin Wall: on the one side the communist countries under the influence of Moscow; on the other the West under the umbrella of America. The two alliances, NATO and the Warsaw Pact, are both heavily armed with nuclear weapons, strategic, theatre and tactical – numbering between 10,000 and 15,000 missiles in position.

Massive ground, air and naval forces are also deployed on both sides. Army-limitation talks, especially on the Strategic Arms Limitation Treaty, are deadlocked and arms expenditure is now planned to rise still further. The military establishments controlling these forces and this technology are funded on a large scale, command huge industrial resources, and are getting more and more powerful inside each nation that sustains them and, as a result, are getting harder and harder to control politically. Meanwhile, in the background the two superpowers have problems of their own, which greatly influence their respective approaches to Europe.

Both the superpowers have their own interests in Europe, but the division of our continent is not quite as sharp and clear as might be supposed. Yugoslavia and Albania, each under a communist government, stand apart from their neighbours in COMECON (Soviet-led Council for Mutual Economic Assistance).

And the West is not monolithic, either, for, even allowing for further enlargement to include Spain and Portugal, the EEC does not include Sweden, Norway, Finland, Austria or Switzerland. The complex pattern of European systems is a product of the past: the First World War, the Russian Revolution, the growth of fascism, the Second World War and the subsequent tension which has persisted since.

The dominant factor in European politics today remains fear of attack by both East and West from each other. In the West the Soviet control of East Germany, Czechoslovakia, Poland, Hungary, Bulgaria and Romania is widely interpreted as clear evidence of Soviet intentions to expand its control over the whole of Europe, and the military arsenals of the Warsaw Pact, with their heavy preponderance of ground troops, add to those fears.

In Moscow the situation must look very different. Given Russia's past experience, the hostility of China, and the immense technical, industrial and economic superiority of the US, the Kremlin calculates the balance of military forces on a different basis, which must look a great deal less favourable to them.

But unless Europeans are content to remain pawns in a superpower chess game, we must seek to make our own judgements of what is happening, and why. It is necessary for us first to consider whether we really believe the warnings that issue from Washington about Moscow's intentions; or from Moscow about Washington's plans. My judgement is that both the Pentagon and the Kremlin are mistaken if they believe that the other is seriously planning for world domination.

Each appears to be behaving exactly as Great Powers have always behaved – determined to safeguard their own homeland and vital interests; and seeking to extend their influence and interests and their ideology as far as they have the power to do so. That certainly was Britain's posture during the heyday of the Victorian empire, and it even led Britain into an invasion of Afghanistan in the nineteenth century.

But it is not credible to believe, in the age of nuclear weapons, that either superpower is preparing for expansion by war. And if either were to attempt it, by non-nuclear means, their plans would encounter such violent hostility worldwide and in the countries they occupied that they could not hope to succeed. Some judgement of the intentions of the superpowers has to be made, if Europe is to look to its own future in its own right.

For as soon as we have cleared our own minds we can plan accordingly. For those who believe that it is only a matter of time before the Red Army marches on the West, preceded by a bombardment from SS20 missiles, then mass mobilisation together with a crash programme of nuclear rearmament and civil-defence measures is the proper course. And if Russia really expects a direct attack on her security system she will activate her troops in Poland, establish military regimes in every Warsaw Pact country, and expand her nuclear-weapons programme. The reality is, of course, very different.

Despite the renewal of the Cold War and the escalation of the arms race, the real Europe does not behave as if it believes in the inevitability of war. Nor does the pattern of life in Europe, as it is, correspond with the rigid division between East and West which superpower strategists seek to impose upon it in their speeches and writings. It becomes clear as soon as any of the simple litmus tests are applied to the real world.

First, is it true that the conflict can be clarified in terms of ideology? Are we facing a holy war between 'Christian capitalism and atheistic communism'? Those who argue that case would have a difficult task to sustain it. There is too much evidence which points the other way.

The second untruth is that the Iron Curtain is impenetrable. Look at the Ostpolitik of the Federal Republic of Germany and the human contacts that have been allowed. Look at the special relationship between Austria and Hungary that benefits both countries. These contacts are also developing in the Balkans.

Consider the pattern of trade between East and West. In 1978 Western Europe as a whole exported US $18 billion worth of goods to Eastern Europe and imported US $20 billion worth in return. And in 1980, in spite of the increase in international tension, intra-German trade remained high and profitable. Even in energy, which is of vital importance to the world economy, Soviet gas exports and Polish coal exports to the West, though temporarily reduced, are a part of the economy of the real Europe and play an important role in its mutual prosperity. Europe needs an energy plan worked out, in detail, between East and West.

And, following the Helsinki Accords, there is growing contact in cultural matters and exchanges of visits and delegations, although they could be increased still further. BBC World Service plays an important part in the process. Many Western countries have technological agreements with the USSR and Eastern Europe. France pioneered them, then Germany, and I signed many of them myself as the British Minister of Technology in the 1960s. Later, my own direct experience as secretary of state with responsibility for nuclear matters taught me that there is even a close accord on the issue of proliferation of nuclear weapons, to which the Soviet Union is as strongly opposed as is the USA.

Even the denial of human rights is by no means confined to the communist countries, as memories of Franco's Spain, Salazar's Portugal and today's Third World dictatorships backed by the West remind us. Europe is living together, and working together, and changing its prospects by doing so. The restoration of democracy in Portugal and Spain is very significant in this context.

This is the reality to which we must turn our eyes. Europe is a huge continent. Excluding the USSR, the traditional Europe consists of twenty-nine countries: ten in the EEC; eleven outside the EEC; and eight in COMECON. Its total area is nearly 6 million square kilometres and its total population is over 500 million. Together its national income added up in 1978 to US $27,700 billion. To speak of the continent as a whole will be so strange to the ears of many people, and to consider plans for its future, in cooperation, may seem visionary at this moment.

But despite all that has happened, there is a strong common interest on which to build. The surest starting point must be the demonstrable desire of all the people of Europe for the achievement of certain minimum necessities of life itself.

The people of Poland, like the people of Portugal; or the inhabitants of the two Germanies; or of Britain and Czechoslovakia — must necessarily hope and pray for peace for themselves and their families. Everyone wants work and good housing, healthcare and adequate schooling, opportunities for the young, dignity in retirement, and a fair distribution of wealth. The majority would like to enjoy full human rights political and trade union freedom so that they can organise and express themselves openly and without fear of victimisation. Women want equality, and ethnic and cultural minorities want safeguards. Everybody would prefer to live in circumstances which allow them a real say over those who govern them. And the demand for regional self-determination is to be found in many countries. Unfortunately nowhere in Europe today are *all* these rights achieved or aspirations met.

But for anyone who seeks to uphold these rights it is clear that there is a stronger common interest among common people in detente and disarmament than in tension and the arms race.

If that is all true – and it is so obvious as to be beyond argument – we have to turn our minds to those policies which might move us towards their realisation. Any serious attempt to identify such policies must begin with the problems of security. Every government, of whatever political complexion, always makes security its first priority. That was the foundation upon which both the League of Nations and the United Nations based their charters. We must then ask ourselves how that security is to be achieved, and whether the balance of nuclear terror satisfies that requirement.

There are powerful voices around the world who still give credence to the old Roman precept – 'If you desire peace, prepare for war'; this is absolute nuclear nonsense, and I repeat – it is a disastrous misconception to believe that by increasing the total uncertainty one increases one's own certainty.

A growing number of Europe's half-billion population would share that judgement, and I am one of them. How can we reverse the drift to nuclear war? The most hopeful initiative that has emerged in Europe has been the growing demand for European Nuclear Disarmament to make our whole continent a nuclear-free zone.

It has been canvassed by ministers over the years in both East and West, in speeches by Poles, Czechs and East Germans. The Irish government touched on it in 1959 and the Swedes and Finns have also promoted it.

Last year the European Nuclear Disarmament movement began to gather momentum in West Europe, including Britain, and an appeal for support was launched in several capitals, and it has met with an encouraging response. This groundswell of opinion is growing as the arms race threatens to grow. It would be a mistake to present this argument in terms of pacifism.

For many who are not pacifists now see nuclear weapons as a recipe for mass destruction, and not as a defence policy at all. Others – like the British Labour Party – have decided to oppose all military strategies based upon the threat or use of nuclear weapons, and favour a non-nuclear defence policy, rejecting Trident, and cruise missiles, and the deployment of the neutron bomb. We want a defence policy that would defend our homeland and its people, not one which threatens to obliterate it. Here is a campaign which really does offer a future with some hope, instead of the acceptance of fear as the main driving force for security. Moreover, experience since 1945 strongly suggests – as Vietnam and Algeria established, and Afghanistan and Poland may prove yet again – that a determined people is the best guarantee against permanent domination from outside. Decisions about peace and war cannot be subcontracted to a man in a bombproof shelter with control over a nuclear button.

The Swedes and the Swiss have certainly founded their defence strategy upon 'dissuasion' rather than 'deterrence' and it makes a lot more sense to examine that option carefully. Both have a large citizen army that can be mobilised very quickly and would inflict immense casualties on any invader, without nuclear weapons or creating a military elite that could organise a domestic coup. But security is not entirely an external problem.

Internal security must necessarily rest in the end upon a foundation of popular consent. For example, the French Revolution, with its battle cry 'liberty, equality and fraternity', overthrew the *ancien régime* of the Bourbons, which did not enjoy that consent. The appeal for popular support for socialism was defined in 1848 in these words: 'The free development of each is the condition for the free development of all.'

And in El Salvador last July the present Pope said: 'Any society which does not wish to be destroyed from within must establish a just social order.'

These beliefs, and the commitment to achieve them, inspired the British trade unions, when they demanded the vote for the working class in Britain more than a hundred years ago, just as the Polish trade unions have raised the same cry today. And it is the same voices from the Third World which are now demanding social justice and a new world economic order through the UN.

The achievement of domestic justice and domestic security is a great deal easier when no external threat can be used as an excuse for internal repression. That too points to the desirability of detente, rather than a nuclear arms race.

It also points to the importance of stimulating trade and commerce between East and West, and seeking to interlock the economies of the two blocs so tightly that interdependence makes conflict increasingly difficult, and ultimately impossible. In this context we have to decide whether it is in our interests in the West for the economy of Eastern Europe to fail or to succeed.

State communism and its international system must be transformed from the inside, and it is in our interests to allow that to happen. These internal reforms are much more likely to succeed if they can take place within a framework of growing European cooperation and detente, and without raising the spectre of a security threat for the Russians, which their military leaders might then use as an excuse for intervention. But pressure for internal reform is not confined to Eastern Europe.

The Western economies are stagnating, with high and chronic unemployment and cutbacks in essential services. There are today 8.5 million unemployed in the EEC; and, allowing for two dependants in every household, this means that nearly 25 million people in the Common Market are now living in homes where the breadwinner is out of work and the family income is dependent upon social benefits, the real value of which may be eroded by inflation.

The challenge to this generation is how to return to full employment without rearmament and war. It is against this background that the whole philosophy of the Treaty of Rome, which entrenches and sanctifies market forces, will now be judged.

The most telling critique of that treaty which is now emerging is based not upon national interests, but upon its inherent defects and the undemocratic nature of the Commission itself, which operates against the true interests of peoples in all member states.

As the Community changes by enlargement – or withdrawal – the pressure for a much looser and wider association of fully self-governing states in Europe is likely to be canvassed and could transform the whole nature of European cooperation in the West.

It is not too soon to begin thinking about Europe in the twenty-first century, which lies less than nineteen years ahead.

Our vision must be of peace, jobs and freedom, achieved between fully self-governing states within a security system ultimately replacing both the Warsaw Pact and NATO. We must envisage a multi-polar world well disposed to America and Russia, but under the control of neither. Europe must play a full part in the UN to realise the aims of its charter, and respect the demands for self-determination and independence in Third World countries, with whom we must establish a constructive dialogue.

It is a vision for our children and our children's children, and in that spirit I commend it for your consideration.

20
The Falklands Factor

As a long-time peace campaigner, on 21 December 1982, Benn spoke in the House on the dishonesty surrounding the reasons for the conflict and the political lessons to be learned. This was not a last imperial sortie but an electoral strategy to bolster the image of the 'Iron Lady'.

Millions of people in Britain of many political allegiances, and of none, opposed the task force and the government's handling of the situation in the Falklands from the beginning. It is right that our voice should be heard in this debate.

The real lessons of the Falklands are political, not military. The first lesson is that the future of the Falklands should have been settled years ago by negotiations under the auspices of the United Nations, as the United Nations decided it should be on 16 December 1965. All governments – two Conservative and two Labour – since 1965 can be criticised for not taking those negotiations seriously. For example, the Argentine claim and its historical basis have never been presented to Parliament or to the British people as having any serious basis. That is not the view of the majority of the United Nations.

Secondly, Parliament and the public were never told of the islands' dependence for their life support upon Argentina in respect of trade, transport, education and health. The true cost of replacing that support is only now becoming apparent. Successive governments have failed to think through the future of those outposts of empire such as the Falklands, Hong Kong and Gibraltar, which have been left as anachronisms in our post-imperial circumstances.

The armed invasion by Argentina, which was a clear breach of international law and which the United Nations recognised as such, drew from the government the first serious British peace proposals. These were published on 20 May and withdrawn on the same day. I have alluded to those proposals before. I shall refer to them again briefly.

The government, the Cabinet and the prime minister published those proposals for a mutual military withdrawal, or a United Nations administration with British and Argentine participation, and for real negotiations under the United Nations about the sovereignty and administration of the islands. If those proposals had been offered at any time since 1965, they would have settled the issue without bloodshed. They would have carried the full support of the United Nations and still would. The House should not forget that they will have to form the basis for any permanent settlement.

Instead of following that course, the government deliberately chose a military solution. To justify the war, they adopted a policy that has brought discredit on the government and on Britain.

The proposals that the government issued on 20 May deliberately left the issue of sovereignty open. My Right Hon. friend the Member for Cardiff South-East, who was once Foreign Secretary, will know, as will every other Foreign Secretary since 1965, that they would very much have liked an agreement with Argentina but that one of the factors involved was fear of public criticism if they were to come out openly with the plans that were known to be in discussion in the Foreign Office.

I should like to deal with the way in which the government justified the military action that they took. The first argument was that it was a war against fascism, but they armed the junta right up to the last moment. They supported a fascist junta in Chile, just as they supported fascist governments all over the world, including Turkey and South Africa.

Even now, the government appear to be assenting to a big bank loan to the Argentine government.

The government pretended that the task force was sent to strengthen our hand in negotiations, but from the start it was intended to reoccupy the islands by force.

The third lesson is that the government have isolated Britain in the world by their actions. There was full United Nations support for Britain on 3 April, but after the 4 November debate in the United Nations, even the United States was on the other side. The Hispanic world has remained united against us, France and Germany, our major partners in the EC, have renewed arms supplies to Argentina, and British communities all over Latin America have been in danger.

The fourth lesson is that, in the process, the government have undermined the role of the United Nations as a peacemaker, when our only real hope of avoiding a nuclear war is by international action under the United Nations.

The fifth lesson is that the government committed hundreds of millions of pounds – probably billions of pounds – to an enterprise that is doomed to fail, in that Argentina will, in the end, acquire a leading position in the control of the Falklands. The figure now quoted – we have only been allowed the information in dribs and drabs – is £2 billion to £3 billion. Each year, £400 million – more than £1 million a day – is to be spent on the garrison. A further £30 million to £35 million has been allocated for development. Between £1 million and £2 million per Falkland Islander has been spent on this enterprise, the lessons of which the retiring secretary of state says are only military. The government caused untold human suffering for those courageous men who died and for the families whose sons were killed or maimed in an enterprise that cannot achieve its prime purpose.

I shall go further and say what I know will not be popular among Conservative members. I deeply feel, as do others, that the government used the sacrifices of the dead and wounded to boost the political standing of the Conservative Party in general, and of the prime minister in particular. They invented and exploited the 'Falklands factor', and it has been paid for in blood and bereavement. That view is widely shared throughout the country.

The next charge that I level against the Cabinet is that it deliberately released the poison of militarism into our society. They praised war and killing and suggested that that dangerous virus was the best remedy for our national ills and that it would in some way restore our pride and self-confidence. In that campaign to reawaken militarism in Britain, Fleet Street, the BBC and the ITN played a considerable part in spreading the poison.

I have made grave charges against the government, but more and more people in Britain know that those charges are true, and the verdict of history will confirm them. After all that has happened, the government have failed because everyone in the world knows that in the end the Falkland Islands will go to Argentina, just as China will recover Hong Kong and Spain will recover Gibraltar, however many warships and aircraft we build.

There are, however, two more hopeful lessons to be learned for the future. First, nuclear weapons were unusable in this case and will be in any modern war because no country dares to use them. There is no doubt that there were nuclear weapons on board the ships, despite the government's denials, but even if the Argentine army had secured a military success those weapons could not have been used.

The second point has a broader political bearing. If all the money, the human effort and the planning by governments that now go into war were devoted to fighting poverty, disease, ignorance and injustice, those scourges could be ended once and for all in Britain and throughout the world. That argument is well understood by many people who do not follow detailed defence debates. If the *QE2* can be requisitioned to take troops to the South Atlantic, it can be used to take food to the starving peoples of Asia. The methods of war can be used to meet the underlying problems of people in this country and throughout the world.

Let anyone who doubts that recall that in 1945, after the horrors of the Second World War, the British people chose peace, reconstruction and social justice and rejected Mr Churchill, who was arguably the greatest war leader in our history. I believe that the British people will act in the same way when the real lessons of the Falklands tragedy sink in, and in so doing they will reject the leadership of the present prime minister, who has inflicted so much suffering on our people and so gravely damaged our national interest.

21

After Enniskillen

The Remembrance Day bombing in Enniskillen, Northern Ireland, on 8 November 1987 by the IRA killed twelve people. It was seen as a turning point in the Troubles. Benn was an adamant peace campaigner and throughout his career he believed that there was a political solution to the Irish question. Even in this article in the aftermath of the attack, he was willing to see the possibilities of the Good Friday Agreement, which came a decade later.

People were shocked by what happened at Enniskillen; but also by the response to it. For a while we were told it was not possible to discuss the question of Ireland. Another purpose of this treatment is to distract people's attention from the long historical background, without which it is quite impossible to understand what has happened. If we're going to make progress – and I think we are – we must excavate some of the background to the struggle.

One of the things missing in modern British politics is the radical tradition that goes back to before the birth of socialism: the opposition to militarism, the opposition to imperialism, the opposition to the dictatorship of the mind. This is readily apparent when discussing the 'Irish question', as it is called.

After Enniskillen

I think that it's important to root this in history. Those who forget history are condemned to repeat the mistakes of history. The continued British occupation of Ireland takes away the liberties of the British people as well as those of the Irish people – their rights to live a full life in independence and unity. We therefore have a common interest in finding a way to end this mutual tragedy as soon as possible.

Public opinion in Britain is well ahead of the political leadership on this matter as on so many others. Millions of people realise that if there is ever to be peace there must be a negotiated settlement to the war – after the decision to withdraw has been taken. The violence in Northern Ireland indicates the urgency for a negotiated settlement.

The partition of Ireland was itself the product of a British government policy of the ballot and the bullet under which the Black and Tans were sent in to undermine the clear majority vote for Irish independence after the First World War – a policy opposed by Labour then as it should be now.

The question we have to face is not whether, but when, how soon and under what conditions British withdrawal takes place. The starting point must therefore be the setting of a fixed date for that withdrawal to which we would adhere and for discussion to begin with everyone in the north to work out what will happen once Britain has withdrawn.

That is why the Campaign Group of Labour MPs has decided to present a bill in the House of Commons to terminate British jurisdiction in Northern Ireland, to campaign around that bill with working people in both our countries so we can all liberate ourselves to build a decent and fair society in Britain and Ireland.

That's a summary of our position. Now let's look at some of the objections we will face when advocating this view. The first problem is that there is a basic contradiction in the position of those who say we are there because we are involved and it is part of the UK. There's an awful lot of ignorance in Britain about Ireland, encouraged by the media. And it's an awful thing to say but when there's no violence, there is no discussion – and when there is violence, you can't discuss it. If anyone tries, they're greeted with a yawn or a broadside.

Another argument used by Labour people is the argument about democracy. That the republican movement in the north is a denial of democracy. Of course, the reality is that Lloyd George denied the democratic vote by the use of enforced partition.

There has been no vote, and none is contemplated, in which the Irish people as a whole would be involved – or the British people for that matter.

We are told that there should be no talks with republican leaders, but everyone knows that even the Conservatives have had talks with republican leaders. A recent PLP meeting was designed to be a drumhead court martial to deal with Mr Ken Livingstone. Yet Clive Soley, our former frontbench spokesperson, met Sinn Féin; Merlyn Rees met Sinn Féin. We are misled into assuming that there have never been talks – it's an important point to make.

Then there is the argument that you cannot talk to terrorists. The word 'terrorists' is a term of abuse to describe those with whom you disagree. According to Mrs Thatcher the ANC are terrorists. According to President Reagan the Contras are freedom fighters. According to the British Establishment the people in Afghanistan are freedom fighters. Our history has it that the Free French in the Second World War who blew up restaurants with German soldiers in them were freedom fighters. The term doesn't stand up as an argument.

If you want to get rid of violence you have to deal with the political problem that underpins it. To argue that anyone who wants to hold talks with republicans is stimulating violence is to speak an absolute untruth. That is doing the opposite of what has to be done – to seek a political solution.

The other argument is that Dublin doesn't want unity. But, of course, partition creates two states whose structures depend on the border. The politics based on the border lie at the root of many of the problems which face Ireland.

Then there's the argument that there would be bloodshed if Britain withdrew. The fact is that there has been bloodshed for many centuries. When the troops went in in 1969 there was a proposal from Dublin that a UN peace-keeping force be sent in.

Then we come to the Anglo-Irish Agreement, which I voted against. It was a fraudulent agreement which pretended to be all things to all people. It hinted that it recognised an all-Irish dimension and at the same time recognised the veto. My opinion is that, although I opposed it and think it won't work, it confirms the recognition by this government of a special position there. But also, it was done to win the support of the US and the EEC to the partition of Ireland and the fact that this was thought to be necessary is an indication of the weakness of Britain's international position. I think the deal will soon be shunted into the long list of failures on Ireland.

Now I come to the position of the Labour Party itself on Ireland and right back at the beginning we had a position of outright opposition. After a war we got dragged into a bipartisan position on Ireland. Many efforts were made to drag us out of that position and we did make a move towards a break with bipartisanship but now with support for the Anglo-Irish Agreement we're back in a bipartisan posture.

It is time for us to renew the campaign for British withdrawal. We've always been told you can't raise the Irish question because it is difficult and divisive, but if we had adopted a clear position a long time ago we would have made some real progress.

We must remember that Northern Ireland has been a testing ground for weapons and methods of repression that we've seen employed in the UK. About ten years ago *Time* magazine had an interview with a British officer who said that all British soldiers must be brought here to prepare them for what must be done on the mainland.

The military's minds are now on the instruments of domestic control. We saw that in the Miners' Strike. It is only when this is made clear to people that we will make progress.

What we need now is a clear decision to withdraw. Some want this done immediately. Personally I think we need to set a date and adhere to it. The bill we are going to propose is based on the Palestine Act of 1947. That is the only precedent where a British government unilaterally decided to terminate its interest in Palestine. There was a date fixed and it was adhered to. The terms of the bill are based on those of 1947, designed by the best parliamentary draughtsmen of the time to be most appropriate for the protection of British servicemen during withdrawal.

I don't doubt for a moment that there would be problems in pursuing such a course. But I think that is what we should go for. I think the reaction would in general be a positive one, but if there were peace-keeping problems the one army in the world least equipped to deal with them would be the British Army whose withdrawal we would be announcing.

In campaigning for this we should see it as a joint enterprise. We are campaigning for the liberation of Ireland/Britain and of Britain/Ireland. We should get away from the bloodshed which has characterised our relationship and move to one of cooperation for the development of a decent society there and here.

I'm absolutely certain that, whatever the reaction of the media and the Establishment, before the end of this century we shall see that withdrawal take place.

22
Why We Should End Nuclear Weapons

In January 1992, following the dissolution of the USSR, Benn stood up in the House to debate the continued threat of nuclear warfare. He argues that it is now the time to seek political solutions rather than military ones.

When the election comes, I shall present myself to the people of Chesterfield as a candidate who is committed to the ending of nuclear weapons and bases in Britain. I shall do that because that is what I put to the electors in 1987 and 1984. I know that this is not a debate about individual records, but I resigned from my frontbench in 1958 – thirty-four years ago – because I could not support a policy of using nuclear weapons. That is my position. When people ask, I shall also make clear to them the fact that there is a wide measure of agreement – if not total agreement – across the House about what should be done.

At the end of the Cold War, it is necessary for those of us who take the view that I take to restate our position, given contemporary circumstances. One of the things that has happened in the past twelve months is that British, American and other forces have killed 200,000 Iraqis and have almost certainly caused the deaths of 150,000 children under five in Iraq. That was done with modern conventional forces, using more weapons and dropping more bombs than were dropped in the whole of the Vietnam War.

Despite that, the government still stress the importance of nuclear weapons. I opposed the Gulf War, and nothing that I have heard today has convinced me that it would have been better if we had had more powerful weapons.

When I listened to the secretary of state's arguments, I became even more convinced of the rightness of what I have been saying. The Soviet Union had nuclear weapons on a huge scale, but they did not protect the Soviet Union. It collapsed. Indeed, it collapsed partly because it had wasted so much money on nuclear weapons but I shall return to that point in a moment. Nuclear weapons do not guarantee the integrity of a state against either internal or external enemies.

If it is really true that some nuclear weapons are now in the hands of hungry, riotous and underpaid soldiers and are being serviced by nuclear scientists who are not receiving any money, what effect can a British deterrent have?

I put it to the secretary of state that it was the policy of the West to bankrupt the Soviet Union. Ken Coates, who is a member of the European Parliament and a friend of mine, has just returned from a mission to the Soviet Union. I asked him for his best estimate of the amount of gross national product that the Russians spent on defence. He said that it was between 30 and 70 per cent. I do not know the exact figure and I have no doubt that the Ministry of Defence has a better figure than that, but the fact is that the Soviet Union was bankrupted by its military expenditure. That, more than anything else, probably explains why changes have occurred in the Soviet Union.

I hope that no one thinks that what has happened in the Soviet Union happened because people in Moscow went around whispering to each other, 'The British government are ordering Trident: we had better abandon communism.' That had nothing to do with what happened. The Soviet people wanted freedom. What happened had nothing to do with the threat from the West.

I must say something else so that it is put on the record before it passes into history. The Western intelligence agents used Islam to undermine communism. There is all the evidence in the world to show that Khomeini was brought to power because it was thought that the fundamentalists in Iran would help to encourage rebellion in the Soviet Union. Nationalism was also encouraged.

We are also told that it is wicked for Russian scientists to leave the Soviet Union to get more money elsewhere. I thought that that was what market forces are all about. The Conservative Party says that one cannot interfere with market forces, but if a Russian scientist goes to Tehran to work on nuclear matters Conservative members say that that must be stopped – if necessary by having more Trident missiles. What nonsense the whole business is. Turning to arms sales, are we not the world's second-largest arms exporter? But if the Russians cannot get enough food and sell a few weapons to buy food, Conservative members say that that must be stopped.

I fear that at the end of this period we shall see a repetition of the Gulf War – against Libya and Cuba and, possibly, the toppling of Castro and Gaddafi – because the Soviet Union's weakness has led the Americans to believe that they can run the world. That is what the new world order is about.

I should now like briefly to rehearse some of the arguments against nuclear weapons because people listening to the debate or reading the Hansard of it should know.

My position is unilateralist and always has been. The hon. gentleman has asked a very silly question because a substantial number of people in this country share my view – far more than might be suggested by the number of their parliamentary representatives.

Let us start with the argument that the Cold War was ended by the nuclear deterrent and that we did not have a war because of that deterrent. It was not until I went to Hiroshima that I learned that, far from the bomb being dropped there to bring the Japanese to the peace table, they had offered to surrender weeks before.

The bomb was dropped on Hiroshima to tell the Russians that we had such a weapon. That all came out at the war crimes tribunals in Japan.

As those who know anything about me will know, I have never had any sympathy with the Soviet system and its lack of democracy, but I never believed that the Russians were threatening to invade Western Europe. Like, I am sure, most people in this country, I never believed that. Does anyone honestly think that the Russians, with all their domestic problems, planned to take over West Germany, Italy and France and come to London to 'deal with Ken Livingstone' or go to Northern Ireland to 'deal with Ian Paisley'? Does anyone honestly think that that was their strategy? That threat was the most convenient political instrument ever used in domestic politics because those who criticised the Conservative government were regarded as agents of the KGB.

Indeed, when the Secretary of State for Defence talks about the Campaign for Nuclear Disarmament, he ought to know. His department ordered the bugging of CND and treated its members, who were honest, decent people, as though they were enemies of the state. Cathy Massiter resigned from MI5 because she would not go along with its KGB tactics. So of course the secretary of state knows a lot about CND. He probably knows a lot about what we say to each other on our telephones today. I hope that he does, because my telephone is the only remaining link that I have with the British Establishment. So I speak clearly and I hope that those who are listening understand what I am saying.

The second argument against nuclear weapons is that we cannot afford them. I am one of probably only two or three remaining members of Parliament who heard Aneurin Bevan make his resignation speech from the place where the Right Hon. Member for Guildford [Mr Howell] now sits. He made it in 1951 when the big defence budget was introduced. It is worth reading what Nye said. He said that we could not afford it. When we look back at the reasons why the British economy has been weak in the past forty years, one of the main ones is that we have wasted too much money on weapons of war that are not necessary.

I think that I am right in saying that six out of ten scientists in Britain still work on defence or in defence-related industries. Let us consider the country which now has the most powerful nuclear arsenal in the world – America. Bush has to go to Japan to plead with the Japanese to buy a few more gas guzzlers from Detroit. Why is Japan so rich? Because it has not wasted all that money on nuclear and other weapons. Neither have the Germans. We would not let them do so at the beginning. But the shops are full of Japanese cameras, videos, cars and Japanese this and that. All that we can offer to sell is a few missiles to a sheikh. That is our major export drive as a major arms supplier. We cannot afford those weapons. That is a powerful reason for not having them.

The third argument against nuclear weapons is that they do not deter anyone. Has anyone re-examined the deterrent argument? Argentina attacked a nuclear state – Britain – when it went into the Falklands. Did nuclear weapons deter Galtieri? Not on your life. He knew that we could not use them against him. Saddam Hussein defied an ultimatum from two nuclear states – the United States and Britain. Did nuclear weapons deter him? Not on your life. He dropped some Scuds on another nuclear state – Israel. Did nuclear weapons deter him? Not on your life. The whole deterrent argument is a fraud.

I watched the Hon. and learned Member for Fife, North-East [Mr Campbell], the spokesman for the Liberal Party, dancing on a minefield with the skill of a ballet dancer. He was really saying that unless a country says that it will use nuclear weapons first, it is not worth having them.

I now come to another point, and perhaps I may put on another hat. I was the minister responsible for Aldermaston from 1966 to 1970. Like most people, I have had a chequered career. We do not have our own nuclear weapons. Since the Vulcan and the early bombs, we have depended on the Americans. Aldermaston may not even be able – I do not claim inside knowledge; if I had it, I would not speak in this way – to refurbish the weapons that the Americans give us. We do not have a nuclear deterrent and if we did we could not use it without the American worldwide satellite network which provides communication.

The Labour Party was never unilateralist in Parliament. I challenge anyone to find one motion tabled in the House of Commons in which the Labour frontbench advocated unilateralism. It simply talked about it at conference and then came back and did nothing about it. But can anyone imagine a more absurd democratic fiasco than that there should be election after election in which we discuss whether we should, or should not, have what we do not have anyway?

I tell the House solemnly one thing that the Americans would do. If Boris Yeltsin said, 'I will take my nuclear weapons away from the Ukraine if you will take them away from Britain', the Americans would be wise to do so, because the Ukraine is more of a threat than Britain. The Americans could take our weapons away simply by cutting off the supply.

My last point is dear to my heart. Simply having nuclear weapons destroys democracy. When a country has them, ministers – of all parties – lie. No minister has ever told the truth about any central question of nuclear policy. We heard that today. We were told that the government could not say when they would use nuclear weapons. If we ask whether they exist in any one location, the government say that they cannot confirm or deny it. Every party has done the same. I am not making a party point. Mr Attlee built the atom bomb without telling Parliament. When Aneurin Bevan made that speech, he may have known – although I doubt it – that atomic bombs were being built. But Parliament did not know.

I think that there were some nuclear weapons on HMS *Sheffield* when it went down in the Falklands, but that has never been admitted. Then there was Chevaline and all the rest of it. To lie about nuclear weapons in the interests of defending one's country undermines what one is defending.

If the world continues spending money on weapons, the problems will worsen. As my Hon. friend the Member for Islington North [Mr Corbyn] said, the real problem of the world is poverty. The dangerous thing about hungry soldiers with nuclear weapons in Russia is that they are hungry. The dangerous thing about the third world is that it does not have enough to eat. If nuclear weapons would give a country a little more territory or something else, it might well be tempted by them. I do not believe that the world would be a safer place if we had more nuclear weapons.

Of course, any leader of a Third World country who reads the speech of the Secretary of State for Defence will be able to use it in his own assembly to say, 'If the British say that, it must be right for Iran, Libya and everywhere else.' The secretary of state made the most powerful case for nuclear proliferation. We are proliferating with Trident. It represents a major addition to our armoury.

Britain is a small country, but we have such pretensions – we speak as though we were a superpower. We are a tiny country, and the idea that our deterrent will somehow determine whether Kazakhstan will agree to inspection is misleading. If one continues misleading people, in the end it will catch up with one. That is what Russia learned. It is time that we came to terms with the fact that we are a small island off the west coast of Europe. We depend on a new association across the whole of Europe. That is a better way of dealing with the problem of Russia. We should bring them into a pan-European association rather than building up our own weapons, which is what the Liberal Party has policies for. We must seek political solutions to problems which we are still told are best dealt with by military means.

23
Iraq: A Speech against Bombing

On 17 February 1998, Benn made one of his most famous speeches against the invasion of Iraq. On a rare occasion Parliament was voting whether to bomb strategic targets, regardless of the lack of support of the UN. His references to the former prime minister Sir Ted Heath are a reminder to the post-war consensus to avoid war at all costs.

If this debate is to make sense, we should understand the area of total agreement and where differences of opinion exist. First, no one in the House supports the regime of Saddam Hussein, who is a brutal dictator. I shall come to the support he has had from the West, but he is a brutal dictator and nobody in the House defends him. Secondly, no one in the House can defend for one moment the denial by the Iraqi government of the implementation of the Security Council resolution which said that there should be inspections. The third issue on which there is major agreement, but little understanding yet, is the sudden realisation of the horror of modern chemical and biological weapons, which do not depend on enormous amounts of hardware – previously only available to a superpower – but which almost anybody, perhaps even a terrorist group, could deliver.

The disagreement is on how we deal with the matter. The former prime minister, the Right Hon. Member for Huntingdon

Iraq: A Speech against Bombing

[Mr Major] – whose speech was listened to with great attention – was talking about a preventive war. I shall read Hansard carefully, but he talked about a preventive war. There is no provision in the UN Charter for a preventive war. If we are realistic – we must not fool ourselves – that huge American fleet of thirty ships and 1,000 aircraft is not in the Gulf waiting to be withdrawn when Saddam makes a friendly noise to Kofi Annan. The fleet has been sent there to be used, and the House would be deceiving itself if it thought that any so-called 'diplomatic initiatives' would avert its use.

This is a unique debate as far as I am concerned. I have sat here with the Right Hon. Member for Old Bexley and Sidcup [Sir Edward Heath] through four wars – the Korean War, the Suez War, the Falklands War and the first Gulf War. I cannot remember an occasion when any government asked the House to authorise, in a resolution, action which could lead to force.

The reason is that the right to go to war is a prerogative power. The government are inviting the House – I understand why – to share their responsibility for the use of force, knowing that force will be used within a week or two.

We are not starting afresh. I opposed the Gulf War. We should have asked why Saddam got into Kuwait and why he was not stopped. We had the war. The equivalent of seven and a half Hiroshima bombs was dropped on the people of Iraq – the biggest bombardment since the Second World War. Some 200,000 Iraqis died. Depleted uranium bullets were used. I have had two or three letters from Gulf War veterans in a mass of correspondence in the past week, one of whom has offered to be a human shield in Iraq because he feels that he was betrayed by the British government and does not want the Iraqi people to suffer again.

All the evidence confirms my view that sanctions are another instrument of mass destruction. They destroy people's lives, denying them the food and medicines that they need. It is no good saying that Saddam took the money for his palaces. If that is the case, why does the United Nations Children's Fund now say that there are 1 million children in Iraq starving, along with 500,000 who have died?

Bombing the water supply and the sewerage plants is like using chemical weapons, because the disease that spreads from that bombing contributes to disease in the country. And, at the end of all that, Saddam is stronger than he was at the beginning. Nobody denies that. People ask why we have to go back seven years later. It is because the previous policy inevitably made him stronger. We know that when a country is attacked, leaders wave their fists and say, 'We will never give way.' It happened in Britain, it happens when we are dealing with bombings from Ireland – it happens all the time. Are we such fools that we think that if we bomb other people they will crumble, whereas when they bomb us it will stiffen our resolve? The House ought to study its own history.

The government's motion would not be carried at the Security Council. I asked the Foreign Secretary about that. Why is he asking us to pass a resolution that he could not get through the Security Council? On the basis of his speech, the Russians and the Chinese would not vote for the use of force. Why involve the House of Commons in an act that runs counter to what the Security Council would accept?

I regret that I shall vote against the government motion. The first victims of the bombing that I believe will be launched within a fortnight will be innocent people, many, if not most, of whom would like Saddam to be removed. The former prime minister, the Right Hon. Member for Huntingdon, talked about collateral damage. The military men are clever. They talk not about hydrogen bombs but about deterrence. They talk not about people but about collateral damage. They talk not about power stations and sewerage plants but about assets. The reality is that innocent people will be killed if the House votes tonight – as it manifestly will – to give the government the authority for military action.

The bombing would also breach the United Nations' Charter. I do not want to argue on legal terms. If the Hon. and learned Member

Iraq: A Speech against Bombing

for North-East Fife [Mr Campbell] has read articles 41 and 42, he will know that the charter says that military action can only be decided on by the Security Council and conducted under the Military Staff Committee. That procedure has not been followed and cannot be followed because the five permanent members have to agree. Even for the Korean War, the United States had to go to the General Assembly to get authority because Russia was absent. That was held to be a breach, but at least an overwhelming majority was obtained.

Has there been any negotiation or diplomatic effort? Why has the Foreign Secretary not been in Baghdad, like the French foreign minister, the Turkish foreign minister and the Russian foreign minister? The time that the government said that they wanted for negotiation has been used to prepare public opinion for war and to build up their military position in the Gulf.

Saddam will be strengthened again. Or he may be killed. I read today that the security forces — who are described as terrorists in other countries — have tried to kill Saddam. I should not be surprised if they succeeded.

This second action does not enjoy support from elsewhere. There is no support from Iraq's neighbours. If what the Foreign Secretary says about the threat to the neighbours is true, why is Iran against, why is Jordan against, why is Saudi Arabia against, why is Turkey against? Where is that great support? There is no support from the opposition groups inside Iraq. The Kurds, the Shi'ites and the communists hate Saddam, but they do not want the bombing. The Pope is against it, along with ten bishops, two cardinals, Boutros Boutros-Ghali and Pérez de Cuéllar. The Foreign Secretary clothes himself with the garment of the world community, but he does not have that support. We are talking about an Anglo-American preventive war. It has been planned and we are asked to authorise it in advance.

The House is clear about its view of history, but it does not say much about the history of the areas with which we are dealing. The borders of Kuwait and Iraq, which then became sacrosanct, were drawn by the British after the end of the Ottoman Empire. We used chemical weapons against the Iraqis in the 1930s. Air Chief Marshal Harris, who later flattened Dresden, was instructed to drop chemical weapons.

When Saddam came to power, he was a hero of the West. The Americans used him against Iran because they hated Khomeini, who was then the figure to be removed. They armed Saddam, used him and sent him anthrax. I am not anxious to make a party political point, because there is not much difference between the two sides on this, but, as the Scott Report revealed, the previous government allowed him to be armed. I had three hours with Saddam in 1990. I got the hostages out, which made it worth going. He felt betrayed by the United States, because the American ambassador in Baghdad had said to him, 'If you go into Kuwait, we will treat it as an Arab matter.' That is part of the history that they know, even if we do not know it here.

In 1958, forty years ago, Selwyn Lloyd, the Foreign Secretary and later the Speaker, told Foster Dulles that Britain would make Kuwait a Crown colony. Foster Dulles said, 'What a very good idea.' We may not know that history, but in the Middle East it is known.

The Conservatives have tabled an amendment asking about the objectives. That is an important issue. There is no UN resolution saying that Saddam must be toppled. It is not clear that the government know what their objectives are. They will probably be told from Washington. Do they imagine that if we bomb Saddam for two weeks, he will say, 'Oh, by the way, do come in and inspect'? The plan is misconceived.

Some hon. members – even opposition members – have pointed out the double standard. I am not trying to equate Israel with Iraq, but on 8 June 1981, Israel bombed a nuclear reactor near Baghdad. What action did either party take on that? Israel is in breach of UN resolutions and has instruments of mass destruction. Mordechai Vanunu would not boast about Israeli freedom. Turkey breached UN resolutions by going into northern Cyprus. It has also recently invaded northern Iraq and has instruments of mass destruction.

Lawyers should know better than anyone else that it does not matter whether we are dealing with a criminal thug or an ordinary lawbreaker – if the law is to apply, it must apply to all. Governments of both major parties have failed in that.

Prediction is difficult and dangerous, but I fear that the situation could end in a tragedy for the American and British governments. Suez and Vietnam are not far from the minds of anyone with a sense of history. I recall what happened to Sir Anthony Eden. I heard him announce the ceasefire and saw him go on holiday to Goldeneye in Jamaica. He came back to be replaced. I am not saying that that will happen in this case, but does anyone think that the House is in a position to piggy-back on American power in the Middle East? What happens if Iraq breaks up? If the Kurds are free, they will demand Kurdistan and destabilise Turkey. Anything could happen. We are sitting here as if we still had an empire – only, fortunately, we have a bigger brother with more weapons than us.

The British government have everything at their disposal. They are permanent members of the Security Council and have the European Union presidency for six months. Where is that leadership in Europe which we were promised? It just disappeared. We are also, of course, members of the Commonwealth, in which there are great anxieties. We have thrown away our influence, which could have been used for moderation.

The amendment that I and others have tabled argues that the United Nations Security Council should decide the nature of what Kofi Annan brings back from Baghdad and whether force is to be used. Inspections and sanctions go side by side. As I said, sanctions are brutal for innocent people. Then there is the real question: when will the world come to terms with the fact that chemical weapons are available to anybody? If there is an answer to that, it must involve the most meticulous observation of international law, which I feel we are abandoning.

War is easy to talk about; there are not many people left of the generation which remembers it. The Right Hon. Member for Old

Bexley and Sidcup served with distinction in the last war. I never killed anyone but I wore uniform. I was in London during the Blitz in 1940, living where the Millbank Tower now stands, where I was born. Some different ideas have come in there since. Every night, I went to the shelter in Thames House. Every morning, I saw Docklands burning. Five hundred people were killed in Westminster one night by a land mine. It was terrifying. Are not Arabs and Iraqis terrified? Do not Arab and Iraqi women weep when their children die? Does not bombing strengthen their determination? What fools we are to live as if war is a computer game for our children or just an interesting little *Channel 4 News* item.

Every member of Parliament who votes for the government motion will be consciously and deliberately accepting responsibility for the deaths of innocent people if the war begins, as I fear it will. That decision is for every hon. member to take. In my parliamentary experience, this is a unique debate. We are being asked to share responsibility for a decision that we will not really be taking but which will have consequences for people who have no part to play in the brutality of the regime with which we are dealing.

On 24 October 1945 – the Right Hon. Member for Old Bexley and Sidcup will remember – the United Nations' Charter was passed. The words of that charter are etched on my mind and move me even as I think of them. It says: 'We the peoples of the United Nations determined to save succeeding generations from the scourge of war, which twice in our life-time has brought untold sorrow to mankind.'

That was that generation's pledge to this generation, and it would be the greatest betrayal of all if we voted to abandon the charter, take unilateral action and pretend that we were doing so in the name of the international community. I shall vote against the motion for the reasons that I have given.

24

The Crisis in Kosovo

Extracted from a speech on 19 April 1999 in the House, on the legitimacy of intervention in the conflict in Kosovo, a supposed humanitarian action. The government's refusal to put this to a parliamentary vote, Benn argues, was a dangerous undemocratic move by a belligerent prime minister.

If ever there were a case that justified the House of Commons, it is today's debate. There is disagreement – I shall try to vote against the war tonight – so we should be clear about what we agree on.

There are no apologists for Milošević in the House. Nobody here could conceive of endorsing, supporting or accepting ethnic cleansing. There are people who are concerned about not only the refugees in Kosovo, but the 300,000 Serb refugees from Krajina, who are now being bombed in their refuge in Yugoslavia, and the Serbs who have left Kosovo because of the Kosovo Liberation Army. The Foreign Secretary told us in January that the KLA had killed more Serbs than the Serbs had Albanians.

The argument is not even about force. I favour the use of force, but not by NATO. I want to be specific and clear about that. As I have said in earlier debates, I am of a generation for whom the United Nations' Charter was the great hope of the world. The charter said clearly that force could be used, but only by the Security Council. When NATO was formed, article 1 of its constitution – I looked it up to remind myself of its words – said that its members 'shall refrain in their international relations from the threat or use of force ... in any ... manner inconsistent with the Purposes of the United Nations'.

NATO is breaking its own constitution. I shall turn in a moment to what hope NATO might have of achieving anything. The House is, if I may say so, ill-informed by the media and the government. The annex of the Rambouillet Agreement says that NATO personnel would be permitted to enter into Yugoslavia from any border – Bosnia, Croatia, Hungary, Macedonia – with machinery, arms, ammunition and men. Furthermore they have to be given all assistance from the military and civilian authorities throughout Yugoslavia, and would be able to leave their arms in Yugoslav army depots, or where they so choose. That was not an agreement; it was an ultimatum. It said to the Serbs, 'If you don't accept this, we will bomb you.'

What was the Serb response? We are so ill-informed that I only discovered it in an article from the *New York Times* of 8 April, which somebody sent me in one of the thousands of letters that I have received. In that article Steven Erlanger from Belgrade said: 'Just before the bombing the Serbian parliament rejected NATO troops in Kosovo ... it also supported the idea of a United Nations force to monitor a political settlement there': the argument is about whether the answer is NATO troops or an international force.

We all speak from experience. I was a member of the House at the time of the Suez crisis. The only other member who can say the same, the Right Hon. Member for Old Bexley and Sidcup [Sir Edward Heath], was then the government chief whip. I was advising Hugh Gaitskell, who did not, as leader of the opposition, have a television set. He came to my house to watch Eden's broadcast. I sat with Gaitskell at his house in Hampstead for the whole of Sunday 4 November 1956 and helped him, as a young member would help a party leader, with his broadcast about Suez. He said:

There is no doubt about it that the large-scale invasion of Egypt was an act of aggression ... We should have been acting on behalf of the United Nations with their full authority ... It is not a police action; there is no law behind it. We have taken the law into our own hands. What are the consequences? We have violated the Charter of the United Nations. In doing so we have betrayed all that Great Britain has stood for in world affairs.

The sound and other technicians were listening, riveted, to that broadcast. That represented my commitment, which is that force can be used only by the UN.

We are facing a long war; there is no doubt about that.

The war has already spread to Macedonia, Montenegro and Albania and, for all I know, it will spread beyond that. I do not know what the Russians will do. I am told that earlier this afternoon Yeltsin said that Russia would not allow Yugoslavia to be defeated. We cannot rely on Yeltsin – he may be seeking a foreign crisis to get him off a hook, but so may President Clinton.

How will the situation end? With ground troops? The Hon. Member for Tatton [Mr Bell], who speaks from great media experience of war, is right – bombing will not work. Troops will therefore be sent in, but if we do that, will it be an occupation, a partition or a protectorate? How will the refugees return? The opposition properly asked those questions. The Right Hon. and learned Member for Folkestone and Hythe [Mr Howard] exercised his responsibility as a party spokesman to ask questions that simply have not been answered. Who will pay for the villages to be rebuilt? Those questions are simply brushed aside.

Who wants the war? President Clinton wants the war because he runs NATO. The prime minister is continually repeating his commitment to the war. We see pictures of him in the cockpit of aircraft, which make clear his intent. NATO wants the war because it will make it credible. Many times I have heard people say, 'NATO must be credible', and I realise that the war is not so much about the refugees as about NATO's credibility. The KLA wants the war because we are arming it. We joined in a civil war, and armed the KLA. I will not say that the arms trade wants a war, but there is big business to be made from replacing the armour that has been used.

As for the media, there are daily press conferences. I personally think that it is an insult to our intelligence to personalise all conflicts as if, somehow, shooting Saddam Hussein and Milošević would return peace to the Middle East and the Balkans. What folly to engage in such schoolboy politics. There are complex historical conditions. If Milošević were shot, somebody else would come along who is just the same, because the Serbs are united. The history is ignored.

The Serbs are demonised. There is demonisation of the enemy in war; we must make out that every Serb is a criminal and it is therefore our duty to kill him. The Serbs are people; people know that they may not like their own government. The Hon. Member for Tatton [Mr Bell] said that many Serbs want to get rid of Milošević, yet they are all demonised.

Critics are denounced as appeasers — I have heard that before. I was accused by Bernard Braine, whom I dearly love, of being 'Nasser's little lackey' during Suez. He apologised so many times afterwards that I felt quite sorry for him. Critics were always accused of being an agent of the Kremlin, a supporter of the IRA, in favour of Adolf Hitler. That is no way in which to conduct a conflict of this kind.

The peace movement is, of course, ignored. What is the role of Parliament in this war? We are being told by the government's two chief press officers what is being done, and then told that all parties agree. The Right Hon. and learned Member for North-East Fife [Mr Campbell] was fair in saying that he shared my view about the role of Parliament.

There is to be no vote tonight. My whip has told me, on this great historic occasion, 'Your attendance is requested' — with one line under it. Is it not important to the government to indicate their support? When all we can do is vote on the closure motion, I do not think that many will vote with us – they probably will not – but at least others will be given an opportunity to abstain. I am not so sure whether the government do not want a vote because, although they might not yet find many against them, many – even from the Conservative Party – might not want to go into the lobby.

We are responsible people. Being a member of Parliament is a great honour, but it carries responsibility: the responsibility for deciding whether one agrees with the government of the day. This is an ill-thought-out policy. It is not legal in character; it is not moral in its implication. I do not make much of the convoy, because war is bloody and indiscriminate – it always has been and always will be. Hon. members who want to be spectators of their fate ought to consider very seriously whether, even by abstention, and certainly by not voting, they are assenting to a policy which, in my serious judgement, will not succeed, but which will inflict terrible damage on the Balkans, with which we shall have to live for many years to come.

25
On the Real Nature of Global Capitalism

A speech in the House on 9 December 1999 on the state of global trade and the supernational power of the World Trade Organization (WTO). Benn was a lifelong critic of the unelected and unaccountable, none more so than the instruments of global capital.

This debate was arranged to celebrate another triumph for free trade, and it has turned out to be a long-overdue – and, in my case, very welcome – debate about the real nature of global capitalism. It is from that point of view that I want to address the House.

Free trade and global capitalism are accepted almost unanimously among important people in Britain. Multinational companies demand free trade because it gives them freedom. The City needs it to prosper as a financial centre. Speculators depend on it. Most newspaper proprietors and editors are committed to it. The BBC is so devout about free trade that it broadcasts share values and currency values every hour, entirely replacing the daily prayer service. Teachers explain free trade in business, study courses, and some trade union leaders believe that free trade is bound to come about.

All frontbench members are utterly committed to global capitalism and free trade. Conservative members, whether pro or anti the

On the Real Nature of Global Capitalism

single currency, are utterly committed to capitalism. The Liberals, with their Gladstonian tradition and the Manchester School, are committed to capitalism. I say with the greatest respect that I have never heard a more powerful speech for world capitalism than that just made by my Right Hon. friend the Secretary of State for Trade and Industry (Stephen Byers), who occupies an office that I once held.

Third-way philosophers line up to support capitalism and free trade. Modernisers and focus groups yearn for more of it, and business-friendly ministers think of nothing else. Labour members had an important letter from four Department of Trade and Industry ministers on 24 November, and the contents of that letter were reproduced in the minister's speech.

The truth is that the benefits of capitalism and free trade are not really being seen in the world at all. We are told, for example, that the best way to narrow the gap between rich and poor is to have free trade and world capitalism. Ten years ago, the world had 147 dollar billionaires; five years ago, it had 274 dollar billionaires, and that number increased recently to 447. Those billionaires have a combined wealth equivalent to the annual income of half of the world's population.

We must consider also what the World Health Organization says about the health of the world. One-fifth of the world's children live in poverty; one-third of the world's children are under-nourished, and half of the world's population lack access to essential drugs. Each year, 12 million children under five die, and 95 per cent of them die from poverty-related illness; more than half a million mothers die in childbirth, and more than 1 million babies die of tetanus. What contribution have globalisation and free trade made to solving those problems? The theory that wealth trickles down and that the richer Bill Gates gets, the richer people in Asia will get is one of the most ludicrous illusions that could possibly be imagined.

What the secretary of state did not say is that the one thing that globalisation has done is to make multinational companies more powerful than countries. That is why so many Third World countries are worried. Fifty-one of the largest hundred economies in the world are now corporations: Mitsubishi's is bigger than that of Indonesia; General Motors's is bigger than that of Denmark; Ford's is bigger than that of South Africa; and Toyota's is bigger than that of Norway. The sales of the top 200 corporations are greater than one-quarter of the world's economic activity.

Multinational corporations want free trade because they are trying to get governments off their back so that they can exploit the profits that they can make with the minimum of interference. They think that global capitalism and free trade will end redistributive taxation and, although this has not been mentioned so far, gradually turn health and education into market-related activities.

A restricted paper circulated to World Trade Organization delegates was brought to my attention by one of the members of the European Parliament who received it. It asked, 'How can WTO members ensure that ongoing reforms in national health systems are mutually supportive and whenever relevant market-based?'

It will not be long before some countries can say to others, 'You are discriminating against us because you have a health service and our workers have not, so you must cut back your health service so that you are not taking unfair advantage.'

The Secretary of State for International Development [Clare Short]: There are many myths about the WTO, partly because the negotiations are so complicated that people can make up anything that they like. There is an agreement on trade in services. Some developing countries need banking and other financial services to get their economies going, but the agreement says that each country will open whatever sectors it wants to the market, and there is no compulsion for it to open any sector that it does not want to open.

Mr Benn: There may be no compulsion, but the WTO would like health to be market-related.

Clare Short: No, that is not true.

Mr Benn: Well, it said so in the document, and my Right Hon. friend must have seen it. This is a debate marking the end of the millennium, and I do not want to get into a party argument at all; I want to try to understand what is happening. Not long ago, Richard Whelan from the Institute of Economic Affairs said, 'Africa should be privatised and leases to run individual countries auctioned off.' That is serious. In the *Financial Times*, James Morgan, the BBC economics correspondent, said: 'If some countries, especially in Africa, were to be run along the lines of commercial enterprises rather than states, investors might find them much more attractive.'

That is what the multinational companies are thinking about. When the secretary of state drew a comparison with the Luddites, he reminded me of the leading article in the *Economist* on 26 February 1848 – a year or two before I entered the House – in which the slave trade was discussed. The article said:

> If in place of entering into Treaties for the suppression of the Slave Trade, we made conventions to ameliorate the conditions of the existing race of slaves – to establish and regulate on unquestionable principles the free emigration of Africans ... we might, with a tenth of the cost, do a great substantial good to the African Race.

I can imagine Ofslave being set up, with Chris Woodhead in charge, naming and shaming the captains of slave ships on which the sanitary arrangements for slaves are inadequate. For God's sake, surely we must take some account in this debate of the worry of the enormous number of people in the world who have not got rich through free trade.

Global capitalism empowers companies to move money freely, but it does not allow workers to move freely. If someone owns a factory in London, but the wages are so high that he cannot make a profit, he can close it and open it in Malaysia, where wages are lower. If, however, someone from Malaysia tries to come to London where wages are higher, immigration laws would keep him out.

Globalisation has nothing to do with internationalism. At least in the European Union there is a free movement of capital and labour.

We are not talking about letting workers move in search of higher wages, but only of companies moving in search of higher profits. Global capitalism allows big business to run the banana republics. It involves risks to the protection of the environment, and we are told that it is inevitable.

We have had free trade in Britain for a long time, but it has not solved the problems of poverty automatically. There was terrible poverty in Dickensian Britain and, even today, the gap between rich and poor is wider, even though Yorkshire cannot impose bans or tariffs on goods from Derbyshire.

Let us look at the matter from another point of view that is all the more important. Global capital is eroding political democracy. Power has already been transferred to Eddie George [Governor of the Bank of England]. I do not know which constituency he won at the election; I could not find his name anywhere on the list. Nonetheless, he has more power than the Chancellor of the Exchequer. The European Central Bank will have more power than either of them.

None of the representatives of the International Monetary Fund, the World Bank and the WTO is elected. Who elects the Secretary General of NATO and the Director General of the WTO? Nobody. Our political democracy has been decapitated in the interests of worship of money. As Keir Hardie said at the beginning of the century, we must choose between worshipping God or Mammon, and there is no doubt on which we decided.

That brings me to another matter. People outside the House know that there is a massive coalition in this Parliament in favour of capitalism, and they are therefore becoming cynical and disillusioned with the political process. One of the reasons why people do not vote is that they think that there is one view inside the House – that all the leaders are huddling together in coalitions and patriotic alliances – and that they are excluded from it.

The minister who made that point clear [Peter Mandelson] is now the Secretary of State for Northern Ireland. He said in Bonn on 3 March last year, 'It may be that the era of pure representative democracy is coming slowly to an end.' That was a more candid account of what is happening than the praise of trade in this debate.

The prime minister [Tony Blair], if I may quote him with approval, said when leader of the opposition during a debate on the Halifax Summit in June 1995, 'Is not the central issue the revolution in the globalisation of the financial and currency markets, which now wield massive speculative power over the governments of all countries and have the capacity seriously to disrupt economic progress?' [*Official Report*, 19 June 1995; vol. 262, c. 23–4].

That idea inspired many of the people who went to Seattle. The churches were there, many concerned about world poverty; there were environmentalists, animal-welfare groups, trade unionists and those who campaign for the cancellation of Third World debt. All were immediately denounced as anarchists, extremists, members of the mob and so on. The police in Seattle put up a pretty good show of organising a Tiananmen Square operation without the killings. When I saw the police in their *Star Wars* outfits and the arrest of 500 people who wanted only justice for their own people, it gave me an indication of what it is all about.

The Internet plays a very important part in these matters because through it, all the groups sent out their messages. They could not get their messages across through Rupert Murdoch, CNN or the BBC, but they could communicate directly. They have no leaders to be demonised by the press; groups turned up with their own faith.

In the next century, people want cooperation and not competition in self-sustaining economies, working with other nations. They want security in their lives – and that does not mean more nuclear weapons. They want to plan for peace as we have always planned for war, with a single-minded determination to meet our needs. They want democratic control over their own destiny. That is the real lesson that this century must teach the next one.

I shall finish with a quote that, in a way, sums up what I feel on this issue:

We have lived so long at the mercy of uncontrolled economic forces that we have become sceptical about any plan for human emancipation. Such a rational and deliberate reorganisation of our economic life would enable us, out of the increased wealth production, to establish an irreducible minimum standard which might progressively be raised to one of comfort and security.

Those are the words of Harold Macmillan in his book *The Middle Way*. I sat in Parliament with that man – the great-grandfather of the wets, who was well to the left of the present government.

If as a democrat, an internationalist and a committed socialist I may endorse that view, I suspect that I would be doing so with the support of most people in the world, who do not benefit from the worship of money that we have been celebrating in this strange religious festival that we call a debate.

26
After the Bombing

Three days after the 9/11 attacks, Benn warns of rash actions in relation to the atrocity in an article for Morning Star.

The huge tragedy of wholly innocent people caught up in the bombing of New York and Washington has quite properly occupied the attention of everyone in Britain. The messages of sympathy that have been sent are real and moving. No one could ever have imagined that they would see pictures showing such devastation in America, which is by far the most powerful nation the world has ever seen.

We are used to watching television news bulletins showing Hanoi being bombed, or Baghdad or Belgrade, but America we all thought was exempt, and now that has changed and the world will never be the same again. For what was destroyed was not just the World Trade Center and the Pentagon, but the illusion that any nation great or small could act without consequences. The old ideas about defence have been shattered.

Traditionally nations protected themselves from attack by threatening to kill their enemy, but that does not work when you are up against a suicide bomber who is ready to die and take you with him, and however many smart bombs a country may have they don't help either.

It is not hard to imagine a situation in which chemical or biological weapons are smuggled into any country, however well defended, and the assumed supremacy that we associate with industrial muscle and atomic warheads may just be an illusion.

Indeed, one of the surest casualties of this tragedy has been the Star Wars project, which would have been no help at all against such an attack. Whereas if the $60 billion cost of it was diverted to help reduce world poverty that might just help to reduce the risk of conflict.

Predictably President Bush warns of retaliation, but against whom and with what? For no one can be sure who is responsible, and the suicide bombers themselves were engaged in retaliation since they may well have been the sons or brothers of civilians who were killed when Iraq was bombed, as it has been for the last ten years – most recently a week ago.

Osama bin Laden is the suspect most often mentioned, but we are not often reminded that he was trained and financed by the CIA when President Bush's father was in charge of it. Bin Laden was sent to Afghanistan, his headquarters built for him by the Americans, to be a 'freedom fighter' against the Russians who then occupied that country. In Moscow at the time he was seen as a terrorist, which is how he is now seen in Washington.

After the attacks on the US embassies in Africa three years ago Clinton launched a massive missile attack on a factory in the Sudan, which everyone now knows had nothing whatsoever to do with the original assault. For all I know the suicide bomber this week may have seen what he did this week as a retaliation for that.

There can be no end to revenge killings, and when the White House advises Israelis and Arabs to call a ceasefire and start peace talks it is right – and maybe they should take their own advice now. Certainly Israel, which has an immensely powerful army itself, is learning that its forces cannot quell the Palestinian intifada, and America too may have to learn that lesson.

The prime minister's grave warnings and pledges of full support for the president suggest that if the United States does strike back with force, British planes may be made available to join them. When Parliament meets today I hope that the danger of that is spelled out in the debate. It is right that the House of Commons is being recalled, as was the US Congress, because we need to gather experience and wisdom from all over the world if we are to respond in the right way to this tragedy. This is why the UN General Assembly should also meet in an emergency session, in which the real underlying causes of this crisis can be explored.

Whether this situation is going to be made worse by the impending world recession we do not yet know, but anxiety and fear are now widespread and we know from experience that such fear can easily breed hatred and bring far-right governments to power, justifying their authoritarianism by identifying scapegoats who have got to be eliminated.

All this points to the need for serious discussion by serious people, drawn from every continent, to avoid escalation. We owe it to the Americans who have suffered, as well as to ourselves and the rest of the world, to think before we take immediate military action that might just escalate into a world conflict that no one can control.

Sometimes good can come out of evil, and maybe the scenes we have been watching on our TV screens over the last three days will bring people to their senses; but it depends on what we do, too, and there can be no peace without social justice. Labour Action for Peace at its own meeting in London, just after these appalling attacks, strongly warned against US unilateral military retaliation and urged the summoning of a special UN meeting to discuss the international situation as a whole.

I hope the labour and peace movements take up this call.

V. The Radical Tradition

27

Christianity as a Revolutionary Doctrine

Benn's interest in the radical potential of Christianity is often overlooked. Despite his professing atheism, the fascinating relationship between religion and Marxism comes to the fore in this essay from 1980 that first appeared in Marxism Today.

When Jesus was asked by one of the scribes, 'What commandment is the first of all?' St Mark's Gospel (Ch. 12, v. 29) records his answer thus:

> The first is: Hear, O Israel: The Lord our God, the Lord is One: And thou shalt love the Lord thy God with all thy heart, and with all thy soul, and with all thy strength. And the second is this. Thou shalt love thy neighbour as thyself. There is none other Commandment greater than these.

Any serving student of the teachings of the historical Jesus – and I lay claim to be such a student and no more – must take that passage as his starting point in the search for their revolutionary consequences.

In his history of the world, H. G. Wells – himself an atheist – wrote this about the revolutionary nature of Jesus's teachings:

In view of what he plainly said, is it any wonder that all who were rich and prosperous felt a horror of strange things, a swimming of their world at his teaching? He was dragging out all the little private reservations they had made from social service into the light of a universal religious life. He was like some terrible moral huntsman digging mankind out of the snug burrows in which they had lived hitherto. In the white blaze of this kingdom of his there was to be no property, no privilege, no pride and precedence; no motive indeed and no reward but love. Is it any wonder that men were dazzled and blinded and cried out against him? Even his disciples cried out when he would not spare them the light. Is it any wonder that the priests realised that between this man and themselves there was no choice but that he or priest-craft should perish? Is it any wonder that the Roman soldiers, confronted and amazed by something soaring over their comprehension and threatening all their disciplines, should take refuge in wild laughter and crown him with thorns and robe him in purple and make a mock Caesar out of him? For to take him seriously was to enter upon a strange and alarming life, to abandon habits, to control instincts and impulses, to essay an incredible happiness.

This radical interpretation of the message of brotherhood and its clear anti-Establishment agitation has surfaced time and again throughout our history. Wycliffe and the Lollards were engaged in it. So was the Reverend John Ball, whose support for the Peasants' Revolt cost him his life in 1381. The belief in the 'priesthood of all believers', which lies at the root of Congregationalism, and the Quakers' 'inner light' were – and remain – profoundly revolutionary in their impact upon the hierarchies of the church itself. Nor was this revolutionary agitation confined to the church.

The 'divine right of kings' asserted by King Charles I as a defence of his powers was overthrown, along with the king himself, and in the ensuing revolution a furious debate began about the legitimacy of the organs of both church and state power.

The Levellers expressed their political philosophy in Christian terms:

> The relation of Master and Servant has no ground in the New Testament; in Christ there is neither bond nor free. Ranks such as those of the peerage and gentry are 'ethnical and heathenish distinctions'. There is no ground in nature or Scripture why one man should have £1000 per annum, another not £1. The common people have been kept under blindness and ignorance, and have remained servants and slaves to the nobility and gentry. But God has now opened their eyes and discovered unto them their Christian liberty.

Gerrard Winstanley – the true Leveller, or Digger – went further and defined the Creator not as God but as 'Reason', and on that basis rejected the historical justification for the doctrine that 'one branch of mankind should rule over another':

> In the beginning of Time, the great Creator, Reason, made the Earth to be a Common Treasury, to preserve Beasts, Birds, Fishes and Man, the lord that was to govern this Creation; for Man had Domination given to him, over the Beasts, Birds and Fishes, but not one word was spoken in the beginning, that one branch of mankind should rule over another.
>
> And the reason is this, every single man, Male and Female, is a perfect Creature of himself; and the same Spirit that made the Globe dwells in man to govern the Globe; so that the flesh of man being subject to Reason, his Maker, hath him to be his Teacher and Ruler within himself, therefore needs not run abroad after any Teacher and Ruler without him, for he needs not that any man should teach him, for the same Anointing that ruled in the Son of Man, teacheth him all things.
>
> But since humane flesh (that king of Beasts) began to delight himself in the objects of the Creation, more than in the Spirit Reason and Righteousness ... covetousness, did set up one man to teach and

rule over another, and thereby the Spirit was killed, and man was brought into bondage and became a greater Slave to such of his own kind, than the Beasts of the field were to him.

In this way a bridge was constructed that carried the message of brotherhood and sisterhood from Christianity to secular humanism, a bridge that carried the ethics across but left the creeds behind. Across this bridge there is now a growing two-way traffic of people and ideas. Christians involved in political action cross it one way. Humanists can cross it to go back to the teachings of Jesus and study them. There are many other examples to cite.

Environmentalists and ecologists assert that we are all stewards of the earth, on behalf of our brothers and sisters and our children and grandchildren, for whose right to live free from pollution we are morally responsible and politically accountable. They are revolutionaries too, in their hostility to exploitation of the planet and its people by feudalism, capitalism or any temporal authority.

The deeply held conviction that conscience is above the law – because conscience is God-given and laws are made by men and women – is also highly revolutionary, yet the struggles to assert it, and those who died to secure it, are the true founders of our civil liberties – including the right to worship in our own way and to hold dissenting political views.

Perhaps the greatest inheritance that this country has derived from the teachings of Jesus has been the heritage of democracy itself – with all the political ideas that are associated with it.

If we are our 'brother's and our sister's keeper', then an 'injury to one is an injury to all' and from that derive most of our contemporary ideas about solidarity and the moral responsibilities of trade unions. The right of each man or woman to vote in elections also stems from their right to be treated as fully human and equal in the sight of God.

So too does the pressure for social justice and greater equality, which the ballot box allows the electors to exercise through their vote. So too does the internationalism which is a part and parcel of socialism that has never accepted any divine authority for nationalism at the expense of others. All this was beautifully summed up in the words of the Great Charter issued by the Chartists in 1842:

> The great Political Truths which have been agitated during the last half-century have at length aroused the degraded and insulted White Slaves of England to a sense of their duty to themselves, their children and their country. Tens of thousands have flung down their implements of labour. Your taskmasters tremble at your energy, and expecting masses eagerly watch this great crisis of our cause. Labour must no longer be the common prey of masters and rulers. Intelligence has beamed upon the mind of the bondsman, and he has been convinced that all wealth, comfort and produce, everything valuable, useful, and elegant, have sprung from the palm of his hand; he feels that his cottage is empty, his back thinly clad, his children breadless, himself hopeless, his mind harassed, and his body punished, that undue riches, luxury and gorgeous plenty might be heaped in the palaces of the taskmasters, and flooded into the granaries of the oppressor. Nature, God, and Reason have condemned this inequality, and in the thunder of a people's voice it must perish for ever.

These are some of the reasons why so many democratic socialists in this country look back to the teachings of Jesus as a major and continuing source of political inspiration over centuries of thought and effort. For many Christians such openly secular interpretations of the teachings of Jesus may seem to separate those who hold them completely from the creeds of Christian faith. It is argued that without the acceptance of a personal God whose fatherhood is ever-present, the brotherhood and sisterhood of men and women loses its meaning and the teachings of Christ degenerate into mere ethics.

In order to consider that argument it is necessary to look back into history and consider how, in the past, Christianity came to terms with the then equally threatening challenge of the natural sciences.

In past centuries the faith of a Christian would have been defined in such a way as to require him or her to deny the validity of all scientific enquiry into the nature of the universe or the origins of man if they conflicted with the Book of Genesis. Galileo fell foul of the church.

Darwin was denounced for his *Origin of Species* and so were all those who challenged the most literal interpretation of the words of the Old Testament. Indeed, Darwin was forced to admit in 1870: 'My theology is a simple muddle. I cannot look upon the universe as the result of blind chance. Yet I can see no evidence of beneficent design, or indeed of design of any kind in the details.' Darwin became an agnostic, was buried in Westminster Abbey, and today few Christians would find difficulty in reconciling his theories of evolution with their Christian faith.

Scientists who study the working of nature are now accepted as they are, without being seen as heretics. Today Christian fundamentalism remains as a respected position to occupy, and since fundamentalists no longer have the political power to persecute science, science has no interest in discrediting fundamentalism. They co-exist in peace. That struggle is over. It was a struggle against the church and not against the teachings of Jesus.

But how should Christians respond to the challenge of completely secular socialism and Marxism, which for over a century have consciously disconnected their view of brotherhood and sisterhood from the church and its creeds and mysteries? Such socialists believe that the continuing denial of our common humanity does not derive solely, or even primarily, from the sinful conduct of individuals, but is institutionalised in the structures of economic, industrial and political power which Christian churches may support, sustain and even bless, while turning a blind eye to the injustices that continue unchecked.

Socialists argue that neighbourly love must be sought in this world and not postponed until the next one. They do not believe that priestly injunctions restricted to matters of personal conduct – 'Be good' or 'Be kind' – are any substitute whatsoever for the fundamental reforms that require collective political action.

The socialist interpretation of the parable of the Good Samaritan would cast many churches and churchmen in the role of the priest and the Levite who passed by on the other side; and would identify the socialist position with that of the Good Samaritan, who was less concerned with the personal salvation of the traveller who was stripped and beaten than with his immediate need for medical treatment, accommodation and food in this world here and now.

Unless Christians can respond institutionally and politically to that socialist challenge, their faith can become an escape from reality and, indeed, an escape from the challenge posed by Jesus himself. In a world characterised by brutal repression and exploitation under regimes of all kinds, Christian escapism is no more acceptable than it was on the road to Jericho.

How should Christians answer this challenge? It is just not good enough to declare a holy war on socialism and Marxism, on the grounds that they are atheistical. That is how, historically, the Catholics treated the Protestants, and the Protestants treated the Catholics – burning each other at the stake. Yet that is the approach advocated by many Christian anti-communist crusaders, which lies behind the harassment of Marxists in many Western capitalist countries, including Britain; and in all countries living under anticommunist military dictatorships.

But before adopting such a position it is necessary to consider one of the interpretations of the true meaning of Marxism. Dr Nathaniel Micklem had this to say in his book *A Religion of Agnostics*: 'Though he disguised his moral indignation under cover of scientific terminology, was it in response to the call of a higher and more lasting justice that Karl Marx repudiated the "bourgeois" inequality of his day?'

This view was echoed by Ivan Sviták in his speech at Charles University during the Prague Spring on 3 May 1968:

Marx was not, and is not, and never will be, the inventor and theoretician of totalitarian dictatorship that he appears today, when the original meaning of his work – true humanism – has been given a thoroughly Byzantine and Asian twist. Marx strove for a wider humanism than that of the bourgeois democracies that he knew, and for wider civil rights, not for the setting-up of the dictatorship of one class and one political party. What is today thought to be the Marxist theory of the State and the Marxist social science imply an ideological forgery, a false contemporary conception, as wrong as the idea that the orbits of heavenly bodies are circular.

Milan Machovec, in his book *A Marxist Looks at Jesus*, carried this argument a stage further forward in assessing the Marxist view of Jesus:

> You can corrupt the heritage, overlay what is best in it, or push it into the background, but those who seek it out tomorrow will find life and new hope beneath the layers of dirt and the petrified outlines – simply because they are attuned to it. Thus in Christianity the dogmatised image of Jesus Christ has never been able thoroughly to banish the image of the man, Jesus of Nazareth.

That view of the relationship between the teachings of Jesus and the writings of Marx merits very serious consideration. If that view prevails – as I believe it may – a century from now the writings of Marx may be seen as no more threatening to the teachings of Jesus than the writings of Darwin are now thought to be today.

I am not urging a political concordat between the hierarchies of the Vatican, the Kremlin and Lambeth Palace – which, if they merged, all their historical experience of centralised organisation and bureaucracy could pose – it might be argued – the greatest threat to freedom of conscience the world has ever seen.

But I am saying that as the ecumenical movement gathers momentum – and if it remains a mosaic and does not become a monolith – it should extend the range of its dialogue to embrace socialists and Marxists as well as Catholics, Protestants, Jews, Buddhists and Muslims. And there is one compelling reason why it must.

The technology of destruction in modern weapons, and the rocketry to deliver must now require us all to open our hearts and minds to the inescapable need for neighbourly love on a global scale and then build the social, political and economic institutions that can express it, bringing together those who now marshal themselves under different banners of religious and political faith.

I say all this as a socialist whose political commitment owes much more to the teachings of Jesus – without the mysteries within which they are presented – than to the writings of Marx, whose analysis seems to lack an understanding of the deeper needs of humanity. In that sense, too, the teachings of Jesus can be seen as truly revolutionary and to have spread their influence far beyond the bounds of Christendom.

28
Marxism and the Labour Party

Extracted from a longer chapter on 'The Inheritance of the Labour Movement', from Arguments for Socialism, 1979. *In this book Benn accounts for the collapse of the post-war consensus and argues for a new democratic socialism. Here, he shows how the new party must hold onto its intellectual origins.*

Marxism has, from the earliest days, always been openly accepted by the Labour Party as one of many sources of inspiration within the labour movement along with – though much less influential than – Christian socialism, Fabianism, Owenism, trade unionism or even radical liberalism. The party has, of course, consistently opposed the admission of those who belong to other parties calling themselves socialists, where these parties have put up candidates to oppose official Labour candidates in local or parliamentary elections.

This has automatically ruled out the admission of members of the Communist Party, which, in addition to its disqualification on these grounds, has for a long period condoned violations of human rights in the USSR and Eastern Europe under Stalin and others; and even supported the use of Soviet troops against Hungary and other independent countries in the past. But never since the earliest days of the labour movement has Marxism itself been regarded as a disqualification for party membership.

All that is required by way of political allegiance from party members, or paid officials, is that they should accept the policy and programme of the Labour Party and thus commit themselves to advancing socialism through parliamentary democracy. This is a position many are determined to maintain.

The Labour Party has been, is and always will be an extremely tolerant and undogmatic party, deriving much strength and popular support from its refusal to impose a rigid test of doctrine upon its members. The influences that lead individuals to embrace democratic socialism have always been left to the individual conscience, and there are no inquisitions to root out Marxists any more than there are to root out Catholics, atheists or followers of Adam Smith, Sigmund Freud, Leon Trotsky or Milton Friedman.

It is, however, important that the Labour Party's attitude to Marxism should be restated at a time when the Tory Party and the Tory press are campaigning hard to persuade the British people that the Labour Party is dominated by Marxists (which it is not), that Marxism and communism are synonymous (which they are not), and that there is a dominant group growing up within the Labour Party which really believes in violent revolution and the suppression of democratic rights, and the introduction of a one-party state (which there is not). Perhaps the classic text is to be found in *The Labour Party in Perspective* written by Clem Attlee in 1937. Attlee described the Marxist contribution to the party in these words:

> The ideas which called the pioneers to the service of the Socialist Movement were very varied. They were not the followers of a single gospel of one prophet. They did not accept one revelation as inspired. It is this which distinguishes the British Socialist Movement from many of those on the Continent.

Predominantly, the parties on the continent have been built on the writings of Karl Marx. Around his teachings the movement has grown. Different interpretations have been put upon his creed. In some countries other powerful influences have been at work and the characters of his apostles and the circumstances of the countries to which they belong have necessarily caused differences in the method pursued by particular parties, but they have this in common – that they were formed as definite socialist movements, inspired by the word revealed to Marx.

In Britain the history of the movement has been entirely different. Widely diffused as his influence has been, the number of those who accepted Marxism as a creed has always been small. The number of those who have entered the socialist movement as a direct result of his teaching has been but a fraction of the whole. One must seek the inspiration of the majority of British socialists in other directions.

There were, however, three organisations which have been the main contributors to the spread of socialist thought in this country, and to the creation of a political socialist movement. All three have their own characteristics. The first was the Social Democratic Federation. Founded by H. M. Hyndman, it was based definitely on the teaching of Karl Marx.

In 1943 Harold Laski wrote a pamphlet under the title *Marx and Today*. In it, Laski, who was a member of the National Executive Committee of the party and its chairman two years later, identified himself as a Marxist. He went on to write:

> What do we mean today by a Marxist basis? Sixty years after Marx's death, it would be foolish to pretend that Marxism is a body of sacred formulas, the mere incantation of which charms away our danger; Marx himself would have been the first to admit the immense addition to our knowledge since he wrote, the urgency of taking full account of what that new knowledge implies in the fullest perspective we can give it.

And later still, in his pamphlet, Laski wrote: 'The preservation of individuality, its extension, indeed, its ability to affirm its own essence, that is, I believe, the central aim of any ethic that Marxism can endorse.'

Over the years a very large number of members of the party, including some of our most distinguished leaders, have been drawn to socialism by study of Marx. Leaving aside entirely those who have left the Communist Party in order to join the Labour Party, there are many others whose Marxism led them into the Labour Party. Herbert Morrison was one of the most famous. In a recent biography, Morrison's early experience and opinions were set out quite clearly: 'Morrison put a revolutionary Marxist line, liberally spiced with quotations from Marx, whose first volume of *Capital* he brought with him to the meetings. Indeed, he took a copy of *Capital* almost everywhere at this time.' Thus Morrison's biographers describe his early radical days in 1908. But they go on to tell how he became dissatisfied with the SDF as a vehicle to achieve his objective: 'He first began to move away from it for tactical reasons. He wanted it to affiliate to the Labour Party, so as to permeate it with Marxist ideas.'

Herbert Morrison believed therefore that Marxists should join the Labour Party in order to influence its policy. But, like many others before him, and since, his views were later tempered by the experience of working within the mainstream of the movement.

Michael Foot, in his biography of Aneurin Bevan, describes a dinner which he attended with Nye Bevan in Soho in 1952, held at a restaurant where Karl Marx had once found sanctuary:

> At the beginning of the proceedings we drank a toast to the great man's memory and there was no sign then – or at any other time, for that matter, in my knowledge of him – that Bevan wished to disown his debt to Marxism, so long, of course, as the doctrine was undogmatically interpreted.

Indeed, an interest in Marxism has by no means been confined to the present left of the Labour Party. In a letter published in *Tribune* Tony Crosland wrote as follows:

> We conceive the function of *Tribune* to be the expression in popular form, and to as large a public as possible, of the views of the Left and Marxist wing of social democracy in this country. Its policy must be that of those who believe that the present leadership of the Labour Party is not sufficiently socialist.

The contribution made by Marx to social democracy is widely recognised and admired by those who would not wish to call themselves Marxists. In a letter dated 17 March 1972 to Willy Brandt of Germany and Bruno Kreisky of Austria, Olof Palme, then prime minister of Sweden, has this to say:

> I have always found it difficult to understand why elitist thinkers and supporters of revolutionary violence should regard themselves as the standard bearers of a Socialist and Marxist tradition which has its roots in Western Europe and in Western European humanism.

Indeed, though it should not be necessary to have to emphasise this, the role and contribution that Karl Marx has made has been widely recognised by those who would not call themselves socialist at all. For example, in his book *A Religion for Agnostics* Professor Nathaniel Micklem, the distinguished Congregational preacher and former principal of Mansfield College, writes: 'Though he disguised his moral indignation under cover of scientific terminology, it was in response to the call of a higher and more lasting justice that Karl Marx repudiated the "bourgeois" inequality of his day.'

It is not only in the West that Marxism is seen as one of the main sources of democratic socialist philosophy. Marxists have been among the sternest critics of the Soviet control in Eastern Europe. In Czechoslovakia in 1968 the famous Prague Spring was inspired and led by men who declared themselves to be Marxists. For example, in a lecture given by Ivan Sviták at the Charles University of Prague on 3 May 1968, the following passage appeared:

> Marx was not, is not, and will never be, the inventor and theoretician of totalitarian dictatorship that he appears today, when the original meaning of his work – true humanism – has been given a thoroughly Byzantine and Asian twist. Marx strove for a wider humanism than that of the bourgeois democracies that he knew, and for wider civil rights, not for the setting up of the dictatorship of one class and one political party.

What is today thought to be the Marxist theory of the state and Marxist social science is simply an ideological forgery, a false, contemporary conception, as wrong as the idea that the orbits of heavenly bodies are circular.

By contrast, the faithful, historical picture of the real Marx shows the scholar, the European, the democrat, the socialist, the tribune of the people, the humanist, the revolutionary, the internationalist, the giant personality and the messenger of freedom.

The approach to Marxism contained in these quotations may help to explain why even those non-Marxists, who, like myself, are not part of that Marxist tradition, firmly believe that a place for those who are must be preserved within the labour movement – in exactly the same way, and for exactly the same reasons, as for all other streams of thought.

Karl Marx, who worked and wrote in England and about the English working class, has long been recognised in Britain as a towering socialist philosopher who brought methods of scientific analysis to a study of society, and we certainly rank him with the greatest minds in history, along with Copernicus, Darwin, Freud and Einstein. It would be as wrong to blame him for Stalin's tyranny as it would be to lay blame for the Spanish Inquisition on the teachings of Jesus. Marx and Engels, Rosa Luxemburg and Trotsky, together with a whole range of foreign socialist philosophers, have been read by British socialists as we have developed our own home-grown beliefs in freedom, democracy and equality, and this is reflected in the constitution of the Labour Party.

29
The Levellers and the English Democratic Tradition

Benn was always interested in British radical history and often referred to the Levellers, Diggers and Chartists as progenitors of the contemporary movement. Here, in a lecture at Burford Church in May 1976, he shares his passion for the true revolutionaries of the Civil Wars.

The Levellers grew out of the conditions of their own time. They represented the aspirations of working people who suffered under the persecution of kings, landowners and the priestly class and they spoke for those who experienced the hardships of poverty and deprivation.

The Levellers developed and campaigned, first with Cromwell and then against him, for a political and constitutional settlement of the Civil War which would embody principles of political freedom that anticipated by a century and a half the main ideas of the American and French revolutions.

The Levellers' advocacy of democracy and equality has been taken up by generations of liberal and socialist thinkers and activists, pressing for reforms many of which are still strongly contested in our country to this day.

The Levellers can now be seen not only as having played a major role in their own period, but as speaking for a popular liberation movement that can be traced right back to the teachings of the Bible, and which has retained its vitality over the intervening centuries and which speaks to us here with undiminished force. The Levellers found spokesmen and campaigners in John Lilburn, Richard Overton, William Walwyn, Gerrard Winstanley, the True Leveller or Digger, and others. These men were brilliant pamphleteers enjoying a short-lived freedom to print, publish and circulate their views at a time when censorship was temporarily in abeyance.

They developed their own traditions of free discussion and vigorous petitioning and used them to formulate and advance their demands. These demands included the drafting of a major document called 'The Agreement of the People' which outlined a new and democratic constitution for Britain. The preamble to the third draft of this agreement published on 1 May 1649 runs as follows:

> We, the free People of England, to whom God hath given hearts, means and opportunity to effect the same, do with submission to his wisdom, in his name, and desiring the equity thereof may be to his praise and glory: Agree to ascertain our Government to abolish all arbitrary Power, and to set bounds and limits both to our Supreme, and all Subordinate Authority, and remove all known Grievances.
>
> And accordingly do declare and publish to all the world, that we are agreed as followeth,
>
> I. That the Supreme Authority of England and the Territories therewith incorporate, shall be and reside henceforward in a Representative of the people consisting of four hundred persons, but no more; in the choice of whom (according to naturall right) all men of the age of one and twenty years and upwards (not being servants, or receiving alms, or having served in the late King in Arms or voluntary Contributions), shall have their voices.

The Levellers held themselves to be free-born Englishmen, entitled to the protection of a natural law of human rights which they believed to originate in the will of God, rights vested in the people to whom alone true sovereignty belonged. These sovereign rights the Levellers held were only loaned to Parliament, to be elected on a wide popular franchise, who would hold them in trust.

The Levellers also believed passionately in religious toleration and rejected oppression by presbyters as much as by priests, wishing to end the horrific record of executions, burnings, brandings and banishments that Christians had perpetrated on themselves and others that has led to the martyrdom of thousands of good Catholics and Protestants, dissenters, Jews and gentiles alike.

The rank and file within the New Model Army spoke through adjutants, agents or agitators (hence the special odium attaching to that word in the British Establishment to this day) and they wore the sea-green colours that are still associated with incorruptibility.

They demanded and won – for a time – democratic control of the armed forces and secured equal representation on a grand council of the army sharing decisions with the generals and colonels, known to them as the grandees. They regarded the Normans as oppressors of England and the king as the symbol of that conquest who was buttressed and supported by landowners who had seized much land once held in common, land that they argued should be restored to common ownership.

They argued for universal state schools and hospitals to be provided at public expense three centuries before our generation began, so painfully, to construct the welfare state, the National Health Service and the comprehensive school system against so much resistance.

The Levellers distilled their political philosophy by discussion out of their own experience, mixing theory and practice, thought and action, and by doing so they passed on to succeeding generations a formula for social progress from which we can learn how to tackle the problems of our time. They won wide public support among the people as a whole; and though Cromwell and his generals ultimately defeated them, their ideas still retain a special place in the political traditions of the people of England.

Looking back on these ideas from the vantage point of the present, and knowing that they came out of the minds and experience of working people, few of whom enjoyed the formal education available today, it is impossible not to experience again the intense excitement and the controversy that those demands must have created when they were first formulated. It is also a real comfort for us to discover that in our present social, political, human and industrial struggles, we are the inheritors of such a strong and ancient tradition of action and analysis.

Indeed, to understand what the Levellers said, and why, we must delve back far deeper into our own history. For the Levellers drew many of their ideas, and much of their inspiration, from the Bible with its rich Jewish and Christian teaching. Critics of socialism often seek to dismiss socialism as being necessarily atheistical. But this is not true as far as British socialism is concerned. For the Bible has always been, and remains, a major element in our national political – as well as our religious – education. And within our movement Christian socialists have played an important role, along with humanists, Marxists, Fabians and cooperators. The conflict in the Old Testament between the kings and the prophets – between temporal power and the preaching of righteousness – has greatly affected our own ideas about society; and of course lay at the heart of both arguments in the English Revolution, the one between the king and Parliament, and the other between Cromwell and the Levellers.

For example, in the Bible, it was the prophet Amos who said: 'But let judgment run down as waters, and Righteousness as a mighty stream' (Amos Ch. 5, v. 24).

And the Prophet Micah proclaimed the same message from God: 'He hath shewed thee O man what is good; and what doth the Lord require of thee, but to do justly, and to love mercy, and to walk humbly with thy God' (Micah Ch. 6, v. 8).

The deep conviction to be found in the Old Testament that conscience is God-given, or derives from nature or reason, and must be supreme over man-made law has its origins in these Bible teachings, and is still passionately held today.

Later, when Jesus Christ the Carpenter of Nazareth was asked by one of the scribes 'What commandment is the first of all?' St Mark's Gospel Ch. 12, vv. 29–31, records his answer:

> The first is Hear O Israel; the Lord our God, the Lord is one: And thou shalt love the Lord thy God with all thy heart, and with all thy soul, and with all thy strength.
> The second is this: Thou shalt love thy neighbour as thyself. There is none other commandment greater than these.

Jesus's classic restatement of the Old Testament teaching of monotheism, and of brotherly love under one God which flowed from it, was absolutely revolutionary when uttered in a world which still accepted slavery.

This passage also underlines the idea of man's relationship with God as a person-to-person relationship, neither needing, nor requiring us to accept the intervention of an exclusive priestly class, claiming a monopoly right to speak on behalf of the Almighty, still less of a king claiming a divine right to rule.

These ideas lie at the root of religious dissent, and gave birth to the idea of the priesthood of all believers which is central to nonconformity. H. G. Wells, himself a non-believer, writing of Jesus in his *History of the World* recognised the revolutionary nature of Christ's teachings which led to his crucifixion. Wells's words must rank as one of the most remarkable tributes to Christ ever to have come from a non-Christian.

No wonder that many bishops and clergy of the church in England before the Reformation feared that the Bible – if available to be read widely – might undermine the priestly hold over the minds of their flock. They therefore punished those like Wycliffe and the Lollards who translated the Bible into English, and encouraged the lay to read it, thus undermining the authority of the bishops and the priesthood, the king and the landlords.

In this same church, here in Burford 120 years before the Levellers were shot, there was a gruesome example of the sort of punishment meted out to the Lollards. The history of Oxfordshire tells us that a Burford Lollard paid £1 for an English Bible so that he could read it with his friends, many of them weavers. One of them, John Edmunds, told a Witney man 'to go offer his money to God's own image which was the poor people, blind and lame'. He and his followers were forced to kneel on the altar steps here in Burford Church, throughout the whole of morning service in 1522, with faggots on their shoulders. These faggots were no doubt burned to heat the branding irons with which this group of Bible readers, twelve men and nine women, were all branded on the cheek at the end of prayers to teach the congregation not to read the Bible. For then, as now in many parts of the world, the Bible was seen as a revolutionary book, not to be trusted to the common people to read and interpret for themselves.

It is no wonder then that the Levellers should regard the Bible as their basic text. The Leveller pamphlets abound with religious quotations. Divine teaching – as they read it – expressly prohibited the domination of man by man. One historian summarised the views being advanced by the lower classes at the beginning of the Civil War. The Diggers, or True Levellers as they described themselves, went even further and in Gerrard Winstanley's pamphlet *The True Levellers' Standard Advanced*, published 26 April 1649, these words appear that anticipated the conservationists and commune dwellers of today, that denounced the domination of man by man, proclaimed the equality of women and based it all on God and nature's laws. The plain advocacy of absolute human equality – and the emphasis on the common ownership of land and natural resources – speaks to us today with the same power as when those words were written by Winstanley.

But some Levellers went beyond the authority of the Bible and began to develop out of it, and from their own experience, a humanist buttress for their social philosophy without losing its moral force. The Levellers were, in a special sense, bridge-builders; constructing a bridge that connects Christian teaching with humanism and democratic socialism.

Those who crossed that bridge did not blow it up behind them as converts to atheism might have done. That bridge is still there for anyone who wishes to cross it in either direction. Some use it to go back to trace one of the paths leading to the Bible. Others like the modern Christian pilgrims – for example the Catholic priests and others in Latin America – whose experience of modern-world poverty, persecution and oppression has spurred them on to cross that same bridge from Christianity to social action and democratic socialism, have based it on their Christian faith, and the inspiration of saintly Christians who have pioneered along the same path. The moral force of Bible teaching, and the teachings of Jesus, is not necessarily weakened by being secularised. Indeed it can be argued that humanism may entrench them more strongly, for those who cannot accept the Christian faith.

But however we choose to explain this theological paradox, Christian, humanist and socialist morality has in fact co-existed and cooperated throughout history and they co-exist and cooperate today most fruitfully and not only within the Christian socialist movement itself. The British trade union and labour movement, like Anglicans, Presbyterians, Catholics, Methodists, Congregationalists, Baptists, Jews and campaigners for civil rights, has gained inspiration from these twin traditions of Christianity and humanistic socialism.

We should certainly not allow the horrors of persecution perpetrated at various times in history by societies proclaiming themselves to be Christian to blind us to the true teachings of Christ. Nor should we allow the horrors of persecution perpetrated more recently by societies claiming to be socialist to blind us to the true social morality of socialism.

We owe a deep debt of gratitude to the Levellers for building that bridge and for defending the people from the abuses of power of which some priests and commissars may be equally guilty because they falsely claim to be the interpreters of some truth revealed solely to them. The pure and principled stance of the Levellers on these matters explains the survival of their ideas.

The ideas of the Levellers were thought to be so dangerous because of their popularity then, that, as now, the Establishment wanted to silence them. By 1650 the Levellers' movement had been effectively crushed. Cromwell's Commonwealth represented a formidable advance compared to the reign of King Charles which preceded it. But it did not – and in terms of its historical and industrial development probably could not – adopt the principles that Lilburn, Overton, Walwyn, still less Winstanley were advocating. Ten years later came the Restoration of Charles II. In 1688 Britain witnessed the shadowy beginnings of a constitutional monarchy which, as it emerged at that time, had practically nothing whatever in common with real political democracy.

But the elimination of the Levellers as an organised political movement could not obliterate the ideas which they had propagated. From that day to this the same principles of religious and political freedom and equality have reappeared again and again in the history of the labour movement and throughout the world.

The American colonists inscribed these principles clearly in their Declaration of Independence. The document was drafted by our American cousins but the ideas were taken straight from the English Levellers a century and a quarter before. The Americans had also drawn heavily on the writings of Tom Paine.

The English reformers of the early nineteenth century also drew many of their ideas from that mysterious mix of Christian teaching, religious and political dissent, social equality and democracy. This fired the imagination of generations of Congregationalists, trade union pioneers, early cooperators, socialists, and the Chartists who also used language the Levellers themselves might have spoken. We can find the same aspiration in the moving words of Clause 4 written in 1918, which set out the objectives of the Labour Party in a positive way, thus:

> To secure for the workers by hand or by brain the full fruits of their industry and the most equitable distribution thereof that may be possible upon the basis of the common ownership of the means of production, distribution, and exchange, and the best obtainable system of popular administration and control of each industry or service.
>
> Generally to promote the Political, Social and Economic Emancipation of the People, and more particularly of those who depend directly upon their own exertions by hand or by brain for the means of life.

The same ideas are expressed in the present commitment of the labour movement: 'To bring about a fundamental and irreversible shift in the balance of wealth and power in favour of working people and their families'. The massive impetus of these ideas, with variations deriving from their own traditions, has influenced all the working peoples of the world who are a part of this same movement, uniting those once separated by barriers of narrow nationalism but all facing degrading poverty, deprivation and persecution.

If the Levellers were here today they might be surprised to find so much attributed to their movement, which for them must have seemed to have ended in abject failure. They would be pleased at such progress as we have made since 1649, but, being analysts of the nature of society, they would also see that much of the power structure within the social and political system has survived unscathed despite the outward appearance of reform.

What would the Levellers say to us if they were here today? I hope this question will start a debate and lead on to a fuller examination of the nature of our present society.

For my part I think the Levellers would have much to say about the issues which concern us here in England in 1976 – and I have selected ten issues which I believe would concern them.

First The Levellers would surely concentrate their attention on the huge accumulation of financial power in our society; and the continued exclusion of working people from effective democratic power over it, and link the present maldistribution of wealth, here and worldwide, to the maldistribution of power. They would champion all those in Britain and throughout the world who experience poverty.

Second The Levellers would view with deep suspicion the power of the military establishments to be found worldwide, sometimes incorporating political police forces which seem to believe that they have a divine right to secrecy served by a network of spies and agents, using bribery and corruption to serve their purposes without regard to moral principles.

Third The Levellers would immediately see the relevance of industrial democracy, by workers' control or self-management, as a natural extension of the political franchise to replace the power of the new industrial feudalism which has long established itself through the growth of giant companies.

If the Levellers were to describe shop stewards, in this context, as *agitators* they would be restoring an ancient and honourable word to its proper meaning, just as each Sunday Anglicans pray for 'the whole state of Christ's church *militant*, here on earth' – despite the popular odium now attaching to all 'militants'.

Fourth The Levellers might see in the immense influence of the educational establishment, under the titular leadership of the universities, a new class of rulers in a self-perpetuating hierarchy, aiming to establish a claim to the 'private ownership of knowledge' which by rights is part of 'the common store house' belonging to us all.

The Levellers and the English Democratic Tradition 231

Fifth The Levellers might see in the mass media a modern secular church seeking to control the minds of the people by standard sermons from television pulpits, day after day, and night after night, keeping out dissenters or spokesmen for the common people, imposing a technical monopoly censorship that frustrates the right to free speech because it denies the equally important right to be heard.

Sixth The Levellers would uphold the rights of constituents to recall and replace their parliamentary candidates, on the same basis, and for the same reason, as dissenting chapels claimed the right to appoint and dismiss their ministers, and because of the inalienable sovereignty of the people which no parliament has any right to usurp.

I imagine that for the same reason they would deeply suspect the lawmaking powers of the Brussels commissioners who are not accountable to electors with power to remove them.

Seventh The Levellers, and still more the Diggers, would add a new and moral dimension to the movement for conserving the earth's limited resources by reminding man of his duty to his fellow citizens and his descendants not to squander the earth's 'common treasury' – because it is God's gift to each generation in turn, a powerful argument for common ownership and a classless society.

Eighth The Levellers would demand a far greater public accountability by all those who exercise centralised civil, political, scientific, technical, educational and mass-media power, through the great bureaucracies of the world, and would call for the democratic control of it all.

Ninth The Levellers would warn against looking for deliverance to any elite group, whatever its origins, even if it came from the labour movement, who might claim some special ability to carry through reforms by proxy, free from the discipline of recall or re-election. They would argue that all real reform comes from below, and that the self-confidence of the common people in organising for themselves – in their unions, trades, crafts, local communities and civil and human rights groups, enlarging their own horizons by their own efforts, distilling their own wisdom from their own experience, and breeding their own collective leadership in the process – offered the only real guarantee of advance.

Tenth The Levellers would argue passionately for free speech and make common cause, worldwide, with those who fight for human rights against tyrants and dictators of all political colours, not sparing Stalinists who falsely seek to justify uniformity as a necessary defence for socialism.

To summarise all those lessons the one connecting thread that united the Levellers to each other, and unites us to them, is a passion for democracy advocated for moral and practical reasons, both because it recognises the rights of man, and because democracy imposes responsibilities on those who exercise those rights. True the Levellers believed in original sin. But for them the most dangerous sin was the corruption of political power for personal gain. They would have reconciled the problem of entrusting responsibility through the ballot box to a people prone to sin.

30
Listening to the New Generation

Originally published in Melody Maker *in 1970, this was written in response to an article by Mick Farren, the head of the Yippies (Youth International Party), active in the US anti-war movement. Benn separates the overblown appeals to drug-taking from the truly revolutionary youth movement.*

Mick Farren's article 'Rock as a Political Force' was certainly one of the most interesting statements from his generation addressed to my own, that I have yet to read.

There can be few parents who will not have felt, from the other side of the age barrier, the alienation that he describes and attributes to the fact that 'rock is not something you understand, it is something that you feel in your body and you know'.

Every new generation has always thought its parents were old-fashioned and out of touch and limited in their vision and hidebound in their ideas. But the gap today seems wider, and is wider, for two new and important reasons. First, the rate of change is now so rapid that the old now, for the first time in history, find it harder to understand the world than their own children do.

And secondly because not only is the new generation rejecting the ideas and values of the past (or seem to be doing so) but some are discovering a new physical awareness that Eldridge Cleaver described as 'a generation of whites getting back into their bodies'.

When Mick Farren calls for 'a real alternative to the life-long, mind-twisting routine of office or factory' he is saying something very important that makes sense to a lot of older people as well. Indeed what he says is directly mirrored in some of the writings of the best management philosophers too.

Robert Townsend, the American management consultant in his recent book *Up the Organisation*, wrote:

> We've become a nation of office boys. Monster corporations like General Motors and monster agencies like the Defence Department have grown like cancer until they take up nearly all of the living working space. Two solutions confront each of us:
>
> Solution One is a cop-out: you can decide that what is must be inevitable, grab your share of the cash and fringes; and comfort yourself with the distractions you call leisure.
>
> Solution Two is non-violent guerilla warfare: start dismantling our organizations where we're serving them, leaving only the parts where they're serving us. It will take millions of such subversives to make much difference.

To work to dismantle bureaucracy thus provides a common interest between the generations which has not been fully developed and has great potential.

However, when Mick Farren says 'our parents are making only meagre attempts to cure the sickness in their society' he opens up a wider range of issues which need to be explored. The argument here is not as simple as an argument between those who want to put society right – the young – and those who don't care – the old.

Society has always been criticised by the young and they have always clamoured for radical change. But up until a generation ago the main remedy appeared to lie in the mobilisation of state power to deal with current social ills. The problem of ill health prompted Nye Bevan to work for a national health service administered by the state. The curse of unemployment suggested the need for public ownership and better central economic planning. The direct threat of fascism called forth a vast national and international military effort. Thus the older generation still tends to think of *national* action to deal with *national* problems.

When the young say that this argument does not go far enough and that national action may lead to greater bureaucracy and create new problems as it solves old ones I think they are partly right. But faced with the enormous accumulation of power in the world in which we live I cannot visualise remedies that don't include the mobilisation of national and international power to make strategic choices and force private centres of power to be accountable.

Where the young are wholly right is in arguing that these policies will not in themselves secure an enlargement of human development unless we revolutionise our relationships with each other.

Here we come near to the central moral argument. Probably the majority of older people do half-believe that we live in a society where moral standards are deteriorating and where society is going 'to pot', literally and figuratively.

My own experience of the new generation does not in any way confirm this general middle-aged pessimism. Indeed I would support Mick Farren's counterattack on the values of an older generation that seems to accept violence as an instrument of policy, guide its life by personal financial gain and tolerate a society where the profit-and-loss account is dominant.

The drug issue is in my opinion much the biggest barrier to an understanding. However illogical the opposition to drugs may seem to be from a society that consumes millions of tons of tobacco and hundreds of thousands of gallons of alcohol, the fact is that most parents are genuinely afraid of them and many, like myself, do not believe that real human relationships can be achieved if they depend upon drugs to get them started and sustain them; and we cannot accept the idea of a wealthy society seeking synthetic pleasure in the midst of a world that faces the problems of starvation.

Contrast this with what Mick Farren says at the end of his article:

> There is now a choice that none of us can ignore. If we carry on as we are now we are a frightened overcrowded species on a dying planet. If we work on the principle (and this is really the only revolutionary principle) that the man next to you really is your brother, and that you need each other in order to survive, then maybe, even at this late stage, we may still have a chance to become a free and dignified people.

If this is the message of the young to the old it is a message of supreme importance. It not only enshrines all that is best, in the greatest teaching from history, but it could well be written into the Preamble of the United Nations' Charter and inscribed in stone lettering in the Houses of Parliament and incorporated into the memorandum of association of every industrial enterprise. It is the doctrine of human responsibility, clearly stated, and if it were really that that took a quarter of a million people to the open-air pop festivals in Woodstock or on the Isle of Wight then it would certainly be one of the most important social movements of our time.

31
A Woman's Place

In a speech to the Yorkshire Labour Women's Rally in June 1971, Benn searches for solidarity between the women's and the labour movements. As his daughter, Melissa, notes, this was an ongoing debate within the Benn family also.

Incredible as it now seems, women were altogether denied even the vote until fifty-three years ago and only won the franchise at twenty-one ten years after that. If we are considering what is still called 'the women's question' we have got to see it against a background of centuries when women were specifically and categorically discriminated against by men, as indeed they still are. In feudal times they were just chattels, as they still are in some parts of the world. But even after some of them escaped from male domination they were denied political representation.

Today, even in Britain, they still suffer from laws passed by Parliament before women had to vote, which are enforced by the courts in such a way as to keep them as second-class citizens. But the problem goes far deeper than that. Public attitudes adopted by many men, and accepted by many women, are now a hundred years out of date.

It is appropriate that the new women's movement which has become active in recent years in America and Europe should have demanded liberation, for that is what the battle is about. In part inspired by the colonial liberation movements, and in part by the powerful pressure groups for racial equality established by those who had suffered discrimination, the new women's movement draws much of its energy from a history of clear injustice, which has not yet ended. And it is growing much more rapidly than many people realise. It is no good ignoring it in the hope that it will go away — because it won't. Moreover it has tremendous and untapped political potential.

Many people mock the women's movement today by picking on some of its tactics just as the feminist movement was mocked at the time the suffragettes began their campaigns. But every struggle for rights by an oppressed group is exposed to ridicule by those who are frightened of the power it generates. Those who are privileged know that if a progressive movement succeeds in its objectives the privileges which they have enjoyed will be threatened. No wonder some men are uneasy at the knowledge that some women are now openly objecting to their arrogance in determining how much freedom women should have. It is also true that the leaders of a new movement for social change are always liable to be accused of being unrepresentative. How easy to dismiss them as a lunatic fringe commanding no real support among their own constituency of women. But just the same was said of the trade union and socialist pioneers or the Chartists in the nineteenth century, who were written off as wild men and agitators in a deliberate effort to separate them from a supposedly sensible body of people who, the public was told, were quite content with their lot.

I have mentioned this because if we are to see this new movement in its proper historical perspective we must see it as part of a much wider movement for human rights and human equality which is being fought for against all sorts of privileges all over the world. It is, in fact, a natural part of our fight for a socialist society. Our campaign for women's rights must include women's right to be fully equal with men as workers and individuals.

One of the most interesting things about the new women's movement is the extent to which it has struck a responsive chord in women of all ages and cuts across class barriers. It is perhaps not surprising that many young women should be profoundly discontented when they come across examples of the discrimination in education and jobs and opportunity that are still tolerated in modern society. But it is equally true that many older women whose first political experience was the fight for the vote should now, sometimes as pensioners, be waking up to the fact that the winning of the vote did not achieve what they expected it would. It was only the first step, giving women the outward form of political freedom with some marginal liberalisation, but leaving the inner substance of human equality beyond their grasp. They find they are excited by the new wave of feeling among their children and grandchildren. They want to see them succeed where they failed. Even though the extreme expressions of views we hear do not command majority support, that movement has already helped to awaken a political feeling among women.

The generalised discontent among women has now assumed the proportions of a real national – indeed international – movement. Whether we support it or not – and I am arguing strongly that we should do – it is a political force to be reckoned with.

The movement towards greater women's rights has remained for too long on the edge of our policymaking. We have not been concerned as we ought to have been with it. We must now integrate it more clearly into our own political philosophy as a movement based upon human equality, and human development.

The polls tell us that a majority of British women vote Conservative. It may be that while so many women are working at home we have failed to relate our pressure for social change to their concerns as women and have allowed their discontents to be exploited by our opponents.

Certainly the Tory Party has consistently tried to win their support. In the post-war period there was the Housewives' League created by Lord Woolton.

It is worth remembering how the 1970 Conservative campaign was mounted. There were the usual posters and leaflets about rises in the cost of living. But then towards the end a new note was introduced. The Conservatives deliberately played on the fact that many women were no longer prepared to vote as their husbands wished. They therefore encouraged them into deliberately voting against the men by playing on trade union wage claims and male selfishness – so it was argued – in keeping the increases to themselves and leaving their wives with the same housekeeping money to cope with rising prices. The assumption that women were *only* interested in their homes and money was a limited one – but this appeal had some effect. The attempt to divide women from an equal concern with men on those issues which the trade unions and Labour Party were fighting for was successful.

The campaign to put the blame for rising prices onto the trade unions is still directed mainly at women, and every strike reported in the press or on the radio and TV will, it is hoped, consolidate political support among women against the labour movement as a whole and the Labour Party in particular. We would be very foolish to ignore this campaign. It is part of the long-term systematic strategy of the Conservatives based on continuing market-research surveys done among women to exploit some discontents that most women feel, diverting them from the issues that have to be settled if real equality is to be achieved.

Thus, not for the first time, the Tory Party hopes to divide two great political movements – the movement for better pay and working conditions which the trade unions are leading; and the movement for women's rights – by trying to get them to cancel each other out. And every time there is discrimination against women by men at work, which there is, or men treat women inconsiderately, this tension helps the right. Even the opposition by some men to family allowances with the 'claw-back' was turned to the political advantage of the Tories.

Against this, superficial Labour propaganda 'aimed at the women's vote' is relatively ineffective. A leaflet on the prices of school meals, or housing, important as these issues are, merely scratches at the surface of the problem of bringing these two movements together so that they can reinforce each other in support of the ordinary family which is held back – men, women and children together – by the privileges we still tolerate in our society. The trade union movement could and should do more to help women in their struggle. Whatever its official policy may be, there is still serious discrimination in practice.

If we are serious in our desire to create this unity we have got to see it against a background of industrial change which sets the framework for all political analysis.

Modern technology has done a lot more than re-equip our factories with new machines and spread car ownership. It has begun a revolution of home life, as well as life at work. Domestic appliances have lifted some of the back-breaking drudgery of keeping a home from those women who can afford to buy them, though millions cannot. For some it has opened up a leisure unknown before these appliances were invented, and could be afforded, when they worked from their childhood into the last days of their retirement, cooking and cleaning and mending and serving their menfolk, without pay.

And with leisure has come a whole new source of information and ideas through the popular press, radio and television. Instead of being locked away in an isolated village kitchen with nothing but gossip to feed them with information, more women today have an opportunity to be better informed. All sorts of new ideas are coming into every household, and there is a massive and entirely justified discontent among women as well as men – all part of the revolution of rising expectations.

Some of these ideas go right to the heart of family life. All of a sudden, instead of an apparently inescapable life of childbearing, more women have now discovered that you can theoretically plan your family, and instead of inevitably occupying all the years of life until you are prematurely aged by having and raising children, free time may be waiting for you round the corner in your early thirties when your youngest child is off at school, or earlier if you have no children.

So many a married woman who is still young and full of energy and ideas will find that she has perhaps thirty years of her life up to sixty-five (and a longer and less exhausting period than her grandmother had after that) in which she can make choices about what she does. In other cases, where husbands are unemployed, disabled or lower-paid workers, many wives have to go out to work to supplement the family income – whether they want to or not. But for women with children, and a home to maintain, who work, the physical strain and effort of this double shift is considerable. They have to fight two battles.

We call leisure 'freedom'. But when you come to look at this freedom it can only be enjoyed if you have been educated to use it and have a sufficient income to allow you freedom from anxiety. Many a woman of thirty-five only then discovers, too late to put it right, that *all* she was encouraged to learn at school was cooking, dressmaking and typing which are now graced under the description of 'domestic science' and 'business studies'. She finds she was only equipped for a life that she may not have to lead – or want to lead. There is also the problem of an 'identity crisis' for some mothers when they discover their children no longer depend on them and they have no education to help them cope. No wonder there is so much combustible material about. No wonder the Conservatives would like to see it directed against the trade unions in case it became dangerously threatening to the fabric of a male-dominated, consumer-orientated capitalist society, and our unfair educational system which is the cause of much of the trouble.

The phenomenon of the women's movement cannot possibly be understood without some attempt to integrate important changes in social attitudes into our political thinking. An extraordinary gap still exists between the accepted national view – about the way that people are supposed to behave and the way in which society has actually been moving.

Parliament, and those who sit in it, is still 'officially' wedded to a view of human relations – which supposes that men will be educated to work, and women will be trained to marry them, and they will then all pair off and produce families and live happily ever after. But rightly or wrongly – and I am not passing any moral judgements at all – that is not what actually happens in many cases.

Some do get married, but things don't work out and they part, and they marry again, and perhaps have children or perhaps not. Some women have children without marrying, and some want to marry and not have children, and some don't like men at all. All this is demonstrable, a statistical fact, and the implications are enormous. It means that a lot of women want to do things, or are doing things, that in a way aren't accepted by society and they find themselves discriminated against because of it. The traditional role of the family as a united partnership for life, which it is for the majority, is not threatened by accepting other lifestyles for the minority, though some try to argue that it is.

Remember one thing. This freedom has been accepted for centuries, but for men only. Men have always been generous to themselves, in approving their own lifestyles. But the old double standards are no longer acceptable. Now new options are beginning to open up for women. This is the stuff of which revolutions are made, because it involves a change of values which threatens the existing pattern of male domination.

But all freedom requires choice. What do people want to do with their freedom? Once anyone gets over the shock of being able to do what they like, they will settle down to work out their own lifestyle that conforms to their basic nature and reflects their values. The right to make our own choices is fundamental. It would certainly be wrong to suppose that the women's movement is against moral standards. It is, if anything, rather puritanical. For many men this is the most surprising thing about it.

Parliament has recognised these changes over the years by passing a number of laws that give people greater freedom to handle these matters for themselves instead of laying down the law from the top. In doing so, Parliament has certainly not approved the behaviour that is now legal under them. We have made it easier for people to make choices for themselves in matters that affect their own lives. It certainly doesn't stop us, as individuals, from arguing against the abuse of the freedom people have won. Not at all. But the fact that the churches have now distinguished between *sin* and *crime* liberated Parliament from trying to legislate on personal moral questions. Some of those who oppose this policy are really trying to close Pandora's box and get women back 'where they belong' as the nice reliable uncomplaining unpaid workforce for men.

It is very difficult to run a modern community successfully and it is particularly difficult to see things changing so rapidly without getting frightened. Yet you and I know that we are aiming for unity in diversity; for letting people lead their own lives so long as they do not make life hell for everyone else.

And if women are to be allowed to lead fuller lives there will have to be a lot of changes made, and most of them will require a complete re-education of men.

To start with we have got to change the whole educational system and completely abandon the conditioning of girls in our schools designed to brainwash them into accepting a subordinate role in life. We have got to break the monopoly of good jobs enjoyed by men. We have also got to open up job opportunities and provide far more day nurseries and other facilities women need to free them for work. We must make provision for women of any age who want to upgrade their level of skill or re-enter the working population if they can't have children or have had their children or for any other reason they want or need to work. Here the second chance of adult education, or the Open University, could be so important for women.

We have got to sweep away all the discrimination against women that clutters up our statute book and tax laws, and that disfigures our working practices in industry, especially the continued denial of equal pay. We must make it clear that a person is a person, whether male or female, black or white, rich or poor. That's what socialism is all about. And in doing so we are no more attacking femininity than we would be attacking masculinity if men were the victims of discrimination. The issue is one of freedom, and where femininity is used as an excuse to deny that freedom it must be exposed as an unfair practice.

But it would be wrong to suggest that the only thing we need is changes in the law. The Labour Party which itself has a long way to go has sometimes been too ready to believe that if you passed a bill you solved the problem. We will have to change the law and we will have to make resources available to advance women's rights. But above all we will have to change attitudes. And there are real conflicts of interest at the heart of this issue that have to be faced and resolved.

In the end the whole character of any society is dictated by its values. You can have any number of laws, but if they don't reflect the spirit of the people they are just dead letters. It is how people regard their fellow creatures and how much responsibility they feel for them that make a healthy society, or a happy family, or a happy person.

Looked at like this the women's movement which is campaigning on such a programme can be clearly seen as a powerful ally in the struggle for human rights which, if it wins, will help to liberate men too.

We are all fighting the same battle. The things that women are fighting against – bad housing, inadequate social services, bad education, discrimination, lack of opportunity and outdated ideas – are the very same enemies that men are fighting. A victory for the one is a victory for us all. And if the women's movement looks as if it is middle class, it is because sensitivity to some advanced forms of discrimination only become apparent when basic problems of poverty have been solved.

If we could only ally ourselves to many of the new movements, what a terrific source of ideas and strength we could tap for democratic socialism in Britain.

32
The Political Struggle for Equality

Benn highlighted the relationship between health and inequality in this speech to the Socialist Health Association in November 1992. Here he restates his famous five questions to ask those in power: What power have you got? Where did you get it from? In whose interests do you exercise it? To whom are you accountable? And how can we get rid of you?

I am the only surviving Labour member who was in Parliament when Aneurin Bevan was Minister of Health. I heard his speech in 1951, when he resigned from the Cabinet on the question of teeth and spectacles and because he believed that the defence burden was too great.

The post-war government was an agency for social, political and economic change. Now we are living at a time when politics have become enormously managerial and I am not attracted by the way in which they are conducted. The argument is all about who can run the status quo better. However, a managerial position without an agitational underpinning never comes off at all. I have in my time been a manager, for eleven years as a Cabinet minister, but on reflection I think agitation is more important than management in bringing about social change. And I am an agitator.

What then are the conditions that bring about change? A political movement without a history and without a vision cannot really make a lot of progress. There is a tendency to live for the day: what will tomorrow's headlines say, what will the public opinion polls say on the eve of an election? But what moves people is more than the fact of being spectators of the political process. I think the developments in America, the defeat of Bush and the election of Clinton, are very important, because they raise in people's minds hope of the possibility of change – and hope is a very big factor in all political change.

What has moved people, it is, of course, ideas. When Cain killed Abel and the Lord had a word with him about it, Cain said: 'Am I my brother's keeper?' He was talking about equality. The idea that I have an equal responsibility for my neighbour or my brother has reappeared in a whole range of different forms over the years – 'am I my brother's keeper', 'an injury to one is an injury to all', 'united we stand, divided we fall', 'love thy neighbour as thyself'.

If you look at the great statements that have been made over the years, that have formed a critical part of the labour movement's philosophy, you come across some very interesting passages which are all about equality. There was clearly no demand for child benefit to be uprated in accordance with the cost of living in the seventeenth century, but there was a demand for equality, and in so far as we have gone wrong, it may be, I rather suspect, because we have forgotten the relevance of equality, which is the core of this conference.

I came across a passage recently by a historian, writing about the English Revolution in Chelmsford:

> The relation of master and servant has no ground in the New Testament. In Christ there is neither bond nor free, ranks such as those of the peerage and gentry are ethnical and heathenish distinctions. There is no ground in nature or scripture why one man should have £1000 a year and another not £1. The common people have been kept in blindness and ignorance and have remained servants and slaves to the nobility and gentry, but God hath now opened their eyes and discovered unto them their Christian liberty.

Now that idea is powerfully entrenched in the collective consciousness of the nation and unless we are prepared to reawaken and use it for the purpose of dealing with the problem of equality, it just becomes a curiosity.

But this concept of equality has been obliterated by managerial solutions to every known problem – we set up a quango to do this; have a tax structure to do that – but the main idea which has really guided and inspired people over many centuries has been put on one side.

The birth of trade unionism was all about giving people equal rights. Trade unionism was about a greater degree of equality between those who invested their money in industry and those who invested their lives in industry.

Here you come to an extremely important element in all successful struggles: you have to have solidarity and effort. Nothing ever comes down from the top. This idea of a good king is one of the great illusions of the Middle Ages – good kings and bad kings. It has to be challenged head-on. When the Combination Acts, which made trade unionism illegal, were repealed it was because there was a huge mobilisation comparable to the one we saw recently in London for the miners, but going on over a very long period. The Chartists' demand for the vote was made because they recognised that the vote was an instrument for political power, to bring about greater equality and the services that were needed. The suffragettes won the vote through a huge, long struggle. They chained themselves to railings, they were arrested, imprisoned, they went on hunger strike, they were forcibly fed. I put up a little monument to Emily Wilding Davison in the crypt of the House of Commons, because on the night of the census of 1911 she hid in the broom cupboard of the crypt. When the census return asked 'What was your address on the night of the census?', she replied 'the House of Commons'. I asked the Speaker to unveil a plaque to her but he refused because, he said, the Lord Chancellor objected to a phrase on the plaque, 'by this means was democracy won for the people of Britain', which he said was open to misunderstanding. But of course it wasn't open to misunderstanding: that was how the vote was won.

One of the reasons why we have not been as successful as we might have been in defending and preserving local government is that we have forgotten that the first examples of progressive politics were achieved through the ballot box in local government. Look at Birmingham under Joseph Chamberlain in the nineteenth century: there was a municipal effort to provide housing, hospitals, water supply, transport, gas, orchestras, museums. And what was the means by which these were achieved? Very simple: it was the essentially egalitarian nature of the vote which gave people power to buy collectively what they could not afford individually. If you do not have the ballot box then power rests entirely with those who own the land, factories, banks and the means of communication. It is all about equality – about giving people the right by the vote to counteract the unjust distribution of money.

That is why democracy has always been more frightening to the Establishment than socialist rhetoric. It is easy to make a socialist speech – I must confess I have done it myself once or twice – but it doesn't really frighten those in power. What frightens them is a challenge to the monopoly of their power, by asking them how democratic it is.

If you meet powerful persons, try asking them these five questions: What power have you got? Where did you get it from? In whose interests do you exercise it? To whom are you accountable? And how can we get rid of you?

It has not been very respectable to struggle – extra-parliamentary activity has been frowned upon. But when I look at the world we live in, all power has been extra-parliamentary. If capitalism in Britain depended on Tory MPs it would end tomorrow. It is there because of the power of business, finance, the media, the administration, the military and so on. And our power has similarly been manifested outside Parliament, in the labour movement. One can write marvellous Fabian pamphlets, but unless you are part of a movement with solidarity, a sense of history, some sort of vision, some recognition that you have power that you can deploy, nothing whatever will happen. We have had to get this across to people – a very difficult thing to do over the last ten years, because there is a view that there is no alternative. I think one of the reasons the miners got such a lot of support was that three weeks earlier speculators had picked up £10 billion of our money, gambling on the currency. Three weeks later they said they were going to sack, in effect, 100,000 people because we are not prepared to pay £100 million a year to make British coal competitive with imported coal.

There is a school of thought that says that Mrs Thatcher changed the culture of our society permanently: that somehow when she came to power history flipped and it would never be the same again. I have never believed that for one moment because I remember the spirit that existed in earlier days – the wartime spirit and so on. In wartime there was less food than there is today, but because of equal distribution through rationing in fact the health of children improved enormously.

We have a cash-related society, without a strategy to deal with the social and health and educational and indeed pension consequences of having such a society.

I have a feeling there is a thirst for the politics of agitation, of principle, of a historical and visionary view. Unless there is, we will never be able to harness all the sort of energy it took forty-five years for us to harness, from Keir Hardie to the election of that 1945 Labour government which gave us the health service, gave us full employment and – the greatest equaliser of all – gave us the welfare state, and probably did more for equality in society than any government in our history.

I have a feeling that the 1990s are going to be quite different. The whole monetarist selfish philosophy is in retreat and we have to see that the vacuum is not filled by the hard right but with the vision of a better society.

VI. Politics after Politics

33
Last Speech to the House of Commons

Benn gave his last speech in the House on 21 March 2001. He was retiring, as he quipped, in order 'to devote more time to politics'. He had been an MP, on and off, since 1950, and in this final moment he pressed for the continued importance of the elected House, and of questioning the legitimacy of those in power.

I ask the indulgence of the House. This may be my last speech, so if I am out of order, Mr Speaker, I hope that you will allow me to range widely.

I support the report of the Procedure Committee and the motion proposed by my Right Hon. friend the Leader of the House. The report is scholarly and historical; it considers all the arguments. My only difference with it is over the question of a secret ballot. I have always understood that if one votes as oneself, it must be secret. Years ago, when I was canvassing in Bristol, I asked a woman to support me and she replied, 'Mr Benn, the ballet is secret.' I thought of her dancing alone in the bedroom, where no candidate was allowed to know about it. However, when we vote in a representative capacity, people must know what we have done, so I shall vote for the amendment. The committee has done very well. I hope that the House accepts the report.

The old system had serious difficulties. Although I disagreed strongly with the Father of the House, he carried out his duties with exceptional skill – with panache! I felt that he was the only member of the House who could have turned the Beefeaters into a fighting force – he showed such passion and commitment to the rules. We got the Speaker we wanted and I hope that, as a result of today's proceedings, we shall get the system we want – the one that I advocated, as the House will recall.

As I have done on previous occasions – when we were electing a Speaker – I want to look a little more broadly at the role of the Speaker. Often, we tend to think of the Speaker in relation only to the chamber, but the Speaker's role is of much wider importance. Relations between the legislature and the executive go through the Speaker of the House.

We live in a strange country: we do not elect our head of state; we do not elect the second chamber. We elect only this House, and even in this House enormous power is vested in the prerogatives. The prime minister can go to war without consulting us, sign treaties without consulting us, agree to laws in Brussels without consulting us and appoint bishops, peers and judges without consulting us. The role of the Speaker today compared with that of Mr Speaker Lenthall is that you, Mr Speaker, are protecting us from the triple powers of Buckingham Palace, the Millbank Tower and Central Office, which, in combination, represent as serious a challenge to our role.

Then there is the link between the Commons and the people. I have seen many schoolchildren taken around the House, and have talked to some of them about how it has been a home of democracy for hundreds of years. In 1832, only 2 per cent of the population had the vote. That may seem a long time ago, but it was only eighteen years before my grandfather was born. When I was born, women were not allowed the vote until they were thirty. Democracy – input from the people – is very, very new. The link between popular consent and the decisions of the House can be tenuous.

Furthermore, nowadays, Parliament representing the will of the people has to cope with many extra-parliamentary forces – very threatening extra-parliamentary forces. I refer not to demonstrations, but to the power of the media, the power of the multinationals, the power of Brussels and the power of the World Trade Organization – all wholly unelected people.

The House will forgive me for quoting myself, but in the course of my life I have developed five little democratic questions. If one meets a powerful person – Adolf Hitler, Joe Stalin or Bill Gates – ask them five questions: 'What power have you got? Where did you get it from? In whose interests do you exercise it? To whom are you accountable? And how can we get rid of you?' If you cannot get rid of the people who govern you, you do not live in a democratic system.

The role of the Speaker has another importance. When the political manifestos are yellowing in the public libraries, a good ruling from the Speaker in a footnote in *Erskine May* might turn out to be one of the guarantees of our liberty.

There are two ways of looking at Parliament. I have always thought that from the beginning – from the Model Parliament – the Establishment has seen Parliament as a means of management: if there is a Parliament, people will not cause trouble, whereas, of course, the people see it as a means of representation. Those are two quite different concepts of what Parliament is about. The Establishment wants to defuse opposition through Parliament; the people want to infuse Parliament with their hopes and aspirations.

I have put up several plaques – quite illegally, without permission; I screwed them up myself. One was in the broom cupboard to commemorate Emily Wilding Davison, and another celebrated the people who fought for democracy and those who run the House. If one walks around this place, one sees statues of people, not one of whom believed in democracy, votes for women or anything else. We have to be sure that we are a workshop and not a museum.

My next point, if I am not out of order, is that all progress comes, in my judgement, from outside the House. I am in no way an academic, but if I look back over history, I see many advances first advocated outside the House, denounced by people in power and then emerging. Let me use a couple of non-controversial examples. Twenty years ago, Swampy would have been denounced as a bearded weirdy; he will probably be in the next honours list, because the environmental movement has won. Similarly, when that madman, Hamilton, killed the children at Dunblane, the then Conservative Home Secretary banned handguns within six months, because public opinion had shifted. So we are the last place to get the message, and it is important we should be connected effectively to public will.

There is a lot of talk about apathy, and it is a problem, but it is two-sided. Governments can be apathetic about the people, as well as people being apathetic about governments. For me, the test of an effective, democratic Parliament is that we respond to what people feel in a way that makes us true representatives. The real danger to democracy is not that someone will burn Buckingham Palace and run up the red flag, but that people will not vote. If people do not vote, they destroy, by neglect, the legitimacy of the government who have been elected.

May I finish with a couple of personal points? I first sat in the Gallery sixty-four years ago, and my family have been here since 1892 – five of us in four generations, in three centuries – and I love the place. I am grateful to my constituents who have elected me. I am grateful to the Labour Party, of which I am proud to be a member. I am grateful to the socialists, who have helped me to understand the world in which we live and who give me hope. I am also deeply grateful to the staff of the House – the clerks, the policemen, the security staff, the doorkeepers, librarians, Hansard and catering staff – who have made us welcome here.

May I finish, in order, by saying something about yourself, Mr Speaker? In my opinion, you are the first Speaker who has remained a backbencher. You have moved the Speaker's chair onto the backbenches. You sit in the tea room with us. You are wholly impartial, but your roots are in the movement that sent you here, and you have given me one of the greatest privileges that I have ever had – the right to use the tea room and the library after the election. Unless someone is a member or a peer, he or she cannot use the tea room or the library, but you have extended the rules by creating the title of 'Freedom of the House', so that the Father of the House and I will be able to use the tea room. You will not be shot of us yet. I hope in paying you a warm tribute, Mr Speaker, that you do not think that I am currying favour in the hope that I might be called to speak again because, I fear, that will not be possible.

34
Anti–Iraq War Speech

After Parliament, Benn remained a campaigner, and he was named the president of the Stop the War Coalition. This is his speech against the Labour decision to go to war with Iraq over weapons of mass destruction. It was held at Hyde Park on 15 February 2003. Police reported that it was the largest protest in the UK, with nearly a million marchers.

Friends.

We are here today to found a new political movement worldwide. The biggest demonstration ever in Britain. The first global demonstration. And its first cause is to prevent a war against Iraq. It must also be about other matters as well.

It must be about the establishment of a Palestinian state.

It must be about democracy not only in the Middle East because there is no democracy in Saudi Arabia or Iraq. But dare I say it: some democracy in Britain that allows the British Parliament to decide.

While we are here, 35 million people die every year of hunger. While 500 billionaires have the same income as half the population of the world put together. That the world in which we live is dominated by the military, the media and the multinationals. And what we are about is getting democracy all over the world. So we can build a world that is safe for our children and grandchildren. That is what it is about.

If there are to be inspectors in Iraq, I would like there to be inspectors in Israel. Inspectors in Britain. Inspectors in the United States. I want to see the United Nations take sanctions against the arms manufacturers who supply weapons all over the world. I want to see the money wasted on weapons of mass destruction diverted to give the world what it needs. Which is food, and clothing, and housing. And schools and hospitals. And to protect the old, the sick and the disabled.

My friends, that is what we are here about today.

We are starting something really big. And our first task is peace in Iraq. But we must not stop until we have achieved the objective that brings us all to Hyde Park this afternoon.

Thank you for listening.

35
The Idealism of the Old

After retirement in 2001, Benn remained committed to his political passions, as a speaker, campaigner and writer. However, age also gave him an opportunity to think about the future. In this article for the Morning Star, *he protests against the idea that growing old means becoming more conservative.*

Young people are often considered as either idealistic or cynical and apathetic, while the old are often pessimistic. To my surprise and delight I am rediscovering idealism as I enter my eighty-fifth year.

Pessimism is understandable when brutality is all around, forever tempting you to believe that all is lost, that the hopes of youth for a better world have been dashed by experience and that those who still cherish those hopes are out of touch with reality. The human race, it is easy to believe, is just a collection of animals fighting for survival, power and wealth, and it will never adopt the policies necessary to build a better world.

It is easy for the old to use their experience to justify their pessimism by saying to the young, 'If you knew what we know, you would stop all this foolish talk about building a better world and come to recognise that we live in a jungle where you will have to fight for your own interests.'

The Idealism of the Old

But this argument cannot be used against old people who retain their idealism despite the experience they have had and, indeed, find that their own experience justifies hope and encourages dreams rather than destroys them. Jack Jones, the trade union leader who died in April 2009, and Helen John, the anti-nuclear activist, come to mind. All real progress throughout history has been made by those who did find it possible to lift themselves above the hardship of the present and see beyond it to an ideal world – some utopia that gave them hope and the strength to carry on.

This hope has been proved real by every struggling group: the trade unionists who were sent as convicts to Australia for swearing an oath to an 'illegal' union; the suffragettes, imprisoned for their campaign to get women the vote; the many leaders and movements which fought for freedom from their colonial masters; those who fought and defeated apartheid in South Africa; and now the environmentalists who are taking on the global Establishment.

This is not to argue for the sort of Panglossian optimism that suggests that you should not worry because everything will end up for the best, because that is the very opposite of the truth. But pessimism is a prison into which you incarcerate yourselves, removing any desire to join in meeting the challenges which face the human race, and thereby handing over all the power to those who now exercise it at your expense – and who have been corrupted by that power.

Every student of history learns about the corruption of power, but don't forget that there is also the corruption of powerlessness, by which I mean that those who think they have no power, from weakness, hand over the real power they do have to the powerful and thus become complicit in their own oppression.

Looking back at my life, I have come to appreciate the crucial importance of encouragement, remembering the teachers who encouraged me, and the experienced MPs who did the same when I arrived as a youngster in Parliament. When you are encouraged you can do so much better, and when you are put down you know the motive – to keep you under control.

That is why the powerful encourage cynicism, because cynicism helps to keep people away from progressive movements. By contrast, those who believe in themselves, and in the justice of their cause, can only mobilise the movements to which they belong by tapping the fuel of hope which carries those movements forward. Hope is essential even if it is often dashed.

From the beginning of time in the hearts of everyone in every civilisation there have always been two flames burning, the flame of anger against injustice and the flame of hope that we can build a better world.

The best thing the old can do is fan both flames. I am happy to confess that the visions I had as a youth – peace, justice and democracy worldwide – have become more important to me, now that I have had eighty-plus years' experience and I cannot be dismissed on the grounds that when I grow up I will see things differently.

If that is the only argument that I have to face, then I am quite content to admit that I have still not decided what to do when I grow up. Even if I live to a hundred I would still be growing up – right to the moment that my body goes up in flames in the crematorium. And my grandchildren can then decide whether I was right or wrong.

36
The Last Interview with Melissa Benn

This was conducted in the year after Gordon Brown lost the 2010 election. The New Labour years were over, and much criticised from the right, and increasingly from the left. Tony was in his increasingly frail mid-eighties.

So, Dad, here we are in 2011, a little over a century since the Labour Party was formed. It feels like crunch time for the Labour Party. Do you think it will survive?

Well, I think it will. When I think of what it was to begin with, it was made up of people who were socialists, who saw the class struggle, in socialist analysis, as the clash of interest between those who created the world's wealth and owned it, and trade unionists who lived out that struggle and socialists. The trade union element was stronger, in the first instance, and the socialist element has moved according to events. At the moment, I think the socialist argument is more and more relevant because what is being done by the present government to the working class is a piece of class warfare.

But what's so striking is that the Labour Party is not saying that. It is currently in a very uncomfortable position, isn't it?

Well, I think the trouble with the Labour Party is it has developed from being what it was when it was set up, a radical party about social transformation, into a group of people who think that they can micro-manage the status quo rather better than the Tory Party.

That would be a good enough description not just of the Blair period but of Callaghan and of Wilson in the 1960s and '70s. Would you not agree?

Well, I think it's moved in that direction. [Rather like the] Liberals in the nineteenth century who were also [alternating in power] with the Tories – and they had good ideas, and sometimes they won, and sometimes they lost. But the Labour Party was intended to be a transformational party, and although most people are not revolutionary in their thinking, when an injustice is done to them, as on the pensions,* their feeling is so clear and so strong that they do support very radical demands.

To play devil's advocate for a moment, I would summarise the current Labour position as follows: you have to bring the 'haves' – or some of the 'haves' – with you; that's the argument, isn't it, about Middle England and the third way and all the rest of it? Indeed, some people might look at you, at the height of your elected power, and effectiveness, and say that you yourself didn't then just represent the disenfranchised, but you represented something bigger. Do you have any sympathy for that argument, that the Labour Party always has to bring with it a wider group?

Well, it has to win power, and the question is: do you win power by being just a micro-management alternative to the Tory Party, or do you win power by saying things that need to be said and arguing changes that need to be made and being seen as the party that, if elected, would carry them through? Because in democracy you have to persuade people if you're going to make progress, and I think that

---

* In 2007 Chancellor Gordon Brown scrapped tax breaks on pensions.

there's been a lack of persuasion in what the Labour Party has done. They haven't argued the case.

People will feel disappointed by that, and they wonder why the Labour Party doesn't defend what it's about, and that's been a general anxiety about the Labour Party on the left for a very long time.

The more I talk to you the more I realise that you really do see national politics as being in a state of constant tension; you see it as a battle between different interests, in which the job of the MP is to be the parliamentary representative of labour as well as the underclass, to stick up for those under-represented groups. Whereas the modern Labour Party doesn't see its role like that at all ... It sees its role as conciliating, as bringing the different classes together. Would you agree that that's quite a different view?

Well, I think the Labour Party doesn't identify with the socialist elements in the trade union movement at all. They see strikes as destabilising society – and they're always trying to come along with a compromise. Trade unionists say we're fighting a class battle and the Labour Party doesn't accept that at all. That's what I meant by saying it has moved from being a party that was committed to the transformation of society, by dealing with some of its fundamentals, into a party that was just hovering about trying to come up with short-term solutions when there were problems.

So how do you think it's going to develop in the immediate future? Could the Labour Party be shaped to become more radical?

Well, events make politics, and when the strike action on pensions develops, I think we shall see a lot of support for it, and then, when support comes, people begin rethinking their own position. I think the Labour Party could be influenced by public opinion because public opinion does shape politics, in the end. I think the Labour

Party would realise not only that there's a strong case for the strike action, but that the strike action has had more public support than they realised, and in that way, the trade union movement, by its action, will be carrying the Labour Party a stage further forward in the understanding of modern society.

How do you resist the 'clubbable' element of Parliament?

Well, Parliament is a club, and there is a sort of common interest between all members of Parliament in maintenance of the club, the ins and the outs and so on, and you can have friends across the House. I think that that is an infective element. You begin to forget you are there for a particular purpose. I was rather proud of being a good parliamentarian, but what that really meant was that you were a good member of the club. You could get too fond of the parliamentary side of politics, the debates in the House, the votes and all the machinery of Parliament. Actually, you were all part of the ruling class in Parliament.

But maybe what really *made you a good parliamentarian was that you came to represent the views of the genuinely unrepresented in an effective way.*

You just had to think about what your duties were, and when your own people came out on strike, you had a clear duty to support them. It's a very difficult thing to go on strike – you lose your money for a day or two, you're vilified in the press, you know ... it's very destructive. So, I drew the conclusion that when the crunch came and people did take action, you had to support them. The Miners' Strike I supported very strongly, and I supported individual acts.

Parliament is not very hospitable, is it, to people who are outside that clubbable consensus? Yet it gave Tam Dalyell a place, didn't it? But someone like Ken Livingstone never fitted in there.

Well, Ken was a strange person. His interest was London; he was brought up in London, led the London County Council, then the Greater London Authority – he was the Alex Salmond of London. But the people, they make their contribution, and I think their contributions are appreciated. I think the people you remember are the people who do something on a clear principle. I have lots of individuals I admire. I try not to think of politics in terms of individuals, but John McDonnell, who's the chairman of the Labour Representation Committee, I greatly admire. Quite a number of my mates have now left. Alan Simpson has left, and Tam Dalyell has left, and so when I look back, I look back at a different Parliament to today's.

What do you think your greatest contribution has been, if you're absolutely honest?

Well, colonial freedom, and freedom of information, and trade union movement, and social justice, and peace. But it's a very modest role. I look back on myself as somebody who played a modest role in all of this, and I do resent the idea that you can be built up as a great personality and so on – I don't accept that.

There is now a view – we could characterise it as a New Labour view – that the '70s and the '80s were ruined by too many strikes and that there's had to be a resettlement of the relationship between management and labour. Are you sympathetic to that?

No. I think the reason we had the Winter of Discontent was that two years earlier, the IMF forced upon a Labour government cuts in public expenditure, which were quite unjustified, and which were all taken out of the wages and income of working people, and the workers and the unions were not prepared to put up with it.

That brings me to another aspect of the contemporary situation. While we sit here and talk, Greece seems to be imploding. I mean, there are riots in Athens, the Greek parliament is split, the new head of the IMF is saying they have to take these austerity measures. It's quite frightening, do you not think? Three years after Lehman Brothers and the last financial collapse, could there be another collapse?

Well, I think capitalism is a very unstable system. They will try to take advantage of every difficulty to advance their own interests, at the expense of working people, and that's what they're doing in Greece. They're saying 'you're bankrupt and you've got to pay the price', but, of course, the guys at the top in Greece will be hardly affected at all.

The conventional view is that the left has always wrecked the Labour Party, whereas in your view the right has always been the more damaging element.

The current view has been that it's been the left of the Labour Party that's always endangered its prospect of winning and made it fail. But, you see, if you go back to Ramsay MacDonald in 1929, when my dad was in the Labour Cabinet, and I remember him once saying, the worse the economic situation got, the more cheerful Ramsay MacDonald became. That was because Ramsay MacDonald was in the process of negotiating with the Tories to get a National Government. My dad wouldn't go along with that and was defeated in the 1931 election. That took Labour out of office from '29 till 1945, a very long span.

Then, if I go to my own time in Parliament, in 1950, I was elected. In '51, the Americans persuaded the Labour Cabinet, Attlee's Cabinet, that there was a Cold War and we all had to re-arm, and so Attlee went in for a rearmament programme, and that meant cuts had to be made in the health service and the welfare state, and that drove Aneurin Bevan into resignation. So we couldn't win the 1951 election: even though we had more votes than the Tories had, we lost the election.

Then there was the SDP, formed in 1981. The left was blamed for producing a bad manifesto and all that, but actually, it was two deputy leaders of the Labour Party, and one or two others, who resigned, and got massive press coverage and support, and they went.*

So, I think you could argue a view different from the current view, that it is the left that is the cause of the trouble.

You made your maiden speech, at the age of twenty-five; you are now in your eighties. How do you think politics, in its general terms, has changed? Is it a completely different world? I'm thinking about the involvement of women in politics; I'm thinking about all those movements for colonial freedom, or gay liberation or the ways that immigration has changed our politics.

Well, undoubtedly, there have been developments, and they've changed everybody's thinking, changed politics generally, not just the Labour Party. But, when I look back over my life, it was my ministerial experience that moved me to the left. Normally, people start on the left and become ministers and end up in the House of Lords, and I've done it the other way round, if you see what I mean.

And you did manage to resist that move to the right, do you think, because you were a very good minister?

Well, I worked very hard at it and so on. But, on the occasion of the public sector cuts in 1976, we had all these meetings of the Cabinet in the autumn of 1976, and the PM, Jim Callaghan, gave me a day in the Cabinet to put the case against cuts and in favour of an alternative economic strategy. I was voted down.

---

* This is the setting for the deputy-leadership race between Benn and Healey in September 1981, where Benn came close to winning. Healey's victory was seen as victory for the status quo.

That's quite something, isn't it: a minister puts forward an alternative economic strategy, it's debated seriously. OK, it's set aside, collective Cabinet responsibility wins the day, but I can't really imagine that kind of process within government now.

Well, that was in the Cabinet where you were actually deciding things, but there were real discussions. For example, a year earlier, the Cabinet met and decided to support our entry into the European Union. There was a very strong argument the other way, but the majority went in favour of Europe. I think Cabinet was an interesting committee, the most interesting committee I ever sat on, because they were people of ability, and the arguments were genuine, and important decisions flowed from it.

I don't get the impression that when Labour was in power under Blair there was anything like that kind of discussion. It was run more from the top, wasn't it?

Well, the tendency for all power to accumulate around the top is very natural, because leaders say, well, if you've asked me to do this job, I've got to have the power to do it, and so the centralisation of power is an anti-democratic tendency, but it goes on all the time.

Just going back to that question about how politics more broadly has changed, do you think that there are more voices in politics now? Do you think there are more working-class voices, more women's voices?

Well, women are much more powerful than they were. I remember my dad saying, when he was elected in 1906, there were no women MPs at all, and they had no vote. He said social issues were discussed with [the kind of] sniggering you get in a men's club, and [then] when women got into Parliament, they immediately gave it all a new perspective. I think women have had a very profound influence, and, anyway, it makes for a fairer society.

Socialists have grown and fallen in influence. Aneurin Bevan was a great socialist, and campaigned from his experience as a miners' representative to be Minister of Health, dealing with the very problem he'd had to deal with as a miner, of accidents in the pits. There have been formidable people.

It's become more international. When I was a boy, the general line was there are only two peoples in the world, the British and foreigners, and there were a lot of foreigners! But when I often tell this story I think of your children at school, with seventy-six nationalities, and if I talk to them about multiculturalism, I always say that I'm not sure they understand what I'm talking about because they've got American friends, Muslim friends, Jewish friends, Jamaican friends.

Whereas, when you were a child, when you were at school, it was just very, very inward-looking.

Yes, and I think the younger generation are aware of the fact that there are no foreigners – we are all members of the human race, and that realisation of the internationalism of everything has had a profound influence on the way we think.

You're eighty-six now. My children – two of your grandchildren – are now seventeen and fourteen. What would you see as the best outcome for their generation? What would you hope for in seventy-five years?

Well, I have a lot of confidence in the younger generation because they are idealistic and energetic and understand things, and I think the future for them, and for the human race, depends on whether the problems of the human race are seriously tackled: the question of peace is a fundamental question, the question of development, the question of meeting the environmental challenges, the shortage of water, food and petrol. The world faces enormous problems that can only be tackled internationally, and we have a very defective instrument in the United Nations. It's the only thing we have and you've got to make it work, but it's got to be changed, absolutely fundamentally. I think my grandchildren are going to live in very, very troubled times.

You don't ever seem to entertain the idea that human nature itself is profoundly destructive. And yet so many countries in the world suffer destruction, greed, corruption ... these are pretty persistent cycles of behaviour. Have you ever succumbed to that view, that human beings are not inherently good?

Well, I think there's good and bad in everybody. I know there is in myself. Your job is to inhibit the bad and encourage the good, but I think you do best by working with the good you see in other people. But, of course, it is true, human beings are what they are.

But they're capable of terrible things.

Oh yes!

I mean, you lived through the Second World War and our understanding of the terrible nature of the Holocaust. That didn't inhibit your generation from trying to make a better world, did it?

Well, no. When I came home in a troop ship in 1945, and I heard the words of the United Nations' Charter, which are written on my heart, they were: 'We, the peoples of the United Nations, determine to save succeeding generations from the scourge of war, which, twice in our lifetime, has caused untold suffering to mankind.'

You have always remembered those words off by heart, Dad – they obviously had a big impact.

They did have a big impact.

Bibliography

The Tony Benn works below contain the materials that comprise this collection.

Arguments for Socialism, Jonathan Cape, 1979 (ed. Chris Mullin)
    II. The Many Faces of Democracy, 9. How Democratic Is Britain?, pp. 108–29
    V. The Radical Tradition, 28. Marxism and the Labour Party, pp. 23–44

The Best of Benn, Hutchinson, 2014 (ed. Ruth Winstone)
    II. The Many Faces of Democracy, 11. Democracy and Marxism, pp. 160–86
    III. Industry, 12. The Case for Workers' Control, pp. 56–8
    III. Industry, 15. Argument for Full Employment, pp. 217–25
    III. Industry, 16. On 'Outsourcing', pp. 279–83
    IV. Britain in the World, 19. European Unity: A New Perspective, pp. 137–55
    V. The Radical Tradition, 27. Christianity as a Revolutionary Doctrine, pp. 118–35
    VI. Politics after Politics, 35. The Idealism of the Old, pp. 323–36

Common Sense: New Constitution for Britain, Hutchinson, 1993 (with Andrew Hood)
    I. The British State, 2. Democratic Rights or Ancient Traditions?, pp. 14–26
    II. The Many Faces of Democracy, 10. Rights under Capitalism, pp. 81–9

Dare to be a Daniel: Then and Now, Hutchinson, 2004
    IV. Britain in the World, 22. Why We Should End Nuclear Weapons, pp. 205–11
    IV. Britain in the World, 26. After the Bombing, pp. 191–7

Fighting Back: Speaking Out for Socialism in the Eighties, Hutchinson, 1988
    I. The British State, 3. The Common Ownership of Land, pp. 193–5
    I. The British State, 4. The Disestablishment of the Church of England, pp. 271–7
    I. The British State, 5. Power, Parliament and the People, pp. 248–54
    III. Industry, 14. The Miners' Strike, pp. 102–5
    IV. Britain in the World, 20. The Falklands Factor, pp. 95–8

Free Radical: New Century Essays, Continuum, 2004
    IV. Britain in the World, 25. On the Real Nature of Global Capitalism, pp. 76–9

Letters to my Grandchildren: Thoughts on the Future, Arrow Books, 2010
    I. The British State, 1. On the Power of the Crown, pp. 56–8
    III. Industry, 17. The IT Generation, p. xx

The Levellers and the English Democratic Tradition, Spokesman Pamphlet no. 92, 1976

V. The Radical Tradition, 29. The Levellers and the English Democratic Tradition

The New Politics: A Socialist Reconnaissance, The Fabian Society, 1970
   II. The Many Faces of Democracy, 6. A Socialist Reconnaissance

Speeches by Tony Benn, Spokesman Books, 1974
   II. The Many Faces of Democracy, 7. Developing a Participating Democracy, pp. 201–7
   II. The Many Faces of Democracy, 8. The Politician Today, pp. 221–4
   V. The Radical Tradition, 30. Listening to the New Generation, pp. 185–7
   V. The Radical Tradition, 31. A Woman's Place, pp. 188–95

A Ten-Year Industrial Strategy for Britain, IWC Pamphlet Series no. 49, 1975 (with Frances Morrell and Francis Cripps)
   III. Industry, 13. A Ten-year Industrial Strategy for Britain

Further Reading

The Case for Party Democracy, IWC Pamphlet Series no. 72, 1980
European Unity: A New Perspective, Spokesman Pamphlet No. 75, 1981
Parliament, People and Power: Agenda for a Free Society, Verso, 1982
The Speaker, The Commons and Democracy, Spokesman Pamphlet no. 94, 2012